Being as Communion

A Metaphysics of Information

D1590310

WILLIAM A. DEMBSKI
Discovery Institute, USA

ASHGATE

Published by
Ashgate Publishing Limited
Wey Court East
Union Road
Farnham
Surrey, GU9 7PT
England

Ashgate Publishing Company
110 Cherry Street
Suite 3-1
Burlington, VT 05401-3818
USA

www.ashgate.com

British Library Cataloguing in Publication Data
A catalogue record for this book is available from the British Library

The Library of Congress has cataloged the printed edition as follows:
Dembski, William A., 1960–
  Being as communion : a metaphysics of information / by William A. Dembski.
     pages cm. – (Ashgate science and religion series)
  Includes index.
  ISBN 978-0-7546-3857-5 (hardcover) – ISBN 978-0-7546-3858-2 (pbk.) –
ISBN 978-1-4724-3785-3 (ebook) 1. Reality. 2. Realism. 3. Materialism.
4. Knowledge, Theory of. I. Title.
  BD331.D34 2014
  110–dc23

                                                                2013051034

ISBN   9780754638575 (hbk)
ISBN   9780754638582 (pbk)
ISBN   9781472437853 (ebk – PDF)
ISBN   9781472437860 (ebk – ePUB)

Reprinted 2014

Printed in the United Kingdom by Henry Ling Limited,
at the Dorset Press, Dorchester, DT1 1HD

BEING AS COMMUNION

Dembski has become widely known for his quest to elucidate the role of information in our understanding of science and scientific processes. In this book he clarifies and develops some of the major themes of intelligent design, particularly reflecting on the "nature of nature itself." Materialism sees matter as basic: information is merely a form of matter. Dembski argues emphatically that the boot is on the other foot: matter is really a form of information. Building on the ideas of John Wheeler and von Baeyer, this is a tour de force of analytical writing, and another serious wound to the hegemony of materialism in modern science and culture.

Colin Reeves, Emeritus Professor of Operational Research,
Coventry University, UK

For a thing to be real, it must be able to communicate with other things. If this is so, then the problem of being receives a straightforward resolution: to be is to be in communion. So the fundamental science, indeed the science that needs to underwrite all other sciences, is a theory of communication. Within such a theory of communication the proper object of study becomes not isolated particles but the information that passes between entities.

In *Being as Communion* philosopher and mathematician William Dembski provides a non-technical overview of his work on information. Dembski attempts to make good on the promise of John Wheeler, Paul Davies, and others that information is poised to replace matter as the primary stuff of reality. With profound implications for theology and metaphysics, *Being as Communion* develops a relational ontology that is at once congenial to science and open to teleology in nature. All those interested in the intersections of theology, philosophy and science should read this book.

Ashgate Science and Religion Series

Series Editors:

Roger Trigg, *Emeritus Professor, University of Warwick, and Academic Director of the Centre for the Study of Religion in Public Life, Kellogg College, Oxford*

J. Wentzel van Huyssteen, *Princeton Theological Seminary, USA*

Science and religion have often been thought to be at loggerheads but much contemporary work in this flourishing interdisciplinary field suggests this is far from the case. The *Ashgate Science and Religion Series* presents exciting new work to advance interdisciplinary study, research and debate across key themes in science and religion, exploring the philosophical relations between the physical and social sciences on the one hand and religious belief on the other. Contemporary issues in philosophy and theology are debated, as are prevailing cultural assumptions arising from the 'post-modernist' distaste for many forms of reasoning. The series enables leading international authors from a range of different disciplinary perspectives to apply the insights of the various sciences, theology and philosophy and look at the relations between the different disciplines and the rational connections that can be made between them. These accessible, stimulating new contributions to key topics across science and religion will appeal particularly to individual academics and researchers, graduates, postgraduates and upper-undergraduate students.

Other titles in the series:

Christian Moral Theology in the Emerging Technoculture
From Posthuman Back to Human
Brent Waters
978-0-7546-6691-2 (hbk)

God and the Scientist
Exploring the Work of John Polkinghorne
Edited by Fraser Watts and Christopher C. Knight
978-1-4094-4569-2 (hbk)

Cyborg Selves
A Theological Anthropology of the Posthuman
Jeanine Thweatt-Bates
978-1-4094-2141-2 (hbk)

"Information is information, not matter or energy."

Norbert Wiener, *Cybernetics*, 2nd edn., MIT Press, 1961

"The most valuable commodity in the world today is information."

James Barham, "On Economic Value," TheBestSchools.org

*To the fellows and staff of Discovery Institute's Center
for Science and Culture, Sirach 42:15–25*

Contents

Foreword

Scholars have long acknowledged that scientific revolutions, along with their paradigm shifts, happen in human history. Yet rarely do we have an opportunity to witness such a shift first hand or to have such a clear and careful explanation of one. William Dembski's painstakingly detailed explication of the shift from the material age to the information age in science and philosophy is a brilliant and rare example. As both a philosopher and a mathematician, Dembski is metaphysically and methodologically able to delineate this shift, having previously written in both areas as well as developed a statistical method for inferring intelligent causation.

This book extends his earlier work and asks the most basic and challenging question confronting the twenty-first century, namely, if matter can no longer serve as the fundamental substance of reality, what can? While matter was the only allowable answer of the past century to the question of what is ultimately real (matter's origin, on its own terms, remaining a mystery), Dembski demonstrates there would be no matter without information, and certainly no life. He thus shows that information is more fundamental than matter and that intelligible effectual information is in fact the primal substance.

Dembski understands information as essentially a decision, in which certain possibilities are realized to the exclusion of others. He represents information using "matrices of possibilities," in which the realization and exclusion of possibilities can be verified through methodical investigation of inductive and deductive evidence. He does not deny the material world or that intelligence and information can be partially described by their material manifestation (DNA, for example).

Rather, his argument is that intelligence creates information, which in turn can manifest itself materially, and that intelligence is thus the preeminent first cause. This puts matter causally downstream from both intelligence and information, making it a subordinate and derivative concept. Dembski points out that matter is too "informationally poor" to act with real purpose, arguing instead that the informational systems we see in nature require a teleology or intelligence of a sort not reducible to matter in what Thomas Nagel calls a "dead [material] environment."

Dembski not only takes information to be the fundamental substance, but also clearly believes (as do I) that this substance ultimately originates with a personal God who intentionally gives being to the world, ordering its material structure and guiding its inhabitants for a purpose. However, Dembski does not try to convince us here; he suggests that this belief is not prerequisite to rejecting the reigning materialist plausibility structure and regarding it as demonstrably false. Here he helpfully brings into the conversation atheist philosophers of science, such as Thomas Nagel and others.

While many scholars see the intelligent design movement, of which Dembski is one of the eminent scholars, as simply a challenge to the reigning materialist evolutionary hypotheses (cosmological, chemical, and biological), this book reveals the movement to have far larger aspirations. The controversy over neo-Darwinian evolution, for instance, is but one minuscule piece of a much larger challenge to the basic assumptions we have held about the fundamental makeup of the world. Dembski extends his proposal that the basic stuff of the world is information by underscoring its comprehensibility via intelligence, purpose, and communication. At its core, information is always communicated, foreshadowing the emergence of human communication and the communication systems of all living things. Hence the title – *Being as Communion*.

Being as Communion challenges the very way we see and think about the world at its most fundamental level. To accept Dembski's notion that information serves as the ultimate source of reality, we must shift paradigms, not unlike the task of physicists when they accepted Einstein's interpretation of space–time, and yet still had to hold in mind the valid insights of Newtonian mechanics. Dembski honors what we know about the material world, and yet he situates this material within the higher and more universal reality of information and purpose.

Dembski takes us step by step through a series of brilliantly written chapters, unveiling both the challenge to the old and the theoretical and scientific possibilities of the new. Although Dembski cuts no intellectual corners, much of this book is remarkably accessible and a pleasure to read. Nonetheless, non-mathematicians, like me, will find some chapters quite challenging (for instance, chapter 7, on the mathematical theory of information). I encourage readers to keep reading or skip the parts that seem on the first read too technical. Dembski paints a big picture, and the important thing is to see that picture first.

He is proposing no less than a revolutionary breakthrough in epistemology. His unification of information under the aegis of intelligence in effect reopens the possibility of the original raison d'être of the early university, namely, that all true knowledge forms a unity that together describes reality.

Each short chapter systematically assembles all one needs in order to make the intellectual shift to this higher rationality. Dembski asks what is the single most fundamental aspect of the universe. He answers that it is not simply matter but intelligently formed information that has a purpose and the capacity to communicate.

Sit back and reconsider the basic assumptions about what is most real.

MARY POPLIN
Professor of Education
Claremont Graduate University
Author of *Is Reality Secular?*

Preface

Being as Communion is the final book in a trilogy. The two earlier books were *The Design Inference* and *No Free Lunch*.[1] In those books, I laid out a statistical method for inferring intelligent causation and then applied that method to the question of teleology in biology. *Being as Communion* is a very different book, which in part accounts for its appearance more than a decade later. The two previous books attempted to provide an information-theoretic underpinning for intelligent design (defined as the study of patterns in nature best explained as the product of intelligent or teleological causation). By contrast, *Being as Communion* attempts to paint a metaphysical picture of what the world must be like for intelligent design to be credible (intelligent design being, frankly, incredible within the materialistic metaphysics that dominates so much of contemporary intellectual life). That picture can, however, be considered on its own terms. Unlike a materialistic metaphysics, which shoehorns nature into preset material categories, the metaphysical picture painted here gives scientific inquiry free rein, allowing science to follow evidence wherever it leads.

What, then, is that metaphysical picture? Briefly, it is this: To exist is to be in communion, and to be in communion is to exchange information. Accordingly, the fundamental science, indeed the science that needs to ground all other sciences, is a theory of communication, and not, as is widely supposed, an atomistic, reductionistic, and mechanistic science of particles or other mindless entities, which then need to be built up to ever greater orders of complexity by equally mindless principles of association, known as natural laws or algorithms or emergent properties or principles of self-organization.[2] Within such a

---

[1] William A. Dembski, *The Design Inference: Eliminating Chance through Small Probabilities* (Cambridge: Cambridge University Press, 1998); *No Free Lunch: Why Specified Complexity Cannot Be Purchased without Intelligence* (Lanham, Md.: Rowman & Littlefield, 2002).

[2] Laws, algorithms, emergent properties, and self-organizational principles, as understood within materialism, are inherently devoid of teleology. Within a broader understanding of nature, however, these could have an intrinsic teleology, though in that case they would not merely characterize matter but a natural order richer than matter. I consider natural teleological laws in chapter 9.

theory of communication, the proper object of study is not particles, but the information that passes between entities—entities in turn defined by their ability to communicate information. Accordingly, the metaphysical picture that I'm painting attempts to make good on the promise of John Wheeler, Paul Davies, and others that information is poised to replace matter "as the primary 'stuff' of the world" and that in information we have "finally arrived at the 'right' metaphor that will unify" the sciences.[3]

---

[3] The quotes in this sentence are from Paul Davies, "Bit Before It?" *New Scientist* 161(2171) (30 January 1999): 3. Davies, in this article, draws inspiration from John Wheeler, who in 1990 suggested that information is the primal entity of the universe, using the phrase "it from bit" to describe the shift to a fundamentally informational view of reality:

> It from bit. Otherwise put, every "it"—every particle, every field of force, even the space–time continuum itself—derives its function, its meaning, its very existence entirely—even if in some contexts indirectly—from the apparatus-elicited answers to yes-or-no questions, binary choices, bits. "It from bit" symbolizes the idea that every item of the physical world has at bottom—a very deep bottom, in most instances—an immaterial source and explanation; that which we call reality arises in the last analysis from the posing of yes–no questions and the registering of equipment-evoked responses; in short, that all things physical are information-theoretic in origin and that this is a participatory universe.

This quote is from John A. Wheeler, "Information, Physics, Quantum: The Search for Links," in W. Zurek, ed., *Complexity, Entropy, and the Physics of Information* (Redwood City, Calif.: Addison-Wesley, 1990), 5.

Although Davies gives expression to the same high hopes for information as Wheeler, he also, in the *New Scientist* piece cited above, puts a damper on information:

> Certainly, the information concept has much to commend it. Science is, after all, an interrogation of nature, yielding data that we try to link into a coherent scheme. But it would be rash to totally discard the earlier metaphors. The Universe isn't a set of harmonious geometrical forms, or a gigantic piece of clockwork, or a decaying heat engine. Nor is it a vast computer. In their own limited way, they all capture some legitimate aspect of physical reality. None provides a complete description. No doubt in another hundred years, a revolutionary new technology will provide scientists with the next conceptual landscape, and the source for yet another unifying theme. Meanwhile, the notion of information is proving a powerful way to discover connections between physics, biology and engineering.

In keeping with Wheeler's enthusiasm for information, I'm less tentative about information than Davies. In my view, we are now in a strong position to assert that information is the "primary stuff" of and the "final metaphor" for science. I come to this view in part because all the other "stuffs" and "metaphors" of science can, as I will show in this book, be recast quite naturally in terms of information. But I also find justification for the finality of information in the Church–Turing thesis, which has been overwhelmingly vindicated and which states that any instance of computability can always be translated, precisely and without remainder, into the computational processes of a Turing machine.

As always with such grand proposals, the devil is in the details. And I will, in this book, provide details. That said, the details here will consist in carefully painting a metaphysical picture of the world in which information plays a fundamental and irreducible role. Conversely, the details will not consist in providing a systematic metaphysical exposition that addresses every point of contention to everybody's satisfaction. In particular, I take seriously Karl Popper's admonition to avoid being unduly distracted by "what is" and "what do you mean by" questions because, as he put it, "they seem to me prone to produce the danger of substituting verbal problems (or problems about meaning) for real ones."[4] To be sure, I will provide definitions where they help to clarify. But I want to avoid the materialist trap in which nonmaterial realities such as intelligence, purpose, and freedom—*and, of course, information!*—must be cashed out in materialist terms. This is a self-defeating game, and one I decline to play.

The title *Being as Communion* is not unique to this book. Eastern Orthodox theologian John Zizioulas wrote a book with the same title three decades ago.[5] His book examines personhood in the context of ecclesiology. Though seemingly confined to certain narrow theological concerns, his book covers much that is of general metaphysical interest. Moreover, Zizioulas provides an insightful historical account of personhood that is congenial with my treatment of intelligence as the ultimate source of information. Even so, there is little overlap between our books. I chose the title *Being as Communion* because it seemed to me singularly apt for this project. Indeed, I came up with it before learning that Zizioulas had written a book with the same title. Happily, titles are not subject to copyright, which allows them periodically to be recycled.

This book is the final fruit of a Templeton award that I received in 1999 for "Exploring the Constructive Interaction of Science and Religion," with

---

Computability, which is the science of manipulating information, thus forms a precise and complete theory (notwithstanding the many interesting open problems within it). Unlike the science of matter and energy, in which new particles and new forms of energy seem to proliferate without end, the scientific basis for information can thus hold no radical surprises—computation will never exceed what is computable on a Turing machine. For the Church–Turing thesis, often simply called Church's thesis, see B. Jack Copeland, Carl J. Posy, and Oron Shagrir, eds., *Computability: Turing, Gödel, Church, and Beyond* (Cambridge, Mass.: MIT Press, 2013), the introduction, titled "The 1930s Revolution." Also, in this book, see chapter 4 by Saul Kripke titled "The Church-Turing 'Thesis' as a Special Corollary of Gödel's Completeness Theorem."

[4] Karl R. Popper and John C. Eccles, *The Self and Its Brain: An Argument for Interactionism* (London: Routledge & Kegan Paul, 1977), 9.

[5] John D. Zizioulas, *Being as Communion: Studies in Personhood and the Church* (Crestwood, N.Y.: St. Vladimir's Seminary Press, 1985).

particular focus on "Evidence of Purpose" and "Expanding Concepts of God."[6] Initially, I planned to write a single volume to address both the science and the metaphysics of information. As I embarked on the project, however, I found that separate books were required—one to address the science, the other the metaphysics. I addressed the science of information in *No Free Lunch* (which is now in need of a second edition[7]). In *Being as Communion*, I deal with the metaphysics of information. Although *Being as Communion* is part of a trilogy, it is also a standalone book that can be read apart from my previous writings. In fact, readers new to my work may wish to read it first because the metaphysical picture I paint here provides a convenient vantage from which to appraise intelligent design as an intellectual and scientific project.

Why did this book take so long to complete? After *No Free Lunch* appeared in 2002 (*The Design Inference* had appeared in 1998), controversy surrounding intelligent design, and especially my contribution to it, heated up. For the next three years, opportunities to write new books and articles developing intelligent design as a serious intellectual project consumed much of my time. After that, my association with Baylor engineer Robert Marks began in earnest. It became clear to both of us that the information-theoretic ideas in *No Free Lunch* needed to be made precise and extended. As a home for this work, Marks launched the Evolutionary Informatics Lab (www.evoinfo.org) in 2007. The research of that lab over the next five years convinced me that any metaphysics of information

---

[6] No reference to the competition for this award is any longer available on the Templeton website. The original announcement of the competition can, however, be found here: http://lists.ucla.edu/pipermail/religionlaw/1998-November/013503.html (last accessed May 14, 2013). The more than 400 people who initially applied were reduced to a shortlist. The proposals on the shortlist were then evaluated by judges so that each received a score. The top seven scorers then each received a $100,000 award. They were: (1) Philip Clayton, California State University in Sonoma; "The Emergence of Spirit: God Beyond Theism and Physicalism." (2) William Dembski, the Discovery Institute's Center for the Renewal of Science and Culture, Irving, Texas; "Being as Communion: The Science and Metaphysics of Information." (3) Noah J. Efron, Bar Ilan University, Israel; "Golem, God and Man: Divine and Human in an Age of Biotechnology." (4) Niels Henrik Gregersen, University of Aarhus, Denmark; "Theology and the Sciences of Complexity." (5) David J. Krieger, Institute for Communication Research, Meggen, Switzerland; "The Self-Organization of Meaning: A New Paradigm for Science and Religion." (6) Michael Ruse, University of Guelph, Ontario, Canada; "Darwin and Design: Science, Philosophy, and Religion." (7) Robert John Russell, Center for Theology and the Natural Sciences, Berkeley, California; "Time in Eternity: Theology and Science in Mutual Interaction." After receiving the award, I learned from the Templeton Foundation that in the ranking of applications, mine had received the highest score.

[7] Such a second edition is in the works, with Robert Marks added as a co-author.

must first be given a sound theoretical basis in the science of information. That, in my view, has now happened, and in no small measure because of the work of the Evolutionary Informatics Lab. Indeed, the lab's breakthroughs in the science of information have given me the confidence to think that developing a metaphysics of information is not a mere intellectual exercise but a project for truly grasping the nature of nature.[8]

My debts to colleagues and institutions are many. Individuals with whom I have been in direct contact and who, through their insights and/or support, have significantly impacted this book deserve my special thanks. They include Jake Akins, James Barham, Michael Behe, Walter Bradley, Jon Buell, Steven Buri, John Camp, Bruce Chapman, Paul Davies, Richard Dawkins, Winston Ewert, Guillermo Gonzalez, Bruce Gordon, Billy Grassie, Charles Harper, Phillip Johnson, Stuart Kauffman, Casey Luskin, Robert Marks, George Montañez, Timothy and Lydia McGrew, Stephen Meyer, Thomas Nagel, Paul Nelson, Denyse O'Leary, Mary Poplin (for her splendid foreword!), Colin Reeves, Jay Richards, Terry Rickard, Robert Russell, John Sanford, Jeffrey Schwartz, Michael Shermer, Robert Sloan, Micah Sparacio, Charles Thaxton, Vincent Torley, Jonathan Wells, and John West. In addition, I wish to thank the Templeton Foundation, whose book award funded this project, and the Metanexus Institute, which oversaw the award and prodded me to complete it. I also want to thank all my friends, both fellows and staff, at Seattle's Discovery Institute—these are some of the most insightful and courageous people I know. I dedicate this book to them. Finally, I thank my family, above all my wife Jana, for their continual love and encouragement.

WILLIAM A. DEMBSKI
Pella, Iowa

Postscript: A full quarter of this book consists of explanatory and reference notes. A careful reading therefore requires attention to these notes.

---

[8]   The theme of nature's nature has captivated me now for well over a decade. Interest in this theme spurred me to help organize a conference titled "The Nature of Nature: An Interdisciplinary Conference on the Role of Naturalism in Science," which took place at Baylor University, April 12–15, 2000. For details about this conference, visit http://www. designinference.com/documents/2000.04.nature_of_nature.htm (last accessed May 14, 2013). That conference, in turn, inspired an anthology that I co-edited: Bruce L. Gordon and William A. Dembski, eds., *The Nature of Nature: Examining the Role of Naturalism in Science* (Wilmington, Del.: ISI Books, 2011).

Chapter 1
The Challenge of a Material World

What does the world look like if the fundamental stuff of reality is not matter but information? That is the question animating this book. We live in an information age. Yet we also live in an overwhelmingly materialist age in which the things that seem to us most solid and inspire the most confidence are material. Information itself therefore tends to be conceived in material terms, as a property of matter.[1] But what if information cannot be reduced to matter? To turn the tables even more sharply, what if matter itself is an expression of information? Such questions have been raised over the last few decades, but fleshing out an answer that convincingly casts information as more fundamental than matter has remained elusive.[2] The aim of this book is to advance this discussion, expanding the reach and significance of information for our understanding of the world.

---

[1]   Materialist scientists regard information as essentially material, and many see the source of information, especially in biological systems, as residing ultimately in chemistry. Nobel laureate and chemist Christian de Duve develops this perspective at length in his book *Vital Dust*. There he lays out seven "ages" in the history of life: (1) The Age of Chemistry, (2) The Age of Information, (3) The Age of the Protocell, (4) The Age of the Single Cell, (5) The Age of Multicellular Organisms, (6) The Age of the Mind, and (7) The Age of the Unknown. The most important transition among these ages, for our purposes, is from the first to the second. Here is how de Duve describes that transition:

> History is a continuous process that we divide, in retrospect, into ages—the Stone Age, the Bronze Age, the Iron Age—each characterized by a major innovation added to previous accomplishments. This is true also of the history of life. ... First, there is the Age of Chemistry. It covers the formation of a number of major constituents of life, up to the first nucleic acids, and is *ruled entirely by the universal principles that govern the behavior of atoms and molecules*. Then comes the Age of Information, thanks to the development of special information-bearing molecules that inaugurated the new processes of Darwinian evolution and natural selection particular to the living world.

Christian de Duve, *Vital Dust: Life as a Cosmic Imperative* (New York: Basic Books, 1995), 10, emphasis added.

[2]   John Wheeler, one of the outstanding theoretical physicists of the twentieth century, described his career as falling in three stages:

> In the first period, extending from the beginning of my career until the early 1950s, I was in the grip of the idea that Everything Is Particles. I was looking for ways to

build all basic entities—neutrons, protons, mesons, and so on—out of the lightest, most fundamental particles, electrons, and photons. This same vision of a world of simple particles dominated my work with Feynman. We were able to formulate electrodynamics in terms of particles acting at a distance on one another without the need for intermediate electric or magnetic fields ....

I call my second period Everything Is Fields. From the time I fell in love with general relativity and gravitation in 1952 until late in my career, I pursued the vision of a world made of fields, one in which the apparent particles are really manifestations of electric and magnetic fields, gravitational fields, and space–time itself ....

Now I am in the grip of a new vision, that Everything Is Information. The more I have pondered the mystery of the quantum and our strange ability to comprehend this world in which we live, the more I see possible fundamental roles for logic and information as the bedrock of physical theory. I am eighty-six as of this writing, but I continue to search.

This quote is from Wheeler's autobiography, John A. Wheeler and Kenneth W. Ford, *Geons, Black Holes, and Quantum Foam: A Life in Physics* (New York: Norton, 1999), 63–4. See also Wheeler, "Information, Physics, Quantum," 5, in which he introduced the catchphrase "it from bit."

In the same vein, mathematician Keith Devlin, for a time, felt that information was poised to revolutionize science:

Perhaps *information* should be regarded as (or maybe is) a basic property of the universe, alongside matter and energy (and being ultimately interconvertible with them). In such a theory (or suggestion for a theory, to be more precise), information would be an intrinsic measure of the structure and order in parts or all of the universe, being closely related to entropy (and in some sense its inverse).

This quote is from Keith Devlin, *Logic and Information* (Cambridge: Cambridge University Press, 1991), 2. Devlin wrote these words in the late 1980s. At the time, he was trying to make good on them, demonstrating the primacy and utility of information in the physical and mathematical sciences and thereby hoping to revolutionize science as a whole.

Today he regards information as a far less promising idea. The problem with information, as he currently sees it, is that the question "What is the information in a signal?" has no univocal answer. Rather, he sees it as heavily context dependent. Devlin therefore no longer focuses on information but on how media interact (hence his association with Stanford University's Media X think-tank; see http://www.stanford.edu/~kdevlin, last accessed May 30, 2013). Interactions among media and not the information inherent in them is now his main interest. By moving to interactions among media, Devlin has operationalized the concept of information, shifting the focus from what information is to what information does. In his new scheme, media interact in ways consonant with materialism. Devlin's approach to information via interactive media therefore presents no challenge to a materialism, much less does it promise to revolutionize science in terms of the concept of information.

Devlin's backing off from information is not the norm. Most researchers, once bitten by the information bug, tend to stay convinced (as Wheeler) that Everything Is Information. For instance, Hans Christian von Baeyer, in *Information: The New Language of Science*, suggests that information is poised "to replace matter as the primary stuff of the universe" and to provide "a new basic framework for describing and predicting reality in the twenty-first century." See

At the moment, however, matter has the advantage over information. The natural sciences, as practiced in our day, attempt to understand the world in terms of their material properties, leaving no remainder for anything nonmaterial. The most striking expression of this impulse that I've encountered appears in Richard Feynman's well-known lectures on physics. Early in these lectures he wrote:

> If, in some cataclysm, all of scientific knowledge were to be destroyed, and only one sentence passed on to the next generations of creatures, what statement would contain the most information in the fewest words? I believe it is the *atomic hypothesis* (or the *atomic fact*, or whatever you wish to call it) that *all things are made of atoms—little particles that move around in perpetual motion, attracting each other when they are a little distance apart, but repelling upon being squeezed together*. In that one sentence, you will see, there is an enormous amount of information about the world, if just a little imagination and thinking are applied.[3]

Hans Christian von Baeyer, *Information: The New Language of Science* (Cambridge, Mass.: Harvard University Press, 2004), the quote being taken from the dust-jacket.

More recent books in this same vein include Charles Seife, *Decoding the Universe: How the New Science of Information is Explaining Everything in the Cosmos, from Our Brains to Black Holes* (New York: Penguin, 2006), Seth Lloyd, *Programming the Universe: A Quantum Computer Scientist Takes on the Cosmos* (New York: Vintage, 2007), Vlatko Vedral, *Decoding Reality: The Universe as Quantum Information* (New York: Oxford University Press, 2010), Paul Davies and Niels Henrik Gregersen, eds., *Information and the Nature of Reality: From Physics to Metaphysics* (New York: Cambridge University Press, 2010), and James Gleick, *The Information: A History, a Theory, a Flood* (New York: Vintage, 2011).

These are all popular science books. Nonetheless, there exist more rigorous attempts to establish the primacy of information over matter. For instance, Roy Frieden, in a research monograph titled *Physics from Fisher Information* (Cambridge: Cambridge University Press, 1998), recasts much of contemporary physics in information-theoretic terms. Christopher Langan, as worried about Wheeler's "informational reductionism" as materialism's "physical reductionism," offers "a conceptual framework in which the relationship between mind and matter, cognition and information, is made explicit." See his "The Cognitive-Theoretic Model of the Universe" (2002), available online at http://www.iscid.org/papers/Langan_CTMU_092902.pdf (last accessed October 3, 2013). Yet despite such projects as well as attempts by scientists to popularize information, Wheeler's high hopes for revolutionizing our understanding of the world in terms of information have remained largely unfulfilled. Nuts-and-bolts reality tends still to be conceived in material terms.

[3] Richard P. Feynman and Robert B. Leighton, *The Feynman Lectures on Physics*, vol. 1 (1963; reprinted New York: Basic, 2011), ch. 1, p. 2, emphasis in original. The reference to "information" in the last sentence of this quote becomes ironic if information is indeed poised to supplant matter as the fundamental stuff of reality.

Feynman was here writing specifically about scientific knowledge, and not about all knowledge as such. Thus this passage might be seen as leaving room for other forms of knowledge. But in our materialist culture, such alternate forms of knowledge, whatever they might be, tend to undergo a materialist reduction. This is simply a sociological fact about how knowledge in our culture is viewed: the world, whatever else it may be, is composed of matter, and it is best understood in materialist terms. This, overwhelmingly, is the received opinion. Accordingly, many thinkers will claim that science (a science whose main task is to study and understand matter) constitutes our best form of knowledge. Of course, the very claim that science is our best form of knowledge is itself nonscientific. No scientific experiment or scientific theory can define what science is. In fact, what constitutes science is not written in stone but has been continually negotiated for more than two millennia (scientists, or natural philosophers as they used to be called, have been around at least that long). Feynman's materialistic understanding of science and of reality in general therefore flows directly out of a materialist worldview.

Opposition to such a materialist worldview is widespread and readily understandable. If the only legitimate way we have to make sense of the world is in materialist terms, then many of the things we value most go by the board or become dim reflections of their former selves. Here we may include such famous triads as God, freedom, and immortality as well as truth, beauty, and goodness. Despite an intellectual culture wedded to a materialist understanding of the world, most people remain, at some level, unconvinced of materialism. Materialist explanations may be fine as far as they go, but for most people they don't go nearly far enough. Mass culture, as opposed to secular intellectual culture, readily believes that some sort of teleology underlies physical reality. We are here for a purpose and the world is an outworking of purpose.[4] Also, in a Western culture still influenced by Judeo-Christian values, we tend to believe that humans are exceptional, having a special dignity found nowhere else in the world.[5] Yet on materialist grounds, none of this makes sense or can be justified.

On materialist grounds, we are simply organized bundles of matter. What we are and what we do depends entirely on this organization. And when this

---

[4]   Witness the phenomenal sales of Rick Warren's *The Purpose Driven Life: What on Earth Am I Here For?* (Grand Rapids, Mich.: Zondervan, 2002), which in its first five years in print sold 30 million copies.

[5]   Pivoting off this fundamental intuition that humans have a specialness that sets them apart from the rest of the animal world is Wesley J. Smith's initiative at Seattle's Discovery Institute: The Center on Human Exceptionalism. See http://www.discovery.org/che (last accessed May 14, 2013).

organization is finally lost at death, so are we.[6] Materialism comes to us with a Promethean challenge, daring us to stare the bleakness of an all-encompassing material reality in the face and accept, whether bitterly or blithely, the ultimate dissolution of all human aspirations. Thus one will find Bertrand Russell lamenting how humanity and all its achievements are destined for extinction as the universe unwinds to a state of maximal entropy.[7] But one will also find Richard Dawkins extolling what a privilege it is for humans to enjoy life and consciousness even if but for a short time.[8] Yet whatever spin one puts on human

---

[6] Benjamin Wiker insightfully traces this materialist understanding of the human person and its consequent rejection of personal immortality through two millennia of Western thought, starting with the philosophy of Epicurus (341–270 BC). See his *Moral Darwinism: How We Became Hedonists* (Downers Grove, Ill.: InterVarsity, 2002).

[7] According to Russell, "the world which Science presents for our belief" is "purposeless" and "void of meaning." He continues: "Amid such a world, if anywhere, our ideals henceforward must find a home. That man is the product of causes which had no prevision of the end they were achieving; that his origin, his growth, his hopes and fears, his loves and his beliefs, are but the outcome of accidental collocations of atoms; that no fire, no heroism, no intensity of thought and feeling, can preserve an individual life beyond the grave; that all the labours of the ages, all the devotion, all the inspiration, all the noonday brightness of human genius, are destined to extinction in the vast death of the solar system, and that the whole temple of Man's achievement must inevitably be buried beneath the debris of a universe in ruins—all these things, if not quite beyond dispute, are yet so nearly certain, that no philosophy which rejects them can hope to stand. Only within the scaffolding of these truths, only on the firm foundation of unyielding despair, can the soul's habitation henceforth be safely built." Quoted from Bertrand Russell's essay "A Free Man's Worship," first published in 1903 and widely reprinted. Available online at http://www.philosophicalsociety.com/ Archives/A%20Free%20Man's%20Worship.htm (last accessed May 14, 2013).

[8] Richard Dawkins, *The God Delusion* (New York: Houghton Mifflin, 2008), 404–5: "[H]ow lucky we are to be alive, given that the vast majority of people who could potentially be thrown up by the combinatorial lottery of DNA will in fact never be born ... However brief our time in the sun, if we waste a second of it, or complain that it is dull or barren or (like a child) boring, couldn't this be seen as a callous insult to those unborn trillions who will never even be offered life in the first place? As many atheists have said better than me, the knowledge that we have only one life should make it all the more precious. The atheist view is correspondingly life-affirming and life-enhancing, while at the same time never being tainted with self-delusion, wishful thinking, or the whingeing self-pity of those who feel that life owes them something."

Spoken like a true twenty-first-century cosseted Western intellectual. Many people suffer so much hardship that something more than this present earthly existence is needed to make life worthwhile. But Dawkins and atheists have nothing more to offer. Contrast Dawkins's view with that of John Hick: "[M]an's story is illumined by heroism, self-sacrifice, love, and compassion. But these gleams of light only throw into darker relief the surrounding, and chronic, human self-centredness from which have flowed so many forms of man-made evil.

existence, it's still the case that on materialist grounds we have no significance beyond the bits of matter that populate our little corner of space and time.

But what are the alternatives to materialism? In the late eighteenth and early nineteenth centuries, idealism was ascendant, identifying mind rather than matter as the fundamental reality. Both materialism and idealism are monistic, locating all of reality in a single principle, matter in the one case, mind in the other. But dualistic options also exist, such as Christian theism, which distinguishes between a nonmaterial God on the one hand and a created order on the other (a created order that includes but is not limited to matter). Many philosophical and religious options exist that fall short of a pure idealism but are also incompatible with a pure materialism. In the last 2,000 years, Aristotelian philosophy has been the principal player to fulfill this role in Western civilization (with Platonism a not too distant second). And yet, with the rise and success of a materialist understanding of science, materialist categories have come to dominate intellectual discourse in the West, and anything that can't be fitted into a materialist framework has tended to be viewed with suspicion.

Even so, compelling reasons to doubt the truth of materialism have existed from the start. Democritus, a pre-Socratic atomist philosopher, was one of the earliest figures of recorded history to hold to materialism. He held all reality to be constituted of atoms, which he understood as tiny indivisible particles. Thus, like Feynman, he embraced an atomic hypothesis: "By convention sweet and by convention bitter, by convention hot, by convention cold, by convention color: in reality atoms and void."[9] Yet Democritus also recognized a difficulty in this position: these very conventions, drawing on appearance and opinion, though ultimately reducible to a materialist substratum, were also the logical and evidential grounds for thinking materialism true in the first place. The deep truths of reality might all be material, but they could only be known through conventional truths provided by the senses.[10] Which, therefore, is more

Cruelty, greed, lovelessness, ruthless ambition, narrow suspiciousness, with their immense production of human misery, are all expressions of the practical atheism that St. Augustine diagnosed as the heart curved in upon itself." Quoted from John Hick, *Evil and the God of Love*, 2nd edn. (1977; reprinted New York: Palgrave Macmillan, 2010), 263.

[9] Democritus's extant writings are only available in fragmentary form. This fragment (as well as the other available fragments of Democritus) appears in Jonathan Barnes, *Early Greek Philosophy* (London: Penguin, 1987), 252–3.

[10] We find a similar distinction in our day between the disparagingly named "folk psychology" and the honorably named "mature neuroscience." The locus classicus for this distinction is Stephen Stich's *From Folk Psychology to Cognitive Science: The Case Against Belief* (Cambridge, Mass.: MIT Press, 1983). A mature neuroscience supposedly invalidates folk psychology and yet seems also to presuppose it. For more in this vein, see Gordon

fundamental, matter or a mind capable of apprehending matter? Democritus understood the tension and put it this way: "Poor mind, do you take your evidence from us [i.e., the senses] and then try to overthrow us [i.e., by reducing all sense impressions to atoms and the void]? Our overthrow is your fall."[11]

Because the work of the pre-Socratic philosophers exists only in fragments, and thus is largely lost to history, it's hard to say just how seriously Democritus took this challenge to atomistic materialism. This challenge raises a self-referential paradox: how can knowing subjects composed only of matter know that they are only composed of matter? Matter, it would seem, has no intrinsic capacity to produce agents that think, much less that can form representations about the world, much less that can know that these representations are true. More recent thinkers such as C.S. Lewis and Alvin Plantinga have developed these thoughts into a full-blown critique of materialism, charging it with self-referential incoherence.[12] One sees in materialism's self-reference problem the possibility of idealism, in which the mind that employs the senses to infer that all objects are composed of atoms comes to regard these very atoms as an expression of mind. It seems, however, that Democritus never took this line. He is regarded, along with Epicurus, as one of the two premiere materialists of the ancient world, a fact underscored by Karl Marx's choice of dissertation topic: "The Difference Between the Democritean and Epicurean Philosophy of Nature."[13] Marx, of course, was himself an avid materialist.

---

and Dembski, *The Nature of Nature*, part vi, which is devoted to evolutionary psychology, neuroscience, and consciousness.

[11]   Barnes, *Early Greek Philosophy*, 255. Barnes, commenting on this tension in Democritus between matter and the senses, writes (p. 254), "Everyone knows that the greatest charge against any argument is that it conflicts with what is evident. For arguments cannot even start without self-evidence: how then can they be credible if they attack that from which they took their beginnings?"

[12]   See C.S. Lewis, *Miracles: A Preliminary Study*, rev. edn. (1960; reprinted San Francisco, Calif.: HarperCollins, 2001), ch. 3, titled "The Cardinal Difficulty of Naturalism." See also Alvin Plantinga, *Where the Conflict Really Lies: Science, Religion, and Naturalism* (New York: Oxford University Press, 2011), ch. 10, titled "The Evolutionary Argument Against Naturalism."

[13]   According to Marx, Democritus and Epicurus largely agreed about the foundations of physics: "Apart from historical testimony, there is much other evidence for the identity of Democritean and Epicurean physics. The principles—atoms and the void—are indisputably the same. Only in isolated cases does there seem to be arbitrary, hence unessential, difference." The difference that Marx finds is in the philosophical consequences they draw from their physics: "However, a curious and insoluble riddle remains. Two philosophers teach exactly the same science, in exactly the same way, but—how inconsistent!—they stand diametrically opposed in all that concerns truth, certainty, application of this science, and all that refers to

Even if materialism raises certain troubling questions about its logical coherence, it nonetheless tends to rule the day. Often it takes the form of a *methodological materialism*, in which materialism is presupposed as the proper working hypothesis for clear-headed people as they try to make sense of their world. Methodological materialism (also known as *methodological naturalism* or *methodological atheism*) doesn't affirm that all reality is material. It simply says that for the purpose of most serious inquiries, notably science, it is best to treat the world as purely material and ignore nonmaterial factors. This view is extremely widespread, and the success of science is said to justify it.[14]

Methodological materialism has become a regulative principle for guiding inquiry throughout the natural sciences. But one also finds it in many unexpected places. Take biblical studies. Among ordinary believers, the Bible is widely supposed to be a supernatural book, supernaturally inspired and describing supernatural events, such as miracles and prophecies, thought actually to have occurred in the way described. Methodological materialism, however, can't go there. For instance, the Gospels present Jesus as prophesying the destruction of the temple in Jerusalem. Because that event didn't happen until 70 AD, many biblical scholars infer that the Gospels were written afterward. Why? Because reliable prediction of future contingent events cannot be squared with a purely material world. Biblical studies these days tend to embrace methodological materialism. As a consequence, the Bible's construction and the supernatural episodes described in it must be explained away naturalistically, that is, without recourse to anything beyond the material world.[15]

A purely material world operates by unbroken natural law. The beauty of matter is that, at the nuts-and-bolts level, material objects fall into a certain number of basic classes within each of which they are all the same. Moreover, within and across these classes they all interact in the same way. One electron is the same as any other electron. One proton is the same as any other proton. Moreover, electrons and protons in the same states interact with each other in

---

the relationship between thought and reality in general. I say that they stand diametrically opposed, and I shall now try to prove it." Quoted from Marx's dissertation at http://www.marxists.org/archive/marx/works/1841/dr-theses/ch03.htm (last accessed April 18, 2013). For his dissertation in book form, see Paul M. Schafer, ed., *The First Writings of Karl Marx* (Brooklyn, N.Y.: Ig Publishing, 2006).

[14]   For methodological naturalism and its relation to other forms of naturalism see Plantinga, *Where the Conflict Really Lies*, 168–74.

[15]   See Jay Wesley Richards, "Naturalism in Theology and Biblical Studies," in William A. Dembski and Jay Wesley Richards, eds., *Unapologetic Apologetics: Meeting the Challenges of Theological Studies* (Downers Grove, Ill.: InterVarsity, 2001), 95–110.

the same way. From a materialist perspective, the same is true for all fundamental units of matter. Such units of matter will assume different states and combine in different ways, but the principles or laws by which they operate and interact are remarkably uniform and invariant. Feynman's earlier statement of the atomic hypothesis is only a slight oversimplification of this materialist picture.

Some laws describing operations and interactions among material objects are deterministic (such as those describing gravitational forces along geodesics) and some are nondeterministic (such as those describing quantum processes that assume a range of possible outcomes). What makes the nondeterministic case an expression of natural law is that well-defined probabilities are thought to characterize the behavior of material objects that behave nondeterministically. Note that the deterministic case can be seen as falling under the nondeterministic case in which probabilities collapse to zero and one (events of probability zero and one being respectively impossible and certain, leaving nothing nondeterministic about them).

"Chance and necessity" thus become the watchwords of a material world ruled by unbroken natural law.[16] Indeed, what other causes can there be in such a world besides chance and necessity? Things happen because they must happen (thus by necessity) or they happen spontaneously within a range of possible outcomes (thus by chance) or by some combination of the two. Given a materialist understanding of the world, this is all that is, and indeed can be, going on at the nuts-and-bolts level of reality. Matter does what it does because it has certain properties and interacts with itself in certain ways—period. Materialism fundamentally affects how we understand the world, not least in how we view human freedom. We turn to this topic next because of its deep connection to information.

---

[16] Compare Jacques Monod, *Chance and Necessity: An Essay on the Natural Philosophy of Modern Biology* (New York: Vintage, 1972).

Chapter 2

Free Will: The Power of No

A materialist worldview leads to certain stark conclusions, notably that humans lack free will. A free will is *responsible* for its actions, that is, it is able to respond rather than merely react to situations. It responds by identifying possible courses of action, deliberating about their probable effects, assessing those effects in light of one's purposes and values, and in the end choosing a course of action. A free will chooses one course of action over others not by being ineluctably determined to do so and not as a matter of pure spontaneity, but as a rational response to a situation. The rationality at play here can be conscious, but it can also operate unconsciously. An act of free will presupposes a rationally controlled ability to do otherwise so that distinct courses of action constitute genuine possibilities or live options not reducible to purely irrational forces.[1]

In consequence, a free will deserves praise or blame depending on the course it chooses. For instance, the same situation may elicit an act of courage from one person, an act of cowardice from another. And so we praise the one and blame the other. Yet, on materialist grounds, neither praise nor blame makes any sense. A ball rolls down an inclined plane (deterministically) and smashes a teacup; a coin is flipped and by landing heads (probabilistically) causes a teacup to fall and smash. No one blames the ball or the coin for the smashed cup. Likewise, on materialist principles, it is groundless to blame a person for moral or any other failure.

To be sure, we do blame people for their failures. We can imagine that they might have done otherwise, and so we feel that they should have done otherwise. But given their material constitution, they could not have done otherwise (and, presumably, given our material constitution, we can't help but assign blame—unless a materialist worldview convinces us to withhold blame, in which case we can't help that either). Yet, on materialist principles, to say that someone should have done otherwise has no logical force (even if it has emotional force).

---

[1] For the understanding of free will described here, known as libertarian free will, as well as the debate over it, see Paul Russell and Oisin Deery, eds., *The Philosophy of Free Will: Essential Readings from the Contemporary Debates* (New York: Oxford University Press, 2013).

And this is the case whether one takes a hard deterministic line, which denies free will entirely, or a soft deterministic line, which tries to understand free will as freedom from outside coercion.

Soft determinism does nothing to soften the internal coercion of a misaligned brain that is behaving badly. In either case (hard or soft determinism), we simply do what our material constitution makes us do. Nor does adding a stochastic element here help to recover free will. A mind that acts on the basis of purely random or spontaneous events is no more free than one whose acts are fully settled in advance. On materialist principles, our minds are limited to the material constitution of our brains (minds transcending brains are simply not an option for materialism), and our brains are simply more complicated arrangements of balls going down inclined planes and coins being tossed. Thus we are not in control, we are not free.

For evidence that we lack the control necessary for genuine free will, materialists often look to neuroscience. Consider, for instance, some widely discussed experiments performed by neuroscientist Benjamin Libet.[2] The upshot of Libet's experiments, as interpreted by the materialist community, is that free will is an illusion.[3] These experiments purport to show that we become conscious of deciding to perform a certain bodily action only after our bodies are neurologically primed to perform it. In the language of these experiments, the *readiness potential* that triggers bodily action has already fired before conscious awareness to perform the bodily action. Materialist neuroscientists regard the firing of the readiness potential before the experience of a conscious decision to act as showing that free will is an illusion: our will has already been co-opted by material forces so that any conscious experience of controlling our actions merely reflects what our material constitutions are determined to do.[4]

Interestingly, Libet himself did not interpret these experiments as contravening free will.[5] Just because we are neurologically primed to perform an action does

---

[2]   For a summary of these experiments as well as for his own interpretation of their significance, see Benjamin Libet, *Mind Time: The Temporal Factor in Consciousness* (Cambridge, Mass.: Harvard University Press, 2004).

[3]   See Daniel M. Wegner, *The Illusion of Conscious Will* (Cambridge, Mass.: MIT Press, 2002), 52–5.

[4]   But note, on the assumption of materialism, free will would be an illusion even if conscious decision could be shown to precede firing of the readiness potential: in that case, some other materialist story would be told about how conscious decision is itself determined by underlying material processes that then, together, also cause the readiness potential to fire.

[5]   For a good summary of Libet's nonmaterialist interpretation of his own research, see Jeffrey M. Schwartz and Sharon Begley, *The Mind and the Brain: Neuroplasticity and the Power of Mental Force* (New York: HarperCollins, 2002), 304–9.

not mean that we will in fact perform it. Subsequent research by Libet showed that even after the readiness potential has fired, we have the power to veto the action that the readiness potential would otherwise have elicited.[6] If you will, the train may have left the station but we can recall it. The relation between the conscious experience of controlling our actions and what our material constitutions seem primed to do is therefore not nearly as simple as materialists would like. Indeed, our power to veto whatever actions the readiness potential is prompting leaves room for our choices to be real after all. This veto power is consistent with the account of free will as "free won't" that I'll describe shortly.

Without the benefit of a developed neuroscience, materialists have historically used a blunter approach to undermining free will. Thus, from the obvious fact that damage to the brain can substantively affect human action, they have concluded that we should think of ourselves as purely material beings.[7] Blows to the head, lobotomies, and neurodegenerative diseases all adversely affect the brain and can profoundly impact cognition and behavior. Yet, from a nonmaterialist vantage, the deleterious effects of brain damage merely point up that what our free will can do is conditioned by our material constitution, not that it is fully determined by it (a point that gains strength in chapter 10 as it becomes clear that materiality is itself ultimately informational). We are embodied beings, and the expression of who we are, including our free will, is limited by our bodies. In any case, to argue that material embodiment precludes free will requires much more than pointing out that brain damage is capable of affecting human action.

For another line of argument that we lack the control necessary for genuine free will, Sam Harris looks to introspection. According to him, introspection destroys free will by showing that we don't consciously choose the train of our thoughts.[8] Thoughts come to us unbidden. One thought hits us and then

---

6   As Schwartz and Begley report, "Experiments published [by Libet] in 1983 clearly showed that subjects could choose not to perform a movement that was on the cusp of occurring (that is, that their brain was preparing to make) and that was preceded by a large readiness potential. In this view, although the physical sensation of an urge to move is initiated unconsciously, will can still control the outcome by vetoing the action." Ibid., 307.

7   See, for instance, the books of Oliver Sacks, such as *The Man Who Mistook His Wife for a Hat and Other Clinical Tales* (New York: Summit Books, 1985).

8   "Free will *is* an illusion. Our wills are simply not of our own making. Thoughts and intentions emerge from background causes of which we are unaware and over which we exert no conscious control. We do not have the freedom we think we have ... [F]ree will doesn't even correspond to any *subjective* fact about us—and introspection soon proves as hostile to the idea as the laws of physics are. Seeming acts of volition merely arise spontaneously (whether caused, uncaused, or probabilistically inclined, it makes no difference) and cannot

another. So how can we be free? The observation that we don't have full conscious control over the train of our thoughts may be disconcerting to those who have never considered the matter, but it is not a threat to free will. At issue here is not free will but personal identity, that is, what it means for a person to be a person. The idea that our personal identity is more than our conscious thoughts goes back well before Freud. Greek admonitions to know thyself and Hebrew teachings about the hidden depths of the human heart suggest that there's more to us than conscious awareness. Indeed, we are often surprised at the things that percolate to consciousness precisely because we did not expect them *and yet* they seem revelatory of our deeper selves.

Still, how can we have the power to choose what to do, and thus have free will, if the very thoughts on which those choices depend are not the product of conscious choice? To answer this question, we need to recognize that even though we may have only limited control over the thoughts that come into our heads, we do have a conscious choice over what to do with them once they've arrived. In particular, when a thought comes to us insisting that we perform some action, we have the power to say no. The power to veto or negate is the power of free will. Free will is "free won't."[9] This connects neatly with information theory, which, as we will see, characterizes information as a reduction or ruling out of possibilities. To be informed that something is the case is to be informed that other things are not the case. Information says yes to some things by saying no to others.

Free will is the power of no. Not only does this understanding of free will resonate with information theory, but it also parallels a Judeo-Christian ethics that locates human freedom in self-denial and obedience. It's no accident that the commands of the Decalogue are stated as negations.[10] Nor is it an accident

---

be traced to a point of origin in our conscious minds. A moment or two of serious self-scrutiny, and you might observe that you no more decide the next thought you think than the next thought I write." Quoted from Sam Harris, *Free Will* (New York: Free Press, 2012), 5–6.

[9] Jeffrey Schwartz elaborates on this conception of free will in a chapter titled "Free Will, and Free Won't." See Schwartz and Begley, *The Mind and the Brain*, 290–322.

[10] Even the commands to keep the Sabbath and honor father and mother can be stated as negations. Restraint, in the sense of saying no, is the mark of freedom not just in the Judeo-Christian tradition. As Jeffrey Schwartz notes, "All five of the basic moral precepts of Buddhism are restraints: refraining from killing, from lying, from stealing, from sexual misconduct, from intoxicants. In the Buddha's famous dictum, 'Restraint everywhere is excellent.'" Quoted from Schwartz and Begley, *The Mind and the Brain*, 308. Nor is the idea that morality consists essentially in restraint limited to religions, theistic or otherwise. For example, the notion of conscience as an "inner check" figures prominently in the moral and political philosophy of the New Humanist authors. See Paul Elmer More, "Definitions of

that Jesus requires that his followers deny their natural inclinations. One of the most widely quoted statements of Jesus asserts that the truth will set us free (John 8:32). But so stated, the quote is out of context. According to Jesus, the precondition for knowing truth and being set free by it is obedience to his teaching (John 8:31). And at the center of his teaching are denying self and taking up one's cross (Mark 8:34). Although such a view of freedom may sound strange in a secular age that regards disobedience to authority and indulgence of self as the mark of freedom (such freedom being compatible with materialism's denial of free will), in fact it makes good sense.

Free will is always exercised as an act of negation, and this applies not just to humans but also to God. Take God in his role as creator. God, conceived in the traditional sense as an all-powerful being, could have created any world whatsoever. All were within his grasp. Yet, in the act of creating this world, God gave up creating others.[11] Creation gives existence to one possibility by withholding existence from other possibilities. Thus, in creating this world, God, far from expanding himself, contracted himself by ruling out other possibilities that he might have actualized. Creation is an act of humility, of self-denial. It is a sacrifice, a gift. Human creativity shares these same characteristics.[12] In general,

Dualism," in *Shelburne Essays, Eighth Series: The Drift of Romanticism* (Cambridge, Mass.: Riverside, 1913) and Irving Babbitt, "Appendix A: Theories of the Will," in *Democracy and Leadership* (Boston, Mass.: Houghton Mifflin, 1924). For more recent discussion, see Folke Leander, *The Inner Check* (London: Edward Wright, 1974) and Claes G. Ryn, *Will, Imagination and Reason* (Washington, DC: Regnery, 1986).

[11] To say that God gave up creating other worlds is not to say that God gave up creating *all* other worlds. It's certainly possible that God created other worlds (for example, worlds causally disconnected from ours and about which God never reveals anything to us). On the other hand, the Judeo-Christian tradition within which I move hardly sanctions that God created all possible worlds. Jesus, for instance, in remarking that it would have been better for Judas never to have been born (Mark 14:21) does not add that in some other possible world that God created, Judas (or an exact counterpart) would have flourished and been the happiest man alive. Some physicists who are more metaphysicians than scientists speculate that all (physically) possible worlds exist. Whatever the merit of such speculation, the Judeo-Christian tradition maintains that some possibilities are never actualized (for example, the pardoning of sin apart from sacrifice).

[12] Diogenes Allen takes these thoughts further. In commenting on Basil's *Hexaemeron* (a sermon series on the six days of creation in Genesis), Allen writes, "the theologian [i.e., Basil] connects the work of his hearers, many of whom were craftspeople, with the productive work of God. The 'productive' arts, such as architecture, especially mirror God's creativity because they endure and continue to show the 'industrious intelligence' of the architect or builder. Basil honors human work as an image of the divine work. Since the productive work of men and women is linked to the restoration of the divine image in us and growth

human freedom is expressed by negating possibilities. In fact, we might say that it's in the refusal to negate possibilities and in the insistence to keep options open that we deny our freedom.[13]

Materialists, of course, don't find in such an analysis of free will a justification for it. So long as matter remains the basic fabric out of which all reality is woven, humans must be conceived as purely material beings, and the items of matter that compose them must be all that there is to them. Thus, even the negation of possibilities that, as I'm suggesting, is essential to human freedom will be conceived not as the responsible activity of a free agent but as the determined outcome of material entities obeying unbroken, and indeed unbreakable, natural laws. Once materialism is presupposed, even if it is untrue, one's options for understanding the world become quite limited. We might even say that they become determined.

---

into the divine likeness, productive work is directly related to our sanctification." Quoted from Diogenes Allen, *Spiritual Theology: The Theology of Yesterday for Spiritual Help Today* (Plymouth, UK: Cowley Publications, 1997), 119.

[13]   Middle-aged people yearning for marriage yet scared of commitment appreciate this point.

Chapter 3
Information as Ruling Out Possibilities

Materialism's appeal these days comes largely from piggybacking on the success of science. Viewed as a philosophical position, however, it has deep flaws, which various philosophers and scholars have ably addressed.[1] Since my interest in this book is not so much to criticize materialism as to develop an information-theoretic alternative to it, I'll forgo recounting these counterarguments to materialism here. I want therefore next to turn to information as such. In everyday life, information is associated with intelligent agents who form statements to convey meaning. Accordingly, intelligent agents convey information to other intelligent agents by making meaningful statements within a system of language. Information, therefore, customarily presupposes intelligence, language, and semantics. That's quite a lot to presuppose, and it comes as no surprise if materialists think that matter constitutes a more parsimonious starting point for reality than information.[2]

---

[1] What I'm calling "materialism" is usually critiqued under the heading of "naturalism." Strictly speaking, naturalism is a doctrine asserting nature's completeness and immunity to any action outside nature (such action would be supernatural). As such, naturalism doesn't stipulate the precise form of nature. But in practice, naturalism tends to devolve into materialism because matter certainly seems an integral part of nature and nothing else seems particularly viable for a hard-nosed understanding of nature. Indeed, what else can there be to nature except matter? Energy, for instance, if not material, promises to become some sort of teleological vital force, which is inconsistent with the sobriety and rigor expected of naturalism. Naturalism is, after all, supposed to keep the world safe from the superstition of supernaturalism. For the deep conceptual problems facing materialism/naturalism, see Michael C. Rea, *World without Design: The Ontological Consequences of Naturalism* (Oxford: Oxford University Press, 2002); William Lane Craig and J.P. Moreland, eds., *Naturalism: A Critical Analysis* (London: Routledge, 2000); Phillip E. Johnson, *Reason in the Balance: The Case Against Naturalism in Science, Law and Education* (Downers Grove, Ill.: InterVarsity, 1995); Stewart Goetz and Charles Taliaferro, *Naturalism* (Grand Rapids, Mich.: Eerdmans, 2008); and Alvin Plantinga, *Where the Conflict Really Lies*.

[2] But note, the principle of parsimony is readily abused. No doubt, explanation should avoid invoking unnecessary or superfluous entities. But it must also be true to the thing it attempts to explain. As Einstein remarked, "It can scarcely be denied that the supreme goal of all theory is to make the irreducible basic elements as simple and as few as possible *without having to surrender the adequate representation of a single datum of experience*." (From

But, in fact, information can make do with fewer presuppositions and is less complicated than the picture just sketched. It's certainly true that intelligent agents are capable of relaying information among themselves by using language. But the core idea underlying information is quite a bit simpler. We can see this by examining human language use and noting an essential feature of it. Suppose Alice tells Bob, "It's raining outside or it's not raining outside." Alice has clearly made a statement and it clearly has a meaning. And yet, we would likely say that Alice hasn't really told Bob anything, that her statement is uninformative. Why? Because her statement is tautological. And why are tautologies a problem for conveying information? Because, by being necessarily true, they don't rule out anything. We don't need to be informed of tautologies because we can figure them out on our own. Bob could know it was either raining or not raining outside without being told so by Alice.

But what if instead Alice had told Bob, "It's raining outside." Again, Alice has made a statement and it has a meaning. But this time, if Bob had not checked on the weather, he would actually have learned something new, namely, that it's raining outside. In this case, he learns something new precisely because Alice's claim that it's raining outside ruled out the opposite claim, namely, that it's not raining outside. In this case, by telling Bob that it's raining and by ruling out that it's not raining, Alice has been informative (unlike the tautological case, where Alice was uninformative).

Now Alice could be still more informative. She might tell Bob, "It's raining outside at a rate of more than one inch an hour." What makes this statement more informative than the simple "It's raining outside" is not that the sentence used to make it is longer or richer in meaning, but that it rules out more possibilities. Indeed, "It's raining outside at a rate of more than one inch an hour or at a rate not exceeding one inch an hour" is longer and semantically richer than "It's raining outside at a rate of more than one inch an hour." But the former statement is far less informative than the latter. Indeed, the former statement is

---

Einstein's Herbert Spencer Lecture at Oxford, June 10, 1933, quoted in Alice Calaprice, *The Ultimate Quotable Einstein* [Princeton, N.J.: Princeton University Press, 2011], 384–5, emphasis added.) This is oft paraphrased as "Everything should be made as simple as possible, but not simpler," the latter being attributed to Einstein, but in that exact form likely to be apocryphal. In any case, the desideratum of parsimony needs always to be counterbalanced against a qualification like Einstein's, to wit, "without having to surrender the adequate representation of a single datum of experience." Insofar as explanation fails to account for some salient fact, it is incomplete and its parsimony can no longer rightly be regarded as an asset. Indeed, the key failing of materialism, as we shall see, is that its parsimony is purchased at the cost of misrepresenting reality.

merely as informative as the simple "It's raining outside." That's because both rule out exactly the same set of possibilities, namely, absence of rain. By contrast, "It's raining outside at a rate of more than one inch an hour" rules out not only absence of rain but also light and moderate rain.

In general, information is about realizing possibilities by ruling out others. Unless possibilities are ruled out, no information can be conveyed. To say "It's raining or it's not raining" is uninformative precisely because this statement rules out no possibilities. On the other hand, to say "It's raining" rules out the possibility "It's not raining" and therefore conveys information. Tautologies, because they cannot be false, can convey no information. Likewise, contradictions, because they cannot be true, can convey no information. We don't need to be informed of them because we can figure them out for ourselves. Information presupposes at least two live possibilities, at least one of which gets ruled out. Writing in the context of human communication, Robert Stalnaker put it this way: "To learn something, to acquire information, is to rule out possibilities. To understand the information conveyed in a communication is to know what possibilities would be excluded by its truth."[3]

Humans are not alone in their ability to rule out possibilities. Nature more generally (and humans are part of nature) is capable of ruling out possibilities. As an example of nature producing information, consider the moon's orbit. Because the moon assumes a stable orbit around Earth, seasons and tides are themselves stable. Yet it's possible, when the moon was formed and started cycling Earth, that it might have assumed an unstable orbit. In that case, Earth would be a very different place. In excluding certain unstable orbits to give the moon its present orbit, nature can therefore be said to have produced information. Nature produces information when it comes down on one side or the other of a contingency (an event is contingent if it is possible but not necessary, in other words, if it can happen but alternatives to it can also happen). In the case of the moon, nature could have come down on the side of an unstable orbit, but it didn't.

As another example of nature sorting among contingencies to produce information, consider natural selection. Natural selection does not so much select for adaptive advantages as rule out maladaptive disadvantages, excluding the latter from survival and reproduction and thus eliminating them from the evolutionary tree. Natural selection is in the business of ruling out possibilities, thereby producing information in the structures and organisms it has retained. An ongoing point of controversy in biology is the extent to which natural selection can generate increases in novel information needed to drive the

---

[3]   Robert Stalnaker, *Inquiry* (Cambridge, Mass.: MIT Press, 1984), 85.

evolution of life. Some see it as biology's primary source of information.[4] Others see its creative potential in producing information as quite limited.[5]

Not everyone accepts that nature, in the absence of intelligence or mind, can produce information. John Horgan, for instance, sees information as presupposing mind:

> The concept of information makes no sense in the absence of something to be informed—that is, a conscious observer capable of choice, or free will (sorry, I can't help it, free will is an obsession). If all the humans in the world vanished tomorrow, all the information would vanish, too. Lacking minds to surprise and change, books and televisions and computers would be as dumb as stumps and stones. This fact may seem crushingly obvious, but it seems to be overlooked by many information enthusiasts.[6]

Horgan is right in thus limiting information if (and this is a big if) information is inherently semantic, requiring minds to extract its meaning. But if information is inherently about contingency, ruling out some possibilities to realize others, then information could make sense in the absence of minds. Of course, one can take the view that nature is the product of mind, and thus that information can never wholly separate itself from mind. But in the dialectic with materialism, one needs a definition of information that materialists themselves can accept. Unlike Horgan's semantic conception of information, defining information in

---

4   Richard Dawkins, Kenneth Miller, and Thomas Schneider all fall within this camp. For the (supposed) information-creating power of natural selection, see Richard Dawkins, *The Blind Watchmaker: Why the Evidence of Evolution Reveals a Universe without Design* (New York: Norton, 1987), 47–50, where he describes his famous WEASEL experiment. See also Kenneth R. Miller, *Only a Theory: Evolution and the Battle for America's Soul* (New York: Viking, 2008), 77–8 and Thomas D. Schneider, "Evolution of Biological Information," *Nucleic Acids Research* 28(14) (2000): 2794–9.

5   Leaving aside intelligent design, well-considered criticisms of natural selection's power to generate biological information have been picking up steam. Consider, for instance, James Shapiro, *Evolution: A View from the 21st Century* (Upper Saddle River, N.J.: FT Press Science, 2011) as well as Susan Mazur, *The Altenberg 16: An Exposé of the Evolution Industry* (Berkeley, Calif.: North Atlantic Books, 2010). The ideas put forward in such books are thoroughly evolutionary and yet also post-Darwinian (rather than neo-Darwinian). In chapter 19 of this book I characterize the inherent limits facing natural selection as a mechanism for generating information.

6   John Horgan, "Why Information Can't Be the Basis of Reality," *Scientific American*, blog entry (March 7, 2011), http://blogs.scientificamerican.com/cross-check/2011/03/07/why-information-cant-be-the-basis-of-reality (last accessed June 5, 2013).

terms of contingency and ruling out possibilities is more metaphysically neutral, to say nothing of being more widely applicable.

Information, as we'll see, is relational and holistic. Matter, by contrast, is individualistic and isolative. With matter, it doesn't matter how many repetitions of it exist, at least not for its identity as a particular type of material object. If the universe, conceived in purely material terms, contains a few more or less electrons than it presently has, nothing will be fundamentally affected. Yes, material objects interact with other material objects. But material objects maintain their identity even as other material objects are added or removed.[7] This helps explain the materialist impulse to analyze matter into its ever finer constituents so that these constituents may then be considered individually. That's why particle accelerators are today's preeminent shrine to the cult of materialism. And that's why so much excitement exists at the time of this writing about the discovery of the Higgs boson at the Mecca of materialism, namely, CERN (the European Organization for Nuclear Research). Indeed, why else do materialists refer to the Higgs boson as "the God particle"?[8]

I'm being a bit facetious, but with the serious intent of underscoring the difference between information and matter. Information is a very different animal from matter. Matter is fundamentally a bottom-up affair. Whether one conceives of matter as particles, fields, strings, branes, or any other structured

---

[7] Quantum interactions seem to provide an exception to this isolative view of matter in that quantum theory can be construed as allowing instantaneous action at a distance, thus introducing a holism and connectedness to matter that is lacking from the conventional particulate accounts of matter (in which material interactions work exclusively by impact, repulsion, and attraction). Some thinkers see this feature of the quantum world as fundamentally changing and challenging the conventional isolative materialism. See, for instance, David Bohm, *Wholeness and the Implicate Order* (London: Routledge & Kegan Paul, 1980) and F. David Peat, *Synchronicity: The Bridge Between Matter and Mind* (New York: Bantam, 1987). The hope of such thinkers is that by embedding matter in a holistic quantum world, everything from consciousness to mystical experience can be recovered. In my view, this puts too much weight on the shoulders of quantum theory, which, by itself, does nothing to explain why the information in nature assumes the particular forms that it does (quantum theory is compatible with a completely uninteresting lifeless universe). In any case, hard-nosed materialists readily embrace quantum theory, seeing quantum effects as applying mainly at the micro level but getting averaged out at the macro level, thereby justifying the conventional view that material objects preserve their identity and integrity in isolation from other material objects.

[8] Nobelist Leon Lederman first referred to the Higgs boson as "the God particle" in a 1993 book: Leon Lederman and Dick Teresi, *The God Particle: If the Universe Is the Answer, What Is the Question?* (New York: Doubleday, 1993). To their credit, some physicists don't like this term, seeing it as misleading and sensationalistic.

bundles of stuff/energy, matter from a materialist vantage is properly understood in terms of such basic constituents, of which the world or reality is then simply an agglomeration. Materialism is essentially in the business of reconstitution, breaking reality down into its elemental parts and then building it back up. As an intellectual exercise, such a project is no doubt interesting. But one has to wonder whether what gets reconstituted is reality as such or a shadow of reality. The breakfast drink Tang broke down orange juice into a powder consisting of "orange juice solids," whatever these might be, and then reconstituted it. Yet Tang was never confused with real fresh orange juice. The material world, as conceived by materialists, however, is continually confused with reality as such.

But we're getting ahead of our story. Our focus here is on information, and the point to recognize is that information makes no sense as a bottom-up, break-it-into-elemental-parts-and-then-reconstitute-it affair. Information, I've said, is about ruling out possibilities. Yet information is not built out of individual possibilities as matter is built out of elemental material parts. In fact, the possibilities associated with information never admit a rock-bottom level of possibility or for that matter a sky-high level of possibility (provided, that is, we disregard tautologies and contradictions). Possibilities can always be refined or coarsened by increasing or decreasing the resolution with which we examine an object of inquiry.

Thus with information we can always, as it were, crank up the magnification on our microscope to discover increasingly fine possibilities. At the same time, with information we can always look through the wrong end of a telescope and find increasingly coarse or low-grained possibilities. "It's raining outside," for instance, can be refined to "It's raining at a rate of one inch an hour" or it can be coarsened to "It's wet outside." Unlike materialism, which sees a virtue in analysis, that is, in breaking matter into its fundamental constituents, from an information-theoretic vantage there is no virtue in breaking possibilities into more basic possibilities.

That's not to say possibilities cannot be analyzed or broken down into subsidiary possibilities (tossing an even number with a fair die can be analyzed into tossing a two, a four, or a six). But with information, the point is not to break down, and then break down further, and then break down still further until one reaches some rock-bottom level of analysis consisting entirely of basic elemental possibilities. Rather, the point is to find the right level of analysis at which to gain insight from an inquiry. If, for instance, one is playing craps, the right level of analysis looks at the top faces exhibited by a pair of dice. At this level of analysis, one doesn't try to keep track of which die is which (there's no need to distinguish the dice in craps), nor does one need to note the precise location where the dice land on the craps table. Such additional information is superfluous for the inquiry at hand.

Inquiry situates possibilities within a reference class of possibilities, with the reference class itself adapted to the inquiry. In the case of craps, for instance, the reference class is all possible tosses of a pair of dice, ignoring the order of the dice faces. Such an approach to possibilities is top down: possibilities only make sense within a larger reference class of possibilities. To be ontologically grounded, possibilities therefore need to play off of other possibilities. But what exactly are these possibilities? And what are these reference classes of possibilities? The next two chapters answer these questions.

Chapter 4

Possible Worlds

What are the possibilities that information alternately realizes or rules out? It is convenient to think of possibilities as existing in possible worlds and a world as consisting of all possibilities realized in it. In our world, the actual world, Barack Obama was reelected president of the United States in 2012, dinosaurs once ruled the Earth, and the Earth resides in a spiral galaxy, the Milky Way. But in other worlds, Mitt Romney defeated Obama in the 2012 election, dinosaurs never arose, and the Milky Way galaxy never formed. A world in which Romney defeated Obama would share more features with, and thus be in some sense closer to, our world than one lacking a Milky Way. And yet, incompatible worlds, however similar they may be to each other in some respects, do not intersect but are wholly separate—each possible world is complete unto itself. Individuation of possible worlds is thus quite different from individuation of matter. From the vantage of materialism, particles are the things most separated from each other but also the things that are most real. From the vantage of information, by contrast, worlds are the things most separated from each other and also the things that are most real.

A theme of this book is to trace how the concept of information turns the fundamental intuitions of materialism on its head. Materialism, as we've noted, is a bottom-up affair: one starts with matter at its most rudimentary (or as close as one can get there), and then builds everything up from there. Information, by contrast, is a top-down affair. Indeed, it cannot be otherwise. The animating principle of information is ruling out possibilities. Information is therefore fundamentally about diminution, about starting with more and delivering less. All things may be possible, but only a relative few are realized. So with information one needs to start at the other end, from the top and work down.

What is the top? The very top presumably would be the collection of all possible worlds, in which case the ultimate act of information would be to identify the actual world, the world we inhabit, to the exclusion of all other worlds. Philosophers and logicians who ponder such imponderables reach different conclusions here. As a Christian theist, I'm happy to regard the collection of all possible worlds as residing in the mind of God and then see

God, in an act of creation, as actualizing one world, ours, to the exclusion of others. To say I'm happy with this prospect is not to say I'm wedded to it or have a slamdunk argument for it. But it seems to me reasonable given my theological presuppositions.

Most theorists who deal with possible worlds, however, would not be happy with this approach since for them worlds are self-contained, and so any god or gods would have to reside inside a world and could not move freely outside or among them. This raises, however, the curious prospect for an infinite God capable of knowing and bringing into existence any particular world (a capacity with which the Judeo-Christian God is traditionally said to be endowed). If such a being is possible (some would even argue that such a being is necessary, existing in every possible world), then this being resides in at least one possible world. But such a world would then contain all possible worlds (even if only as conceptualizations in the mind of God) as well as a supreme being capable of thinking them and choosing among them, who then actualizes one of these possible worlds within the overarching possible world in which this being resides.[1] If, in the foundations of mathematics, sets that contain themselves raise profound conceptual difficulties (cf. Russell's paradox, according to which the set of all sets that do not contain themselves is inherently self-contradictory),[2] how much more so do worlds that contain deities capable of producing every world?

For the purposes of this book, our main focus will be on the actual world, and other worlds assume importance as they relate to the actual world. That does raise the question, however, about the relation between these other possible worlds and the actual world. Are all possible worlds as real as the actual world, as claimed by extreme modal realists, such as the late David Lewis, one of the

---

[1]   And what of the world actualized within this overarching world? It presumably also contains this supreme being, who then creates by ruling out possibilities. In consequence, a world that contains such a God raises the prospect of an infinite nesting of worlds, with an eternal recurrence of transcendence and immanence as God creates a world and then inhabits it. This is where the logic of divine omnipotence combined with possible-worlds metaphysics seems to run, though I personally remain unconvinced that there is much merit to such speculations. There may be a problem here with our conception of divine omnipotence, possible worlds, or both.

[2]   In Zermelo–Fraenkel set theory, the Axiom of Foundation is designed to block this possibility of sets containing themselves. See Kenneth Kunen, *Set Theory: An Introduction to Independence Proofs* (Amsterdam: Elsevier, 1980), ch. 3, which is devoted to well-founded sets. For Russell's paradox, see Michael Potter, *Set Theory and Its Philosophy: A Critical Introduction* (Oxford: Oxford University Press, 2004), secs. 2.3 and 2.4, which are devoted specifically to this paradox.

best-known philosophers to study possible-worlds semantics?[3] In that case, is the only thing distinguishing our world from the others that we happen to inhabit this one? Or are these other possible worlds merely logical constructs consisting of maximally inclusive, logically consistent collections of statements (thus capable of fully characterizing an ontologically real other world if it should exist)? The important thing for our purposes is that these other worlds, whatever their ontological status, serve as useful tools for inquiry into the actual world. As we'll see, they supply conceptual grids for understanding the actual world.

Ordinarily, when we refer to "the world," we mean the actual world. But what is the world, the actual world? When we speak of the world, many of us think in cosmological terms, equating the world with the universe. (Recall Carl Sagan's famous remark, "The Cosmos is all that is or ever was or ever will be."[4]) For our purposes, however, it is best to distinguish the world from the cosmos or universe. By the universe, we usually mean nature in its material manifestation as governed by the laws of physics and chemistry. But who's to say this characterization of the world covers everything that's real or actual? By the world, or actual world, I'll therefore follow what philosophers who study possible-worlds semantics mean by it, namely, the totality of all actual states of affairs (past, present, future, timeless), whatever these may be. Unlike materialism, which prejudices our view of reality, approaching the world in this way has the advantage of allowing reality to be whatever it is.

David Lewis described the actual world as "the way things are, at its most inclusive."[5] The actual world leaves out nothing that is the case, regardless of time or place. This way of characterizing the actual world, however, readily calls to mind other possible worlds because, as Lewis adds, "things might have been different, in ever so many ways."[6] The actual world is all that is the case, and other possible worlds describe counterfactual states of affairs that might have been the case but, because they're counterfactual, are not. Thus, in the actual world, Ronald Reagan was elected president in 1980, whereas in another possible world Jimmy Carter was reelected president that same year.

Unlike materialism, which makes matter the starting point for inquiry, information makes the actual world and the possibilities associated with it the

---

3   David Lewis, *On the Plurality of Worlds* (Oxford: Blackwell, 1986). The first sentence of this book (p. vii) reads, "This book defends modal realism: the thesis that the world we are part of is but one of a plurality of worlds, and that we who inhabit this world are only a few out of all the inhabitants of all the worlds."

4   Carl Sagan, *Cosmos* (New York: Random House, 1980), 1.

5   Lewis, *Plurality of Worlds*, 1.

6   Ibid.

starting point. Information thus allows the world to be whatever it is. Materialism, by contrast, prejudges the world by confining inquiry to paths that ensure everything is conceptualized in material terms. Information therefore provides a more open-ended starting point for inquiry than materialism. We know that a world exists and that it realizes certain possibilities to the exclusion of others, thereby generating information. The question whether the world is a purely material place is logically downstream from whether there is a world at all and whether it generates information. For materialists, matter is the thing they are most sure of. For Cartesians, individual minds are the thing they are most sure of ("I think therefore I am"). For informational realists like me, the actual world, conceived as a cauldron of possibilities, is the thing they are most sure of.

Note that starting inquiry with the actual world rather than with matter doesn't close the door to any view of reality, not even to materialism. Subsequent inquiry may convince us that matter really is all there is to the actual world. But by giving primacy to the actual world rather than to our preconceptions of it, we refuse, rightly, to give any particular view of reality a privileged position. Privilege must be earned rather than arrogated. Thus, by making the actual world rather than matter our starting point, we oblige any particular view of reality to earn its standing based on evidential merit and theoretical insight.

If, as I'm suggesting, information is produced only as possibilities are ruled out, an interesting consequence follows: the ultimate act of information must then consist in separating out the actual world from among all possible worlds. Conceiving of, much less performing, such an act of information is certainly beyond the remit of finite rational agents like ourselves. Nonetheless, finite rational agents are well able to manage subsidiary acts of information as they attempt to understand and influence the world. In practice, we don't try to understand the totality of the actual world as it relates to the totality of all other possible worlds. Rather, we try to understand some aspect of the actual world as it relates to certain limited possibilities residing in other possible worlds. Thus, instead of focusing on the world as a whole, we focus on much more limited informational contexts such as the American presidential election, in which case the informational task is to identify the candidate who was elected as well as those who might have been elected but were not. It's such subsidiary acts of information to which we now turn in formulating a general account of information.

Chapter 5

Matrices of Possibility

Because the actual world is so large and unwieldy, we never grasp it in its entirety. Instead, we only grasp certain limited aspects of it. This we do by situating aspects of the world within *matrices of possibility*. These form conceptual grids for our inquiries about the world. A matrix of possibility (we'll also refer to it as a *possibility matrix*, a *matrix of possibilities*, or a *matrix of possible outcomes*) is a collection of possibilities relevant to an inquiry. It provides a window on the actual world. Just as a window always has a frame, and thus views some things but not others, so a matrix of possibility limits inquiry to some aspects of the world, excluding others.[1]

Choosing a matrix of possibility for a given inquiry is itself an informational act, identifying one matrix, ruling out the rest, and thereby exemplifying the inclusion–exclusion characteristic of information. Choosing a matrix of possibility constrains inquiry, which is a good thing because inquiries must be constrained if they are to advance understanding (a wholly open-ended inquiry lacks a foothold, cannot gain traction, and so goes nowhere). Inquiry by its very nature requires constraint or limitation, looking at "this" to the exclusion of "that," throwing some things into question by holding other things constant. Matrices of possibility are implicit in all human inquiry, limiting the possibilities any given inquiry may consider.

Because information is produced as some possibilities are realized to the exclusion of others, information is fundamentally relational: the possibilities associated with information exist only in relation to other possibilities, and thus within a reference class of possibilities. From an information-theoretic point of view, individual possibilities make no sense on their own but only as part of a reference class. We conceive of such a reference class as a matrix in which some possibilities are born whereas others never see the light of day. The very word

---

[1] Another way to think of a possibility matrix is as a map. A map gives a local representation of some aspect of the Earth at a given level of resolution. Different maps represent different locales or the same locale at different levels of resolution.

matrix, from its Latin etymology, denotes womb, source, or origin. Information, as conceived in this book, comes to birth within such matrices of possibility.[2]

In practice, a matrix of possibility is just a collection of possibilities identified to pursue a given inquiry. To see how this works (and what may go wrong), consider an example from Ivar Ekeland's *The Broken Dice*.[3] Ekeland describes how in the Middle Ages the king of Norway and the king of Sweden cast a pair of dice to decide who would own a settlement on the Island of Hising. High sum was to determine the winner. The king of Sweden went first and rolled double sixes. He was therefore off to a great start, and it would seem that the king of Norway could at best tie him. With six faces on a die and faces numbered 1 to 6, the sum of any pair of faces from the dice could total no less than 2 and no more than 12. The matrix of possible outcomes for the pair of dice could therefore be represented by the set {2, 3, 4, 5, 6, 7, 8, 9, 10, 11, 12}.

This matrix would therefore appear to be the relevant one for characterizing the game the kings were playing. Moreover, because the king of Sweden had just rolled the best possible outcome from this matrix, namely 12, the smart money would be on the Hising settlement going to Sweden. What happened next was therefore remarkable: "Thereupon Olaf, king of Norway, cast the dice, and one six showed on one of them, but the other split in two, so that six and one turned up; and so he took possession of the settlement."[4] Because in this game higher sums beat lower sums, thirteen (= 6 + 6 + 1) beats twelve (= 6 + 6), and so the king of Norway won. Typically, any game with a pair of dice reckons with at most a pair of faces showing on any throw. Given this constraint, the relevant matrix of possible sums for a pair of dice faces will be {2, 3, 4, 5, 6, 7, 8, 9, 10, 11, 12}. Yet given the possibility of a die splitting in two and exhibiting two faces, the matrix of possible sums would have to be expanded to include at least {2, 3, 4, 5, 6, 7, 8, 9, 10, 11, 12, 13} and possibly even more.

---

[2]   What I'm calling a possibility matrix, mathematicians and engineers are more inclined to call a possibility space. What, then, is gained by introducing this matrix terminology? The reference to a matrix here is metaphorical, and yet metaphors can be quite powerful and illuminating in science. Just about anything in mathematics is a space or set, and so to describe something as a space or set is unilluminating. But information, as I'm developing it, is real, indeed the most real stuff we ever encounter. Now information, as it emerges in the world, always involves a kind of yin and yang, an active principle (yang) that causes a possibility to be actualized against the backdrop of a passive principle (yin) in which possibilities exist merely as potential. The matrix metaphor captures this deep truth about information.

[3]   Ivar Ekeland, *The Broken Dice* (Chicago, Ill.: University of Chicago Press, 1993).

[4]   Ibid., 3.

Extraordinary possibilities, precisely because they are extraordinary, are often omitted from the matrix of possibility used in an information-theoretic analysis. Such omissions usually don't impair an information-theoretic analysis because extraordinary events are, by their nature, rare and so tend not to happen, placing them outside the window on reality provided by any matrix of possibility that we are likely to employ. This example of the two kings, however, points up the importance of identifying all relevant possibilities in an information-theoretic analysis and exercising caution in just what possibilities we regard as extraordinary. The king of Sweden was confident that the relevant matrix of possibility comprised {2, 3, 4, 5, 6, 7, 8, 9, 10, 11, 12}. But he omitted what turned out to be a crucial possibility.

In general, we are safer erring on the side of plenty rather than parsimony in assigning possibilities to a matrix. If we err on the side of parsimony, we are likely to omit possibilities that might actually arise, thereby undercutting our information-theoretic analysis (as happened to the king of Sweden, though it seems he can hardly be faulted for his omission). Occam's razor is, as it turns out, a bad rule of thumb for dealing with matrices of possibility. Occam's razor, known in Latin as the *lex parsimoniae*, counsels simplicity in explanation, introducing no more entities than needed to adequately explain some object of inquiry. But with a matrix of possibility, we want to be sure to capture the possibility that does obtain, and so we do better by being generous in the possibilities we take to be relevant.

There is no downside here in preferring plenty to parsimony in setting up a possibility matrix. Because information is about ruling out possibilities, far-fetched possibilities can always be dismissed later in an information-theoretic analysis. Indeed, a matrix of possibility that is richer than we are likely to need is easily handled by focusing on the relevant subclass of possibilities that we regard as "live" or "realistic."[5] Because no information-theoretic analysis can be successful if it omits the possibility that is in fact realized, it's best that the matrix of possibility on which this analysis depends include all relevant, even marginally relevant, possibilities from the start. In contrast to Occam's *lex parsimoniae*, information theory counsels a *lex plenitudinis* in constructing possibility matrices.

Of course, one can go overboard in expanding a matrix of possibility, throwing in too much, even the kitchen sink. A matrix of possibility needs to be full or complete in the sense that it omits no marginally plausible possibility.

---

[5]   Probabilistically speaking, this is a matter of putting all the weight of probability on these live possibilities.

But at some point, possibilities become so remote or far-fetched that they are best not included in the relevant matrix of possibility. Where to draw the line? It is important to understand that a matrix of possibility, as a tool of inquiry, never forces itself on us. Rather, it is we, human inquirers, who must identify the matrix appropriate to our inquiries. This identification of an appropriate matrix of possibility will depend on our background knowledge, assumptions about the world, values, local circumstances, and interests—in short, our context of inquiry. Our context of inquiry determines what possibilities we regard as plausible. In turn, plausibility determines what possibilities we take seriously enough to include in our matrix of possibility.

For the king of Sweden, a pair of dice could show no more than two faces. Given his context of inquiry, the only plausible possibilities for the sum of the faces of a pair of dice would be {2, 3, 4, 5, 6, 7, 8, 9, 10, 11, 12}. This was the matrix of possibility with which the king of Sweden reckoned. The king of Norway, on the other hand, King Olaf Haraldsson, was on his way to becoming a canonized saint of the Roman Catholic Church. Supposedly endued with miraculous powers, he would not be bound to this set of possibilities. Dice splitting in two with faces totaling more than twelve would be entirely plausible within the supernatural world of medieval saints. Thus King Olaf's matrix of possibility would include at least {2, 3, 4, 5, 6, 7, 8, 9, 10, 11, 12, 13}.

Context determines what possibilities we regard as plausible (or not unduly extraordinary), and plausibility determines what possibilities we include in our matrix of possibility. Shift the context, and our matrix will shift accordingly. Within a Newtonian context, freely moving objects proceed in straight lines because spacetime is Euclidean, and thus has zero curvature. Within a relativistic context, freely moving objects proceed along curved geodesics because gravity bends spacetime. This is not to say that all contexts are created equal. Einsteinian relativity corrects serious defects in Newtonian mechanics and thus provides a more adequate matrix of possible motions for objects moving in the actual world. Nonetheless, given a Newtonian context of inquiry, it is entirely appropriate to omit curved paths for freely moving objects since such paths find no place in Newton's theory. In fact, that's precisely what we do in an introductory physics course—we begin by teaching Newton and only later do we bring in Einstein.

A context of inquiry can be problematic in the sense that its aims, methods, and presuppositions may be faulty (Newtonian mechanics mistakenly assumed that space was straight and time absolute). Even so, we can still talk about a matrix of possibility being appropriate or inappropriate to that context. For the king of Sweden, rolling a pair of dice and taking their sum, the matrix represented by

{2, 3, 4, 5, 6, 7, 8, 9, 10, 11, 12} was entirely appropriate. To be sure, the king of Sweden did not reckon with the expanded matrix that was required because his gaming partner, the king of Norway, happened to be a Christian saint blessed with miraculous powers. On the other hand, the king of Sweden would have been seriously misguided to omit one or more of the outcomes from the matrix that he actually chose. Indeed, any such truncated matrix (say, one omitting a dice roll totaling 7) would have been inappropriate to the king of Sweden's context of inquiry. In identifying a matrix of possibility for an information-theoretic analysis, we therefore need to be clear about our context of inquiry and we need to assess the appropriateness of the matrix to that context. Moreover, we want to err on the side of plenitude and include as many possibilities as might plausibly obtain within that context.

In being as inclusive as possible with a matrix of possibility, we can do no better than include all the possibilities that we can for now conceive. What we can for now conceive, however, is not fixed, and what we can conceive down the road may greatly exceed what we can for now conceive. A matrix of possibility may therefore be just fine for a certain line of inquiry at a given time, but at a future time we may have to add new possibilities to it. The prospect of a matrix having to be expanded, however, does not vitiate its present role in inquiry. Possibilities identified and therefore information derived from an earlier matrix remain valid with the addition of new possibilities. In particular, adding new possibilities to a matrix does nothing to diminish the amount of information associated with already realized possibilities.

To see this, consider that the king of Sweden's roll of double sixes continued to make perfect sense in light of the king of Norway's miraculous roll of double sixes plus a one. Moreover, the amount of information associated with a possibility from an earlier matrix can only increase as new possibilities are added. This is because a possibility realized from an earlier matrix rules out not only the remaining possibilities in it but also the new possibilities subsequently added. This suggests that even though the advance of knowledge need not be cumulative (in science a hypothesis or theory can fail to build logically on a previous one—Newtonian mechanics and Einsteinian relativity are, for instance, logically inconsistent), the advance of information may well be cumulative (information gained about the world could continually expand, with new matrices of possibility subsuming the old).[6]

Before closing this chapter, I need to define what these possibilities are that make up a matrix of possibility. For the king of Sweden's context of inquiry, I

---

[6] Compare logical positivism and also Kuhn's *Structure of Scientific Revolutions*.

represented his matrix of possibility as the set {2, 3, 4, 5, 6, 7, 8, 9, 10, 11, 12}. But if this set is a representation, what is it a representation of? And what do the individual members of this set, the individual possibilities, represent? The possibilities that make up a matrix of possibility are, by definition, equivalence classes of possible worlds.[7] To illustrate what this means in the example of the two kings, take the set {2, 3, 4, 5, 6, 7, 8, 9, 10, 11, 12}, but now let each number represent all possible worlds in which the king of Sweden played his game of dice with the king of Norway and rolled that number.

Thus, the number 12 represents all possible worlds in which the king of Sweden played this game and rolled a 12. These possible worlds form an equivalence class because they are each equivalent with respect to the king of Sweden rolling a 12. Note that this equivalence class contains the actual world since the king of Sweden actually did roll a 12 (I'm assuming, for the sake of illustration, that the story is true). But this equivalence class also contains counterfactual worlds, such as a world in which the king of Norway rolled an 11 and thus lost the settlement on the Isle of Hising. With the set {2, 3, 4, 5, 6, 7, 8, 9, 10, 11, 12}, in representing the king of Sweden's matrix of possibility, the number 11 represents all possible worlds in which the king of Sweden rolled an 11 with two dice in his game against the king of Norway. These are all counterfactual worlds since the actual world is not among them (the actual world, we are assuming, is one where the king of Sweden rolled a 12).

In possible-worlds semantics, a proposition is identified with all the possible worlds in which the proposition is true.[8] In the two kings example, the numbers in the set {2, 3, 4, 5, 6, 7, 8, 9, 10, 11, 12} therefore represent the possible worlds in which the following propositions are true: "The king of Sweden rolled a 2 against the king of Norway," "The king of Sweden rolled a 3 against the king of Norway," etc. Thus the proposition "The king of Sweden rolled a 7 against

---

[7] For a precise definition of equivalence classes, see an introductory text on set theory, such as Paul Halmos, *Naive Set Theory* (New York: Springer, 1974), 28. For our purposes it is enough to think of an equivalence class as a collection of items that are all essentially the same with respect to some property and to see different equivalence classes as varying with respect to that property and not overlapping. Equivalence classes are always mutually exclusive, though they need not be exhaustive.

[8] David Lewis writes: "I identify propositions with certain properties—namely, with those that are instantiated only by entire possible worlds. Then if properties generally are the sets of their instances, a proposition is a set of possible worlds. A proposition is said to *hold* at a world, or to be *true at* a world. The proposition is the same thing as the property of being a world where that proposition holds; and that is the same thing as the set of worlds where that proposition holds. A proposition holds at just those worlds that are members of it." Lewis, *Plurality of Worlds*, 53–4, emphasis in original.

the king of Norway" coincides with the equivalence class of all possible worlds where the king of Sweden rolled a combined total of 7 in his game of dice against the king of Norway.

A detailed logical apparatus for possible-worlds semantics and quantified modal logic exists with which one can formalize the preceding treatment of possibility matrices.[9] For our purposes, however, it is enough to treat these matrices as the most convenient sets we can find for representing these equivalence classes of possibilities (or the propositions that delineate these classes). Thus, in the sequel, we shall treat a set like {2, 3, 4, 5, 6, 7, 8, 9, 10, 11, 12} as a possibility matrix characterizing the dice rolling of the king of Sweden even though, technically speaking, the actual matrix consists of mutually exclusive (though not necessarily exhaustive) equivalence classes of possible worlds.

To sum up, as finite rational agents trying to understand the actual world, we consider possibilities in relation to other possibilities, and these, taken jointly, form what we call a matrix of possibility. A matrix of possibility consists of possibilities, possibilities that themselves consist of equivalence classes of possible worlds. Matrices of possibility form the conceptual grids that we overlay on the actual world to understand it.

---

[9]   See, for instance, Nino B. Cocchiarella and Max A. Freund, *Modal Logic: An Introduction to Its Syntax and Semantics* (Oxford: Oxford University Press, 2008).

Chapter 6

Measuring Information

Information is produced as certain possibilities are realized to the exclusion of others within a matrix of possibility. Moreover, the greater the number of possibilities that get ruled out, the greater the amount of information that gets produced (recall chapter 4). It follows that information can be measured. Fred Dretske puts it this way: "Information theory identifies the amount of information associated with, or generated by, the occurrence of an event (or the realization of a state of affairs) with the reduction in uncertainty, the elimination of possibilities, represented by that event or state of affairs."[1]

Although this observation is crucial for formulating a precise measure of information, the most obvious measure of information suggested by it does not work. That measure would be simply to count the number of possibilities that were eliminated and present that number as a measure of information. The problem is that such a simple enumeration of eliminated possibilities tells us nothing about how those possibilities were individuated in the first place. Depending on how possibilities are individuated, the number of possibilities associated with a given inquiry can change dramatically, as will any measure of information based on that number.

Consider, for instance, the following individuation of poker hands: RF (royal flush) and not-RF (not a royal flush, i.e., all other five-card hands). There's a matrix of possibility that consists of RF and not-RF. And to learn that either of these possibilities was realized to the exclusion of the other is to gain information. Yet, to learn that something other than a royal flush was dealt (i.e., not-RF) is clearly to acquire less information than to learn that a royal flush was dealt (i.e., RF). A royal flush is highly specific. We acquire a lot of information when we learn that a royal flush was dealt. On the other hand, we acquire hardly any information when we learn that something other than a royal flush was dealt. Most poker hands are not royal flushes, and we expect not to be dealt them. Nevertheless, if our measure of information is simply an enumeration of

---

[1] Fred Dretske, *Knowledge and the Flow of Information* (Cambridge, Mass.: MIT Press, 1981), 4.

eliminated possibilities, the same numerical value would have to be assigned in both instances since in each a single possibility is eliminated.

It follows that how we measure information needs to be independent of how we individuate the possibilities that make up our possibility matrices. The way to do this is not simply to count possibilities but to assign probabilities to possibilities. For a thoroughly shuffled deck of cards, the probability of being dealt a royal flush (i.e., RF) is approximately .000002 whereas the probability of being dealt anything other than a royal flush (i.e., not-RF) is approximately .999998.[2] Smaller probability therefore signifies not less but more information. Even so, probabilities are not information measures. In the remainder of this chapter, I will describe how probabilities are transformed into information measures, and how information measures are to be properly interpreted. Nonmathematically inclined readers may find this material tough sledding and want to skip it, referring back to it as needed; or they may simply bear in mind that smaller probability signifies greater information, and leave it at that.

Although probabilities distinguish possibilities by the amount of information they contain, probabilities are an inconvenient way to measure information. There are two reasons for this. First, the scaling and directionality of the numbers assigned by probabilities needs to be recalibrated. We are clearly acquiring more information when we learn someone was dealt a royal flush than when we learn someone was not dealt a royal flush. And yet the probability of being dealt a royal flush (i.e., .000002) is minuscule compared to the probability of being dealt something other than a royal flush (i.e., .999998). Smaller probabilities signify more information, not less.

The second reason probabilities are inconvenient for measuring information is that they are multiplicative rather than additive. If we learn that Alice was dealt a royal flush playing poker at one casino and that Bob was dealt a royal flush playing poker at another, the probability that both Alice and Bob were dealt royal flushes is the product of the individual probabilities. On the other hand, it is convenient for information to be measured additively so that the measure of information assigned to Alice and Bob jointly being dealt royal flushes equals the measure of information assigned to Alice being dealt a royal flush plus the measure of information assigned to Bob being dealt a royal flush. There is a straightforward mathematical way to transform probabilities that circumvents both these difficulties, namely, to apply a negative logarithm to the probabilities. Applying a negative logarithm assigns more information to less probability and,

---

[2]   Websites giving poker odds are widespread. See, for instance, http://mathworld.wolfram.com/Poker.html (last accessed May 22, 2013).

Measuring Information 39

because the logarithm of a product is the sum of the logarithms, transforms multiplicative probability measures into additive information measures.

In deference to communication theorists, it is customary, when logarithmically transforming probability to information, to use the logarithm to the base 2. The rationale for this choice of logarithmic base is as follows: The most convenient way for communication theorists to represent and measure information is in terms of bits (binary digits), in other words, as a sequence of 0s and 1s. Indeed, any message sent across a communication channel can be viewed as a sequence of 0s and 1s. For instance, the UTF-8 code (UTF-8 = Universal Character Set Transformation Format, 8-bit) uses sequences of 0s and 1s to represent the characters on a typewriter, with whole words and sentences in turn represented as sequences of such sequences.

All electronic communication may thus be reduced to the transmission of sequences of 0s and 1s. Given this reduction, the obvious way for communication theorists to measure information is in the number of bits transmitted across a communication channel. And since the negative logarithm to the base 2 of a probability corresponds to the average number of bits needed to identify an event of that probability, the logarithm to the base 2 is the canonical logarithm for communication theorists. Thus, we define the measure of information associated with an event of probability p as $-\log_2 p$.[3]

To see that this information measure is additive, return to the example of Alice being dealt a royal flush playing poker at one casino and Bob being dealt a royal flush playing poker at another. Let us call the first event A and the second B. Since randomly dealt poker hands are probabilistically independent, the probability of A and B taken jointly equals the product of the probabilities of A and B taken individually. In symbols, $\mathbf{P}(A\&B) = \mathbf{P}(A) \times \mathbf{P}(B)$.[4] Given that information is a logarithmic transformation of probability, we therefore define the amount of information in an arbitrary event E as $\mathbf{I}(E) = -\log_2 \mathbf{P}(E)$. It then follows that $\mathbf{P}(A\&B) = \mathbf{P}(A) \times \mathbf{P}(B)$ if and only if $\mathbf{I}(A\&B) = \mathbf{I}(A) + \mathbf{I}(B)$. Since in the example of Alice and Bob $\mathbf{P}(A) = \mathbf{P}(B) \approx .000002$, $\mathbf{I}(A) = \mathbf{I}(B) \approx 19$, and $\mathbf{I}(A\&B) = \mathbf{I}(A) + \mathbf{I}(B) \approx 19 + 19 = 38$.[5] Thus, the amount of information inherent in Alice and Bob jointly obtaining royal flushes is 38 bits.

When, as in the last example, events are probabilistically independent, information measures exhibit additivity. On the other hand, if events are

[3] Claude Shannon and Warren Weaver, *The Mathematical Theory of Communication* (Urbana, Ill.: University of Illinois Press, 1949), 32.

[4] Note that within a set-theoretic context we interpret the conjunction $A\&B$ as the intersection $A\cap B$.

[5] I'm using "$\approx$" to represent approximate equality.

correlated, information measures can exhibit nonadditivity. To see how this might happen, consider a different example in which Alice and Bob together toss a coin five times. Alice observes the first four tosses but is distracted, and so fails to note the fifth toss. At the same time, Bob fails to note the first toss, but observes the last four tosses. Let us say the actual sequence of tosses is 11001 (1 = heads, 0 = tails). Thus Alice observes 1100* and Bob observes *1001 (asterisks denote missed coin tosses). Let A denote the first observation, B the second. It follows that the amount of information in A&B is the amount of information in the complete sequence 11001, namely, 5 bits. On the other hand, the amount of information in A alone is the amount of information in the incomplete sequence 1100*, namely 4 bits. Similarly, the amount of information in B alone is the amount of information in the incomplete sequence *1001, also 4 bits. This time information does not add up: $5 = \mathbf{I}(A\&B) \neq \mathbf{I}(A) + \mathbf{I}(B) = 4 + 4 = 8$.

In this example, A and B are correlated. Alice knows all but the last bit of information in the complete sequence 11001. Thus when Bob gives her the incomplete sequence *1001, all Alice really learns is the last bit in this sequence. Similarly, Bob knows all but the first bit of information in the complete sequence 11001. Thus when Alice gives him the incomplete sequence 1100*, all Bob really learns is the first bit in this sequence. What appears to be four bits of information actually ends up being only one bit of information once Alice and Bob factor in their prior information.

All of this can be formalized in terms of conditional probability and conditional information. Thus, if we let $\mathbf{P}(B|A)$ denote the conditional probability of B given A (= $\mathbf{P}(B\&A)/\mathbf{P}(A)$), we can define the conditional information of B given A as equal to $-\log_2\mathbf{P}(B|A)$ and denote it by $\mathbf{I}(B|A)$. In the last example, $\mathbf{I}(B|A)$ signifies the amount of information in Bob's observation once Alice's observation is taken into account. This, as we just saw, is 1 bit. The mathematics confirms this: $5 = \mathbf{I}(A\&B) = \mathbf{I}(A) + \mathbf{I}(B|A) = 4 + 1$. Conditional information shows that there is no more information in two copies of Shakespeare's *Hamlet* than in a single copy.[6]

For our purposes, this is all we need to know about measuring or quantifying information.

---

[6]   Conditional information provides a rudimentary similarity measure for items of information. Paul Vitányi's *information distance* provides a deeper measure in this regard (it is, for instance, useful for identifying plagiarism). See Paul M.B. Vitányi, Frank Balbach, Rudi L. Cilibrasi, and Ming Li, "Normalized Information Distance," in F. Emmert-Streib and M. Dehmer, eds., *Information Theory and Statistical Learning* (New York, N.Y.: Springer, 2009), 45–82.

Chapter 7

Information Theory

When mathematicians and engineers talk of "information theory," they usually have in mind either Shannon's or Kolmogorov's theory of information (the latter also being referred to as "algorithmic information theory"). We'll examine both theories in this chapter. Shannon's theory of information attempts to characterize the transmission of character strings across a communication channel where the characters derive from a finite fixed alphabet (such an alphabet can include numerals, e.g., an alphanumeric character set). The alphabet is assumed to have at least two distinct characters. In case there are exactly two characters, these are typically represented by "0" and "1," and the sequences derived from them are referred to as "bit strings." It turns out that any finite fixed alphabet with n characters can be represented with bit strings of length k provided that $n \leq 2^k$. In fact, all of modern computation encodes the alphanumeric characters on our keyboards in terms of bits (cf. Unicode and the older ASCII).[1]

In the Shannon theory, the matrix of possibility from which information gets produced comprises the different character strings from the relevant alphabet. To convey information within the Shannon theory is therefore to identify a character string within this matrix of possibilities and then send that string across the communication channel. In this way, a possibility is identified, others are ruled out, and information is produced (in exactly the inclusion–exclusion sense of information described in earlier chapters).

---

[1]   Note that alphabets with only a single character can also transmit information, but the mode of transmission here is very cumbersome. With only one character in the alphabet, information is transmitted by counting the number of times that alphabetic character is transmitted (i.e., if the one alphabetic character in question is "x," then all communications have the form "x" or "xx" or "xxx" or "xxxx" ...). To convey information a communication channel must allow a multiplicity of distinct possible signals, any one of which might be sent. This is possible with a unary code, but extremely inefficient. What takes a million characters in unary requires only 20 characters in binary (that is, using bit strings). A billion characters in unary requires only 30 characters in binary. In general, the reduction in number of characters when translating from unary to binary is given by the logarithm to the base 2 (the logarithm to the base 2 of a million is 20 and of a billion is 30).

If the matrix of possible character strings is huge (as it typically is), identifying a single string will exclude a vast number of possibilities and thereby produce a huge amount of information. Theoretical interest in Shannon's theory lies in quantifying the information in such character strings, identifying their statistical properties when they are sent across a noisy communication channel (noise can be represented by a stochastic process that disrupts the strings in statistically well-defined ways), preserving the strings despite the presence of noise (as in the theory of error-correcting codes), and transforming the strings into other strings to maintain their security (as in cryptography).

Shannon's theory starts out as a syntactic theory, focused on combining characters in sequence. Its possibility matrices are therefore composed of character strings from a fixed alphabet. Nonetheless, it readily assumes the form of a statistical theory once one notes that characters (as well as combinations of characters) from the alphabet often have different probabilities of occurrence. For instance, the letters from our ordinary alphabet occur with widely varying frequencies in different languages. Thus, in English, the letter *e* occurs roughly 12 percent of the time, the letter *q* occurs less than 1 percent of the time, and *u* follows *q* with probability one. Such probabilities in turn regulate the quantity of information any given string can convey (see the previous chapter on measuring information).

It is easily shown mathematically that character strings will, on average, convey maximal information if and only if all the letters in the alphabet are equally probable and probabilistically independent (i.e., all letters have the same probability, and the probability of a given letter is unaffected by the occurrence of letters elsewhere in the string).[2] This average of information, denoted by **H**, is called the *entropy* associated with the alphabet. Its precise definition need not detain us here, but it is interesting to note that this information-theoretic entropy measure is mathematically identical to the Maxwell–Boltzmann–Gibbs entropy from statistical mechanics. To make this connection between the Shannon theory and statistical mechanics, alphabetic character strings need to be interpreted as a partition of phase space and the probabilities of occurrence of those character strings in transmission across communication channels need to be interpreted as the probabilities of particles located in those corresponding partition elements.[3] This way of connecting information theory and statistical

---

[2]   Fazlollah M. Reza, *An Introduction to Information Theory* (1961; reprinted New York: Dover, 1994), 83.

[3]   See Hubert Yockey, *Information Theory and Molecular Biology* (Cambridge: Cambridge University Press, 1992), 66–7, but note the errors in formulas 2.27 and 2.28.

mechanics seems quite natural, suggesting that information is getting at something very basic in physical reality.

Like the Shannon theory, the Kolmogorov theory of information incorporates both syntactics and statistics. Where it differs from the Shannon theory is in adding computability. The Kolmogorov theory sits at the intersection of probability theory and computer science. Also known as algorithmic information theory, this theory attempts to characterize what makes a bit string random. Probability theory by itself cannot distinguish bit strings of identical length: if we think of bit strings as sequences of coin tosses ("1" for heads and "0" for tails), then any sequence of n flips has the same probability of occurrence, namely, 1 in 2^n. For example, take the following two sequences of 20 coin tosses: "11111111111111111111" and "10011010101101000101." We regard the first of these as nonrandom and the second random (or at least more random than the first). But as coin tosses, both are equally improbable, having a probability of about one in a million.

Ascribing randomness to a bit string thus requires more than just probability (or improbability) of the string. But what more? According to algorithmic information theory, a bit string is random to the degree that it is incompressible. To make sense of this intuition mathematically, Kolmogorov supplemented probability theory with some ideas from recursion theory, a subfield of mathematical logic that provides the theoretical underpinnings for computation and generally is considered quite separate from probability theory.[4] What he said was that a string of 0s and 1s becomes increasingly random as the shortest computer program that generates the string increases in length.

Since computer programs are themselves encoded as strings of 0s and 1s, we can think of a computer program as a redescription of a sequence of coin tosses. The shorter the redescription, the more a given bit string can be compressed, and therefore the less random it is. Sequences like "11111111111111111111" are less random because they can be redescribed with very short computer programs of the sort "Repeat 1." Sequences like "10110011101101000101," by contrast, which exhibit no obvious pattern, are more random because they can't be redescribed with short computer programs. It is a combinatorial fact that for the vast majority of sequences of 0s and 1s, their computational redescriptions are no shorter than the original sequences themselves.[5] Moreover, since any sequence

---

[4]   See Hartley Rogers Jr., *Theory of Recursive Functions and Effective Computability* (1967; reprinted Cambridge, Mass.: MIT Press, 1987).

[5]   Combinatorics is the mathematics of counting. We usually think of counting as simply laying out a collection of objects in sequence and then doing a straightforward enumeration, saying "1" for the first item in the sequence, "2" for the next, and continuing on

can always be computationally redescribed in terms of itself, most sequences are in fact maximally random in the sense of being algorithmically incompressible. Thus most coin tosses are random in the Kolmogorov sense.

The length of the shortest computer program that produces a given bit string is its Kolmogorov or algorithmic complexity. The lower this number, the less random the bit string. How does algorithmic information theory connect to both the Shannon theory and the more general account of information presented in earlier chapters? First, note that the limitation to sequences of 0s and 1s is not intrinsic to algorithmic information theory. Indeed, just as with the Shannon theory, algorithmic information theory applies to character strings based on arbitrary alphabets (thus, as with bit strings, the character strings can be treated on their own terms or as computational redescriptions of other character strings). Algorithmic information theory is therefore as much about character strings drawn from a fixed finite alphabet as the Shannon theory.

Yet unlike the Shannon theory, which focuses on how character strings traverse communication channels, algorithmic information theory focuses on the degree to which character strings are compressible, interpreting the compressed strings as computer programs within a given programming environment. What then constitutes information—that is, the realization of possibilities and ruling out of others—within algorithmic information theory? In this case, information consists not in identifying individual strings (as in the Shannon theory) but in identifying collections of strings that exhibit the same degree of randomness (gauged in terms of (in)compressibility). These collections are equivalence classes of alphabetic character strings, with strings treated as equivalent if they have the same Kolmogorov complexity. Together, these equivalence classes constitute the relevant possibility matrix for algorithmic information theory.

---

until the last item is accounted for. But in many situations, the number of objects is so large and unwieldy that such an enumeration is not feasible. How many poker hands are there, for instance? As a practical matter, one can't just lay out all the different poker hands on a giant table and then count them. Instead, one needs mathematical techniques to simplify the counting. For poker hands, one therefore considers that the deck has 52 cards and asks how many ways there are of picking five distinct cards from it. Combinatorics tells us that this number is $52 \times 51 \times 50 \times 49 \times 48$ divided by $5 \times 4 \times 3 \times 2 \times 1$, or 2,598,960. Combinatorics is at once a fascinating and deep area of mathematical study, but also one that has an immediate intuitive appeal and very practical applications. For a good overview of combinatorics, see Alan Tucker, *Applied Combinatorics*, 6th edn. (New York: Wiley, 2012). For the actual result stated here, namely, that most sequences of coin tosses are incompressible and thus random in the Kolmogorov sense, see Ming Li and Paul M.B. Vitányi, *An Introduction to Kolmogorov Complexity and Its Applications*, 6th edn. (New York: Springer, 2008), secs. 1.8, 1.9, and 2.4.

Our discussion of Shannon and Kolmogorov information, especially in relation to the general account of information given in earlier chapters, has been quite abstract. Let me therefore offer an example that ties these three conceptions of information together. The example isn't perfect. In particular, its appeal to Kolmogorov information is more in the spirit of Kolmogorov than in keeping with the details of his theory. But the example should nonetheless prove illuminating.

The example focuses on the following sentence: "Play a game of chance in which a wheel having 38 geometrically equivalent slots is spun, slots being numbered 1 through 36 as well as 0 and 00, so that a ball lands in exactly one of the slots, with a payoff of 36 to 1 for betting the ball lands in any of the 38 slots." This sentence is a mouthful. From the perspective of Shannon information, it is simply a string of alphanumeric characters, perhaps coded in UTF-8. Shannon information is not concerned with the meaning of this sentence.[6] It is simply concerned with strings of characters drawn from a finite fixed alphabet. These constitute the possibility matrix, and the sentence in question is one such possibility, perhaps realized as a transmission across a communication channel.

Consider next this sentence from the perspective of Kolmogorov information. Kolmogorov information is concerned about compressibility of character strings. In this case, we can think of compressibility as finding short sentences that have exactly the same meaning as longer sentences. Thus, for the previous sentence, we can find an equivalent shorter sentence, namely, "Play roulette." All character strings with this same meaning (when interpreted as statements in English) would thus be part of the same equivalence class, and such equivalence classes of character strings would then constitute the possibility matrix within this (quasi) Kolmogorov approach to information.

Both Shannon and Kolmogorov information focus on possibility matrices consisting of character strings (or equivalence classes of them, in the case of Kolmogorov). But information can also focus directly on the meaning or intent of such character strings. Thus, with "Play roulette," one can also interpret it as a

---

6   In his preface to Shannon's classic text on information, Warren Weaver writes, "The word *information*, in this theory [i.e., the Shannon theory], is used in a special sense that must not be confused with its ordinary usage. In particular, *information* must not be confused with meaning. In fact, two messages, one of which is heavily loaded with meaning and the other of which is pure nonsense, can be exactly equivalent, from the present viewpoint, as regards information. It is this, undoubtedly, that Shannon means when he says that 'the semantic aspects of communication are irrelevant to the engineering aspects.' But this does not mean that the engineering aspects are necessarily irrelevant to the semantic aspects." Shannon and Weaver, *The Mathematical Theory of Communication*, 8.

recommendation by a casino to its customers. Suppose on a given day the casino urges customers to play roulette (perhaps as the featured game of the day). It might have urged customers to play any number of other games that it offers (craps, poker, blackjack, etc.). The possibility matrix in that case would be the range of games it might have urged customers to play, with roulette being the game actually urged on customers.

But there are other ways to interpret "Play roulette" and position it within a matrix of possibility. For instance, one might interpret "Play roulette" from the vantage of casino patrons, who might be doing other things with their time. Thus the possibility matrix would consist of playing roulette, playing other games of chance at the casino, but also engaging in other activities at the casino, such as going to the bar and ordering a martini or catching a show. The point to realize from this example is that the same linguistic expression can denote different items of information, which in turn can be part of many different possibility matrices, depending on how one makes sense of the expression within a context of inquiry. Mathematical approaches to information, as developed by Shannon and Kolmogorov, have a place within this general information framework but are not coextensive with it.

Chapter 8

Intelligence vs. Nature?

In everyday experience, we distinguish between two sources of information: intelligence and nature. Thus a detective examining a dead body will want to know whether the death resulted from "foul play" (intelligence) or "natural causes" (nature). Likewise, wind and erosion (nature) may account for the rock faces of most mountains, but to explain the faces of presidents etched on Mount Rushmore requires a sculptor (intelligence). More generally, an intelligence, to advance a purpose, may identify one possibility to the exclusion of others and thereby produce information. Alternatively, nature, as a system of causes and effects, may bring about some event to the exclusion of others, and thereby produce information.

These two ways of producing information need not be mutually exclusive. For instance, a human intelligence, to advance a purpose, performs a conceptual act, identifying one possibility to the exclusion of others. Such an act requires thought and consciousness, and yet in humans makes use of neurophysiology, which in turn is part of nature. Human intelligence may therefore be regarded as natural even if it is not purely material.[1] Still, as a matter of practical reason, humans find it important to distinguish between intelligence and nature. Drawing this distinction with philosophical precision, however, is not straightforward. This chapter attempts to shed light on this distinction and to eliminate some long-standing confusions associated with it.

---

[1] For the view that thought and consciousness, which are basic to human intelligence, are natural without being purely material, see Thomas Nagel, *Mind & Cosmos: Why the Materialist Neo-Darwinian Conception of Nature Is Almost Certainly False* (Oxford: Oxford University Press, 2012). Nagel sees a fundamental teleology as undergirding nature, a possibility that's off the table as far as conventional materialism is concerned. See also David J. Chalmers, *The Character of Consciousness* (Oxford: Oxford University Press, 2010). Chalmers takes a nonreductive approach to consciousness, making intelligence natural but, again, not material in any conventional sense. Note that by the conventional sense of matter/ materialism I mean a mechanistic view of matter in which the basic material entities relate to each other by mechanical principles such as attraction, repulsion, impact, changes in energy states, etc.; and all material entities are then built out of these basic ones.

According to information theorist Douglas Robertson, the defining characteristic of intelligent agents (i.e., teleological causes that act for an end or purpose) is their ability to create and communicate information.[2] That's what intelligences do for a living. Assuming Robertson is correct in so connecting intelligence and information (in chapter 20 I'll argue that he is indeed correct), it follows that if nature is itself the act of a creative intelligence, then nature is a form of information and nature's operations may themselves be regarded as intelligent and teleological. Nature's intelligence would in that case be a *derived intelligence*. Its intelligence would thus parallel the intelligence we ascribe to computers when they solve our problems. This is not to say that computers are conscious intelligent agents, nor is it to deny that conscious intelligent agents may be fully part of nature. Yet, insofar as we ascribe intelligence to computers, it is because conscious intelligent agents like us programmed them to engage intelligently with our intelligence.[3]

Because materialism gives primacy to matter, it downgrades the role of intelligence in nature, conceiving of nature in purely material terms, thus making intelligence a byproduct of material nature rather than its source and purpose. Materialism sees matter as fundamentally non-intelligent, and it thus needs to constitute intelligence out of matter. Such an attempt to derive intelligence from matter appears starkly in Darwinian materialism.[4] Darwin's main claim to

---

[2]   Douglas Robertson, "Algorithmic Information Theory, Free Will, and the Turing Test," *Complexity* 4(3) (1999): 25–34.

[3]   Some scientists go so far as to equate nature with a giant computer, albeit without ascribing the computer's origin to God or any outside intelligence (but if the universe is a computer, whence the hardware? and whence the software running on the hardware?). See Hector Zenil, ed., *A Computable Universe: Understanding and Exploring Nature as Computation* (Singapore: World Scientific, 2012). The contributors to this volume are serious scientists and mathematicians, and the volume itself is introduced by the eminent physicist Roger Penrose. Philosophers also are taking the idea of universe-as-computer seriously. Perhaps the best known is Nick Bostrom, who argues that there is a good probability that we are living in a computer simulation. See Nick Bostrom, "Are You Living in a Computer Simulation?" *Philosophical Quarterly* 53(211) (2003): 243–55.

[4]   Deriving intelligence from matter also appears starkly in strong artificial intelligence (AI), which sees human intelligence as reducible to computation, and thus to certain particular arrangements of matter (i.e., those that represent bits and run algorithms). The most extreme form of strong AI takes a transhumanist approach in which technology will, as the transhumanist prophets assure us, so enhance human cognition that in the end we can do no better than to upload ourselves onto a computer and dispense with our "wetware." Ray Kurzweil thinks that this will happen in the next decade or so and that, if he can just keep himself alive long enough, he will in this way achieve immortality. See Ray Kurzweil, *The Singularity is Near: When Humans Transcend Biology* (New York: Penguin, 2006). It is

fame comes from proposing a material mechanism that could create biological information without the need for intelligence (usually, in these discussions, referred to as teleology).[5] Interestingly, he referred to this mechanism as "natural selection." Selection, as understood before Darwin, had been an activity confined to intelligent agents. Darwin attributed the power of selection to nature.[6]

Yet nature, as conceived within Darwinian materialism, is supposed to act without purpose. Indeed, its proponents assure us that the Darwinian process is nonteleological. As evolutionary geneticist Jerry Coyne has put it, "If we're to defend evolutionary biology, we must defend it as a science: a *non-teleological* theory in which the panoply of life results from the action of natural selection and genetic drift acting on random mutations."[7] But why do Coyne and fellow materialists insist that the evolutionary process, to count as science, must be nonteleological or non-intelligent?[8] Where did that rule come from? The wedding of teleology with the natural sciences is itself a well-established science, namely, engineering. Moreover, many special sciences have as their primary aim to discover evidence of purpose (such as the Search for Extraterrestrial Intelligence, archeology, and forensic science). The rule that science refuse

---

a measure of how deeply entrenched materialism is in Western culture that such possibilities are taken seriously. As someone who has followed the unfulfilled promises of artificial intelligence for more than three decades, I see Kurzweil's transhumanism as closer to a Grimms' fairy tale than to sober science. Materialism is adept at transforming illusions of possibility into settled verities.

[5] In chapter 19 we examine whether natural selection, insofar as it successfully executes evolutionary searches, can indeed eliminate from evolution the need for intelligence or teleology. We'll see that far from eliminating teleology, natural selection simply pushes teleology more deeply into the evolutionary process itself, notably into the intelligent programming of the fitness landscape.

[6] Charles Darwin, *On the Origin of Species*, facsimile 1st edn. (1859; reprinted Cambridge, Mass.: Harvard University Press, 1964), ch. 4.

[7] Jerry Coyne, "Truckling to the Faithful: A Spoonful of Jesus Makes Darwin Go Down," posted on his blog Why Evolution Is True on April 22, 2009 at http://whyevolutionistrue. wordpress.com (last accessed April 27, 2009). Emphasis added. "Genetic drift" here refers to random changes in population gene frequencies. It too is nonteleological.

[8] The late Darwinist philosopher of biology David Hull underscored the need to rid science of teleology when he wrote, "He [Darwin] dismissed it [design] not because it was an incorrect scientific explanation, but because it was not a proper scientific explanation at all." David Hull, *Darwin and His Critics: The Reception of Darwin's Theory of Evolution by the Scientific Community* (Cambridge, Mass.: Harvard University Press, 1973), 26. Jacques Monod made the same point: "The cornerstone of the scientific method is the postulate that nature is objective. In other words, the *systematic* denial that 'true' knowledge can be got at by interpreting phenomena in terms of final causes—that is to say, of 'purpose.'" Monod, *Chance and Necessity*, 21.

teleology seems, therefore, less a requirement of science as such than a logical consequence of materialism: if materialism is true, then no fundamental or real teleology can exist in nature for science to study; instead, any teleology or intelligence in nature must result from underlying nonteleological processes.

The question therefore arises whether nature, conceived in purely material terms, possesses the ability to create all the information that we find in it. To answer this question, and indeed to show that a purely material nature is not up to the task of creating all the information that we find in it, requires assessing what is within and outside the reach of the purely material powers of nature. A worry now arises whether this very question may be ill posed. For Aristotelians, for instance, teleology (finality) is fundamental to nature, so to try to divorce teleology from nature makes no sense. For nonmaterialists generally, nature without teleology is not nature, and so bracketing out teleology from nature by focusing purely on its material aspect becomes a fool's errand. Materialists, rejecting a fundamental teleology not reducible to matter, are for this reason ever ready to charge nonmaterialists with embracing dualism, seeing in teleology a second fundamental principle in addition to matter. But nonmaterialists are in their rights to turn the tables on materialists, charging them with embracing what might be called *demidism* (as in a demigod or half god). Demidism, by focusing only on nature's material aspect, makes nature half of what it really is, and thus not nature at all.

Charges of dualism and demidism aside, the question remains to what degree nature, in its material aspect, is able to account for the various things that happen in nature. Materialists, thinking that it cannot but be true that nature in its material aspect is nature as such, tend to regard this question as uninteresting and unnecessary.[9] Nonmaterialists, thinking that nature in its material aspect is not nature at all, tend likewise to discount this question.[10] Yet, if one is forced to answer this question, it seems that, broadly speaking, one will have to do something like

---

[9] Perhaps the most barefaced statement of this unconcern for nonmaterialist alternatives comes from Richard Dawkins in discussing Darwinian materialism. Writing of nonmaterialist "rival theories," he remarks, "Instead of examining the evidence for and against rival theories, I shall adopt a more armchair approach. My argument will be that Darwinism is the only known theory that is in principle *capable* of explaining certain aspects of life. If I am right it means that, even if there were no actual evidence in favour of the Darwinian theory (there is, of course) we should still be justified in preferring it over all rival theories." Dawkins, *Blind Watchmaker*, 287.

[10] For an extended exposition of why teleology in nature is immune to whatever challenges nature in its material aspect might otherwise pose, see Etienne Gilson, *From Aristotle to Darwin and Back Again: A Journey in Final Causality, Species, and Evolution*, trans. John Lyon (South Bend, Ind.: University of Notre Dame Press, 1984). For Gilson,

this: one will need to know what nature in its material aspect can be expected to do and then determine to what extent nature does things outside that expectation. The beauty of matter is that it is supposed to exhibit an unbreakable normativity. In consequence, deviation from that normativity can be taken as evidence for the influence of teleological principles not reducible to material processes.

The logic here proceeds *arguendo*: for the sake of argument, assume that material processes alone are involved in some outcome; and then show that material processes face serious difficulties in bringing about that outcome. At this level of generality, the logic here seems unproblematic. It is the logic of *reductio ad absurdum*: let your interlocutors assume exactly what they want to assume and then show that it leads to a contradiction. Of course, this logic needs to be explicitly laid out and correctly applied. One will need a good grasp of the material processes that might produce the outcome in question (the argument here must be from knowledge, not ignorance). One will have to block appeals to unknown material processes that might have produced the outcome. One will need to be clear about the precise form of the logic to be employed (e.g., statistical, abductive, or deductive, with the exact method of reasoning from premises to conclusion fully laid out). And finally, one will have to identify an actual outcome to which this logic may be applied and for which this logic points convincingly to the insufficiency of purely material processes. Let's call this general schema for refuting materialism the *materialist-refuting logic*.

Just how convincingly the materialist-refuting logic is able to distinguish what's within and beyond the reach of material processes can be debated and will depend on how, specifically, this logic is articulated and to which individual cases it is applied. Topping the list of outcomes to which the materialist-refuting logic has, historically, been applied is the origin of life.[11] My own statistical

---

finality or purposiveness is hardwired into reality, and only faulty (materialistic) thinking can cause us to doubt this.

[11] Many materialist treatments of life's origin give the impression that no right-thinking person questions that life is a direct consequence of the physics and chemistry of matter, and that every right-thinking person accepts that the problem of life's origin, insofar as it is a problem, is simply a matter of sorting through details, finding the right recipe of material entities and how to combine them. Examples of this literature include Robert Hazen, *Genesis: The Scientific Quest for Life's Origins* (Washington, D.C.: Joseph Henry Press, 2005) and Michael Yarus, *Life from an RNA World: The Ancestor Within* (Cambridge, Mass.: Harvard University Press, 2010). Doubts about the ease with which nonliving matter may transition to the living state, however, are widespread and, to varying degrees, employ the materialist-refuting logic. See, for instance, Robert Shapiro, *Origins, A Skeptics Guide to the Creation of Life on Earth* (New York: Summit Books, 1986); Paul Davies, *The Fifth Miracle: The Search for the Origin and Meaning of Life* (New York: Simon & Schuster, 1999); and

method for eliminating chance through small probabilities, when applied to the origin of life, employs this logic.[12] This is not the place to analyze the validity of my particular formulation of this logic, or its cogency in refuting a materialist origin of life.[13] Nevertheless, one can't simply dismiss this logic because it calls materialism into question or might have theological implications. Arguments made according to this logic need to be evaluated on their individual merits. In any case, the materialist-refuting logic is not inherently theistic. Philosopher Thomas Nagel, who is an atheist but also a nonmaterialist, employs this same logic when he challenges materialism's ability to account for life's origin:

> Doubts about the reductionist [materialist] account of life go against the dominant scientific consensus, but that consensus faces problems of probability that I believe are not taken seriously enough, both with respect to the evolution of life forms through accidental mutation and natural selection and with respect to the formation from dead matter of physical systems capable of such evolution. The more we learn about the intricacy of the genetic code and its control of the chemical processes of life, the harder those problems seem.[14]

Stephen C. Meyer, *Signature in the Cell: DNA and the Evidence for Intelligent Design* (San Francisco, Calif.: HarperOne, 2009).

[12] Dembski, *Design Inference*, 55–62.

[13] For a defense of the validity of the materialist-refuting logic as this logic is articulated in my own work and in response to challenges in the work of others, see William A. Dembski, *The Design Revolution: Answering the Toughest Questions about Intelligent Design* (Downers Grove, Ill.: InterVarsity, 2004), pt. V, titled "Theoretical Challenges to Intelligent Design."

[14] Nagel, *Mind & Cosmos*, 9. Nagel has remained an atheist even though the materialist-refuting logic has led him to reject a purely material origin of life. On the other hand, the materialist-refuting logic has led some to embrace theism. For instance, the late Antony Flew, the most prominent atheist in the English-speaking world until Richard Dawkins displaced him, became a theist on account of the inability, as he perceived it, of material processes to account for the intricacies of the cell, notably, its genetic information-processing capabilities. See Antony Flew and Roy Abraham Varghese, *There Is a God: How the World's Most Notorious Atheist Changed His Mind* (New York: HarperCollins, 2007), 75, where Flew writes that DNA "has shown, by the almost unbelievable complexity of the arrangements which are needed to produce [life], that intelligence must have been involved in getting these extraordinarily diverse elements to work together. It's the enormous complexity of the number of elements and the enormous subtlety of the ways they work together. The meeting of these two parts at the right time by chance is simply minute. It is all a matter of the enormous complexity by which the results were achieved, which looked to me like the work of intelligence."

The materialist-refuting logic, taking various guises, has convinced many that materialism can't be right. Nonetheless, this logic has failed to gain the traction that it might in the debate with materialism. Many reasons for this failure can be cited: cultural and intellectual inertia, distaste for creationism, desire to defend the scientific status quo, etc. Yet I want here to focus on a reason for this failure that is not widely appreciated, namely, the muddle wrought by an ancient distinction that promised clarity but, in fact, has been an endless source of confusion. The problematic distinction I have in mind depends on another ancient distinction, the distinction between matter and information. The matter–information distinction is old and was understood by the Ancient Greeks. For the Stoics, for instance, there was matter, passive or inert stuff waiting to be arranged; and there was information, active stuff that did the arranging.[15] Because information seems to flow in, through, and out of matter, this distinction provides a convenient way of thinking about certain basic operations of the world.[16] But if the matter–information distinction is convenient, the next one is pernicious. That's the Aristotelian distinction between nature and design.

Let me be clear that in faulting the nature–design distinction, I am not faulting Aristotle or his use of the distinction. As Aristotle developed it, the nature–design distinction is as convenient and unobjectionable as the matter–information distinction. The nature–design distinction, though originally innocent, has become pernicious because of how materialism redefines its two terms, nature and design. To say that something is pernicious or deadly raises an obvious question: what is it deadly to? The nature–design distinction, as redefined at the hands of materialists, is deadly to teleology in nature. Redefined, the distinction allows materialists to think they've destroyed teleology, showing it to be useless or incoherent, when all they've done is transform the problem of teleology in nature so that materialism wins by default. But perhaps the bigger problem with the nature–design distinction, as redefined by materialism, is that it confuses the role of teleology in nature even for nonmaterialists. I'll address these concerns momentarily, but let me start by laying out the nature–design distinction as Aristotle originally characterized it.

---

[15] See, for instance, F.H. Sandbach, *The Stoics*, 2nd edn. (Indianapolis, Ind.: Hackett, 1989), 72–5. Note that the Stoics were materialists, but not in the modern sense. Thus for them information was a type of active matter, interacting with passive matter that needed to be shaped and ensouled.

[16] Though note, the matter–information distinction bears further scrutiny; as we'll see in chapter 11, matter is itself inherently informational—there exists no information-free substratum for information.

For Aristotle, nature and design represented two different ways of producing information (i.e., getting information into matter). Whereas design produces information externally, nature produces it internally. Consider the difference between raw pieces of wood and an acorn. Raw pieces of wood do not have the power within themselves to assemble into a ship. For raw pieces of wood to form a ship requires a designer to draw up a blueprint and then, by forces external to the wood, to arrange those pieces into a ship matching the blueprint. But where is the designer that causes an acorn to develop into a full-grown oak tree? The acorn develops (if unhindered) into an oak tree not by means of an external hand, as with a ship, but from within. The acorn assumes the form it does through powers operating internal to it.

Thus, on the one hand, Aristotle characterized design as consisting of capacities external to objects that are needed to bring about their form. On the other hand, he saw nature as consisting of capacities internal to objects that enable them to transform themselves without outside help. Accordingly, in Book XII of the *Metaphysics*, Aristotle wrote, "[Design] is a principle of movement in something other than the thing moved; nature is a principle in the thing itself."[17] In Book II of the *Physics* Aristotle referred to design as completing "what nature cannot bring to a finish."[18]

The Greek word here translated "design" is *technē*, from which we get our word *technology*. In translations of Aristotle's work, the English word most commonly used to translate *technē* is "art" (in the sense of "artifact"). Design, art, and technology thus become synonyms. The essential idea behind these terms is that the production of an object occurs by applying information from outside it and that the materials that make up the object lack the power to organize themselves into it. Thus, apart from externally applied information, the object cannot assume the form that it does. Indeed, raw pieces of wood do not, by themselves, have the power to form a ship.

Externalist design thus contrasts with internalist nature, the latter looking to the power within things to express information. Hence, in Book II of the *Physics*, Aristotle wrote, "If the ship-building art were in the wood, it would produce the same results by nature."[19] In other words, if raw pieces of wood had the capacity to organize themselves into ships, we would say that ships come

---

[17]   Aristotle, *Metaphysics*, trans. W.D. Ross, XII.3 (1070a, 5–10), in Richard McKeon, ed., *The Basic Works of Aristotle* (New York: Random House, 1941), 874.

[18]   Aristotle, *Physics*, trans. R.P. Hardie and R.K. Gaye, II.8 (199a, 15–20), in Richard McKeon, ed., *The Basic Works of Aristotle* (New York: Random House, 1941), 250. Note that Thomas Aquinas took this idea and sacramentalized it into grace completing nature.

[19]   Ibid., II.8 (199b, 25–30), 251.

about by nature. The Greek word here translated "nature" is *phusis*, from which we get our word physics. The Indo-European root meaning behind *phusis* is growth and development. Nature produces information not by imposing it from outside but by growing or developing informationally rich structures from the capacities inherent in a thing. Consider again the acorn. Unlike wood that needs to be shaped and fitted by a designer to form a ship, acorns produce oak trees naturally—the acorn simply needs a suitable environment in which to grow.

In setting the stage for Aristotle's nature–design distinction a few paragraphs back, I remarked that this distinction is convenient and unobjectionable. Nonetheless, I omitted to mention that it is prone to a certain fuzziness. Indeed, a little reflection reveals that the boundary between internal nature and external design is not as clear as it might at first seem. To see this, consider which came first, the acorn or the oak tree. An acorn produces an oak tree by powers internal to it. But whence the information inside the acorn that allows it to produce an oak tree? How did that information initially arise? For Aristotle, the universe was eternal and living forms were eternally pregnant in it (arising through either ordinary or spontaneous generation).[20] Aristotle was therefore able to sidestep this question because the information for the acorn was, in some sense, always there. But modern cosmology and geology suggest that life had a definite beginning in the finite past, before which the universe, in its material constitution, was too unstructured to permit life.[21] How, then, did acorns, and life more generally, arise? Even though the acorn develops into an oak tree by internal nature, perhaps external design (space aliens? God?) is required to account for the information that enables the acorn to produce the oak. In this way external design could be seen as upstaging internal nature.

Not to be outdone, a materialist could now attempt to turn the tables, making nature upstage design. The materialist could thus argue that if external design can be plausibly ascribed to the origin of the acorn, so too can internal nature be plausibly ascribed to the origin of a ship. Granted, planks of wood do not have the power to organize themselves into a ship. But planks of wood together with skilled human artisans do have this power. And taken together, these belong to nature (a purely material nature if nature is purely material). Indeed, if humans are the product of natural selection (conceived nonteleologically), would not

---

[20] See James G. Lennox, *Aristotle's Philosophy of Biology: Studies in the Origins of Life Science* (Cambridge: Cambridge University Press, 2001), chs. 6 and 10.

[21] For instance, temperatures of the early universe following the Big Bang would have been in the billions of degrees Kelvin, thus destroying any information-bearing properties of matter. See Steven Weinberg, *The First Three Minutes: A Modern View of the Origin of the Universe*, 2nd edn. (New York: Basic Books, 1993), ch. 5.

ships themselves be an indirect product of natural selection? In this way, ships could themselves be viewed as natural rather than designed.[22]

Thus, whenever an object is ascribed to design because some organizing principle external to the object seems required to explain it, nature can be substituted for design by simply folding that organizing principle into a wider system containing the object. Externalists, as we might call them, may then argue for the external design of this wider system, in which case internalists, as we might in turn call them, can propose a still wider system containing still further organizing principles operating according to internal nature. This competition between internal nature and external design ends when one reaches the limits of nature—the universe, the cosmos, the whole show. It's at this point that either one needs to say that nature is complete on its own terms, requiring no external explanatory principle,[23] or one regards nature as incomplete and in need of an explanatory principle external to it, in which case design takes precedence over nature, though not merely design, because such a principle would, presumably, have to be a first cause, a source of being, a creator—in other words, God.[24]

Leaving aside the fuzziness inherent in the nature–design distinction, I want next to relate this distinction to teleology in general. In the nature–design distinction as Aristotle conceived it, nature and design are both thoroughly teleological. By producing artifacts that exhibit functions and serve purposes, design is obviously teleological. But nature in Aristotle's philosophy operates by final causes, directing nature toward certain ends, and thus is teleological as well. But what happens to this distinction at the hands of materialism? Within materialism, the nuts and bolts of nature are elemental material entities devoid of any inherent teleology. It follows that within materialism any teleology that matter exhibits must result from teleology being imposed on matter and thus by external design. External design, within materialism, thus comes to subsume

---

[22]   In this vein, Richard Dawkins would argue that ships are part of our "extended phenotype." See his *The Extended Phenotype: The Long Reach of the Gene* (Oxford: Oxford University Press, 1982). See also my encounter with David Sloan Wilson described in chapter 17 of this book. In that encounter, Wilson seems happy to attribute to natural selection products of design by intelligent agents so long as those intelligent agents are themselves products of natural selection.

[23]   This was, for instance, the point of Stephen Hawking's *A Brief History of Time*, where he argued that a complete physical theory would obviate the need for God. Stephen W. Hawking, *A Brief History of Time: From the Big Bang to Black Holes* (New York: Bantam, 1988).

[24]   One might say the point of the cosmological argument is to show that nature (broadly conceived) is incomplete on its own terms and requires God to complete it. See William L. Rowe, *The Cosmological Argument* (New York: Fordham University Press, 1998).

all of teleology. Yet because matter is all that exists within materialism, any design will just be one item of matter causing a change in another item of matter. And since matter at root is nonteleological, any teleology associated with such design is, in the end, merely a byproduct of underlying nonteleological material processes. In this way, materialism destroys any fundamental or real teleology in nature.

Nonmaterialists, of course, will reject this conclusion and affirm that real teleology exists and operates in nature. Nevertheless, nonmaterialists can still be tempted to embrace materialism's understanding of the nature–design distinction. Yielding to the temptation, they will then accept that nature is at base material and that all teleology in nature is a consequence of external design. But since the teleology is real, it cannot belong to nature as such, which, because material, is inherently nonteleological. Rather, any teleology in nature will then have had to be put there externally. But this means it had to be put there by a nonmaterial agent, who imposed it on matter (matter, by itself, being incapable of real teleology). Seventeenth-century British natural theologians, such as Robert Boyle, took this approach. Boyle embraced a materialistic understanding of nature, which he called the "mechanical philosophy." Rejecting the immanent teleology of Aristotle and the Stoics, which he saw as idolatrous because it ascribed to nature creative powers that, in his view, belonged properly to God, Boyle made all teleology in nature a consequence of God ordering matter, thereby subsuming teleology under external design.[25]

To his credit, Boyle at least knew what his metaphysical options were and why he settled on the one he did. In his mechanical philosophy, he committed himself to a materialist understanding of nature and to an external-design understanding of teleology. But this is hardly the only way to understand how real teleology might operate in nature. Nature can be more than material and, if idealists are right, may not even be material. Unburdened of materialism, nature can give teleology free rein. Accordingly, teleology could express itself through powers intrinsic to nature and thus apart from external design, or even by some combination of immanent teleology and external design. Yet, in the present materialist climate, to view nature more broadly than matter and to view teleology more broadly than external design requires some conscious effort of thought—it does not, as it were, come naturally. For this reason, the

---

[25] See Robert Boyle, *The Works of Robert Boyle*, vol. 14, eds. M. Hunter and E.B. Davis (London: Pickering & Chatto, 2000), 147–55 as well as Robert Boyle, *A Free Enquiry into the Vulgarly Received Notion of Nature*, eds. M. Hunter and E.B. Davis (Cambridge: Cambridge University Press, 1996).

materialist redefinition of the nature–design distinction helps to confuse the role of teleology in nature even for nonmaterialists.

Nowhere is this confusion more evident than in the debate over intelligent design. Intelligent design is the study of patterns (hence "design") in nature that give empirical evidence of resulting from real teleology (hence "intelligent"). In this definition, real teleology is not reducible to purely material processes. At the same time, in this definition, real teleology is not simply presupposed as a consequence of prior metaphysical commitments. Intelligent design asks teleology to prove itself scientifically. In the context of biology, intelligent design looks for patterns in biological systems that confirm real teleology. The definition of intelligent design given here is in fact how its proponents understand the term.[26] This definition avoids two common linguistic pitfalls associated with it: intelligent design's critics tend to assume that the reference to "design" in "intelligent design" commits it to an external-design view of teleology;[27] moreover, they tend to assume that the reference to "intelligent" in

---

[26]   The textbook definition of intelligent design reads "the study of patterns in nature that are best explained as the product of intelligence." Quoted from William A. Dembski and Jonathan Wells, *The Design of Life: Discovering Signs of Intelligence in Biological Systems* (Dallas, Tx.: Foundation for Thought and Ethics, 2008), 3. *The Design of Life* is, in fact, an intelligent design textbook. Note that right after this definition, intelligence is defined as "any cause, agent, or process that achieves an end or goal by employing suitable means or instruments." This definition of intelligence is, obviously, quite general and consistent with my reference, in the main body of the present book, to "real teleology."

[27]   Thomistic philosopher Edward Feser, for instance, seeing intelligent design as committed to an external-design view of teleology, asserts, "The ID [intelligent design] approach is, for methodological purposes, to treat organisms at least *as if* they were artifacts; and that just is to treat them *as if* they were devoid of immanent final causality, because an artifact just is, by definition as it were, something whose parts are not essentially ordered to the whole they compose." Quoted from Edward Feser, "ID, A-T, and Duns Scotus: A Further Reply to Torley," 2010, available online at http://edwardfeser.blogspot. jp/2010/04/id-t-and-duns-scotus-further-reply-to.html (last accessed October 14, 2013). Stephen Talbott of the Nature Institute, influenced perhaps less by Aristotle than by Johann Wolfgang von Goethe and Owen Barfield, makes virtually the same point: "Although [the term intelligent design] has its legitimate uses, you will not find me speaking of design, simply because—as I've made abundantly clear in previous articles—organisms cannot be understood as having been designed, machine-like, whether by an engineer-God or a Blind Watchmaker elevated to god-like status. If organisms participate in a higher life, it is a participation that works from within—at a deep level the ancients recognized as that of the *logos* informing all things." Quoted from Stephen L. Talbott, "Evolution and the Illusion of Randomness," *The New Atlantis*, 33 (Fall 2011), 37–64, available online at http://www.thenewatlantis.com/ publications/evolution-and-the-illusion-of-randomness (last accessed October 14, 2013). In the body of this chapter, I show why these criticisms fail and, specifically, why intelligent

"intelligent design" makes any such external design the product of a conscious personal intelligent agent.[28] Both assumptions are false.

Granted, intelligent design is compatible with external design imposed by a conscious personal intelligent agent. But it is not limited to this understanding of teleology in nature. In fact, it is open to whatever form teleology in nature may take provided that the teleology is real. The principle of charity in interpretation demands that, so long as speakers are not simply making up meanings as they go along, terms are to be interpreted in line with speakers' intent and recognized linguistic usage. The definition of intelligent design just given, which explicitly cites real teleology and does not restrict itself to external design, is consistent with recognized meanings of both words that make up the term intelligent design. Design includes among its recognized meanings pattern, arrangement, or form, and thus can be a synonym for information. Moreover, intelligence can be a general term for denoting causes that have teleological effects. Intelligence therefore need not merely refer to conscious personal intelligent agents like us, but can also refer to teleology quite generally.[29]

---

design is compatible with a nonmechanistic conception of organisms. Nonetheless, in fairness to Feser and Talbott, their criticisms are understandable because intelligent design advocates, myself included, haven't always been as clear as we might in our use of design terminology, not clearly distinguishing external design from intelligence or teleology more generally.

[28] The most commonly cited such agent in these discussions is, of course, God. Eugenie Scott, an indefatigable defender of Darwinian evolution against intelligent design, regards intelligent design as the "wink, wink, nudge, nudge school of science education. We know what they're saying is God." (The allusion here is to the 1970s British comedy series *Monty Python*.) Quoted from https://www.aclu.org/religion-belief/creationism-new-name-taught-schools (last accessed October 14, 2013). Skeptic Michael Shermer likewise conceives the teleology in intelligent design quite narrowly: "The evolution–Intelligent Design debate boils down to a Humean question of what's more likely: that the diversity and complexity of life we see around us came about by laws of nature that we can observe, or supernaturally by an Intelligent Designer that we cannot observe?" Quoted from Michael Shermer, *Why Darwin Matters: The Case Against Intelligent Design* (New York: Henry Holt, 2006), 49.

[29] It's certainly true that most of the time when we refer to intelligence, we have in mind humans, and hence conscious personal intelligent agents. But the use of the term intelligence is considerably broader. Artificial intelligence refers to computer algorithms displaying behaviors that we would regard as intelligent in humans. Yet I doubt anyone thinks artificial intelligence has, to date, come up with algorithms capable of consciousness or of exhibiting personhood. Nonconscious intelligence is also a theme in some of the astrobiological literature—see, for instance, David M. Raup, "Nonconscious Intelligence in the Universe," *Acta Astronautica* 26(3–4) (1992): 257–61. Nor does intelligence have to be confined to agents, conceived as localized sources of activity capable of interacting with an external environment. The late atheist astronomer Fred Hoyle, in a widely repeated quote, wrote the following about the ability of the universe to produce carbon:

Intelligent design aims to discover solid scientific evidence of real teleology in nature. Typically, it employs some formulation of the materialist-refuting logic to supply such evidence.[30] But that does not mean intelligent design is committed to a mechanistic or reductionistic or artifactual view of life or the universe. In applying the materialist-refuting logic, one must gauge what is within and outside the power of purely material processes, which means looking, temporarily, at living forms mechanistically. But once the materialist-refuting logic has shown that material processes are unable to bring about, for instance, certain biological structures, materialism stands refuted, and so there

---

> Some super-calculating intellect must have designed the properties of the carbon atom, otherwise the chance of my finding such an atom through the blind forces of nature would be utterly minuscule. A common sense interpretation of the facts suggests that a superintellect has monkeyed with physics, as well as with chemistry and biology, and that there are no blind forces worth speaking about in nature. The numbers one calculates from the facts seem to me so overwhelming as to put this conclusion almost beyond question.

This quote is from Fred Hoyle, "The Universe: Past and Present Reflections," *Engineering and Science* (November 1981): 12. Now, my point in repeating this quote is not to argue that Hoyle was a crypto-creationist or that deep down he really held, or should have held, to an external design explanation of the 7.68 MeV resonance state of the carbon-12 nucleus (Hoyle predicted this resonance state in the 1950s—see Fred Hoyle, "On Nuclear Reactions Occurring in Very Hot Stars: The Synthesis of Elements from Carbon to Nickel," *Astrophysical Journal*, Supplement Series 1 [1954]: 121–46). My point is quite the opposite: precisely because Hoyle remained an atheist, his reference to a superintellect is at best analogical with human intelligence and in fact signifies a cosmic intelligence that is not in any straightforward sense conscious, personal, or agentive. At the same time, Hoyle's reference to intelligence here gestures at real teleology. For all these reasons, it seems reasonable to regard intelligence as including among its meanings teleology in general.

[30]   Supporters of intelligent design have developed several different formulations of this logic. For instance, Stephen Meyer, in arguing for intelligent design, develops the materialist-refuting logic as an abductive inference. See Meyer, *Signature in the Cell*, ch. 7. My own approach to the materialist-refuting logic was originally to develop it as a Fisherian statistical inference. For a synopsis, William A. Dembski, "The Logical Underpinnings of Intelligent Design," in W.A. Dembski and M. Ruse, eds., *Debating Design: From Darwin to DNA* (Cambridge: Cambridge University Press, 2004), 311–30. My colleagues and I have since recast this logic in terms of an information measure that incorporates Shannon and Kolmogorov complexity measures. See, for instance, Winston Ewert, William A. Dembski, and Robert J. Marks II, "Algorithmic Specified Complexity," in J. Bartlett, D. Halsmer, and M.R. Hall, eds., *Engineering and the Ultimate: An Interdisciplinary Investigation of Order and Design in Nature and Craft* (Broken Arrow, Okla.: Blyth Institute Press, 2014), 131–51. Lydia McGrew, in arguing for intelligent design, develops the materialist-refuting logic as a Bayesian statistical inference. See her "Testability, Likelihoods, and Design," *Philo* 7(1) (2004): 5–21.

is no need to continue to look at life mechanistically. It is therefore mistaken to think that intelligent design looks at life in the same way as a materialist biology, only that intelligent design sees the hand of a supernatural external designer where a materialist biology sees the hand of natural selection (or some such material mechanism).

Even the predilection of some intelligent design proponents to focus on engineering-like features of living forms needs to be understood as an attempt to find solid scientific evidence of teleology and not as a reduction of life to engineering or external design. The fact is that living forms exhibit structures and functions that could not be understood unless we, as researchers investigating them, were versed in the science of engineering.[31] Organisms,

---

[31]   As an illustration of life's engineering features, consider the following abstract from an article in *Science* that appeared around the time of this writing: "Gears are found rarely in animals and have never been reported to intermesh and rotate functionally like mechanical gears. We now demonstrate functional gears in the ballistic jumping movements of the flightless planthopper insect *Issus*. The nymphs, but not adults, have a row of cuticular gear (cog) teeth around the curved medial surfaces of their two hindleg trochantera. The gear teeth on one trochanter engaged with and sequentially moved past those on the other trochanter during the preparatory cocking and the propulsive phases of jumping. Close registration between the gears ensured that both hindlegs moved at the same angular velocities to propel the body without yaw rotation. At the final molt to adulthood, this synchronization mechanism is jettisoned." See Malcolm Burrows and Gregory Sutton, "Interacting Gears Synchronize Propulsive Leg Movements in a Jumping Insect," *Science* 341 (13 September 2013): 1254. The electron micrograph of the *Issus* nymph in this article leaves no doubt that these are intermeshing gears.

Examples of such machinery abound in biology, especially at the molecular level. For instance, in 2003, *BioEssays* published a special issue on "molecular machines." In introducing that issue, Adam Wilkins, the journal's editor, wrote, "The articles included in this issue demonstrate some striking parallels between artifactual and biological/molecular machines. In the first place, molecular machines, like man-made machines, perform highly specific functions. Second, the macromolecular machine complexes feature multiple parts that interact in distinct and precise ways, with defined inputs and outputs. Third, many of these machines have parts that can be used in other molecular machines (at least, with slight modification), comparable to the interchangeable parts of artificial machines. Finally, and not least, they have the cardinal attribute of machines: they all convert energy into some form of 'work.'" Quoted from Adam Wilkins, "A Special Issue on Molecular Machines," *BioEssays* 25(12) (December 2003): 1146. Six years earlier, Bruce Alberts, president of the National Academy of Sciences, introduced a special issue of *Cell* devoted to "macromolecular machines." See Bruce Alberts, "The Cell as a Collection of Protein Machines: Preparing the Next Generation of Molecular Biologists," *Cell* 92 (8 February 1998): 291.

Taking a more top-down approach, systems biology, a merger of biology and engineering, has in the last decade become an established field of study, and one that promises significant practical benefits: "A new era of scientific research is set to produce a type of engineer unlike

regardless of their essential nature, exhibit artifactual features, and these features certainly suggest teleology. Yet, to say that organisms exhibit artifactual features is not to say that they are artifacts, any more than saying because humans can perform computations, therefore they are computers. Intelligent design looks at life mechanistically as a temporary measure, as part of a *reductio ad absurdum* argument, to refute materialism. Once materialism is refuted, however, intelligent design is able to leave a mechanistic understanding of life behind, looking at life as it is.

To see that intelligent design is open to whatever form teleology in nature may take, consider again the acorn. The acorn does not create its information from scratch, but expresses already existing information, transmitted through previous generations of oak trees. In expressing this information to produce an oak tree, the acorn appears to execute a well-defined step-by-step program. So where precisely does this program reside? Materialists would see the program as residing in the material structure of the acorn. Intelligent design proponents, following the example of Robert Boyle, might agree, but then go further by attributing the program to divine external design imprinted on the acorn's matter. But intelligent design proponents also have the option of seeing the program as residing in a nonmaterial aspect of nature. Accordingly, the acorn could then be viewed as a receiver of information (the program), with this information expressed internally. I mention the latter option, even though it elicits the charge of vitalism, because the evidence supporting it is no worse than the evidence supporting the materialist option. How so?

Unlike a computer program written by humans, where the program's behavior, when executed, can be precisely correlated with its instruction set, we know no exact correlation between an acorn's material structure and its development. To say that its program resides in its material structure is an article of materialist faith, not of independent evidence. Indeed, despite strides in developmental biology, we don't know the "programming language" by which an acorn develops to maturity, so we are unable to identify its "instructions," much less to verify

---

any other and take the UK into what experts claim will be the third industrial revolution after the one in information technology. Biology and engineering groups are converging to develop a new field known as systems biology. It borrows techniques and tools from systems engineering to build and test mathematical models of biological components, such as organs and cells. Experts predict that systems biology will revolutionise the medical sector. Discoveries in health and disease will lead to further research, which could boost the engineering industry with new materials, biofuels and manufacturing capabilities." Quoted from Rebecca Rushmer, "All Systems Go," *Professional Engineering* 20(4) (2007): 37.

that they are faithfully executed.[32] For all we can verify, the acorn could equally be drawing information from nonmaterial sources, and these could operate by immanent teleology or by external design or by some combination of the two. Intelligent design can make its peace with all such options.

It's time to wrap up this chapter, which I titled "Intelligence vs. Nature?" The question mark in the title is there for a reason, and that reason should by now be obvious: pitting intelligence against nature is a *false opposition*. Depending on one's metaphysics, the two can be identical. And when they're not identical, the two nonetheless operate in tandem. Nature, it seems, is ever ready to accommodate intelligence, whatever form it takes. As for the search for evidence of real intelligence or teleology in nature, which is the object of intelligent design, this search needs to be understood not as a denial that nature is inherently teleological or even as a preference for external design over immanent teleology. Rather, this search should be understood as a challenge to the materialist assertion that all of nature is at base nonteleological. For nonmaterialists, the information in nature is there on account of real intelligence or teleology. How intelligence and nature unite to create that information then becomes the interesting question, and one we will explore in subsequent chapters.

Postscript

Before we proceed to the next chapter, I need to say a bit more about the word design. Design, as used by Aristotle, is an engineering term and refers to

---

[32] This is not to say that living things do not engage in computation. For instance, DNA computing is an area of ongoing research, focusing on how to get DNA to solve computational problems of interest to humans. Of course, DNA can also be seen as solving computational problems of interest to the organism in its survival and reproduction. For DNA computing, see Gheorghe Paun, Grzegorz Rozenberg, and Arto Salomaa, *DNA Computing: New Computing Paradigms* (Berlin: Springer, 2010). For computation in biology and nature more generally, see Leslie Valiant, *Probably Approximately Correct: Nature's Algorithms for Learning and Prospering in a Complex World* (New York: Basic Books, 2013). But note, for living things to engage in computing is not equivalent to living things being computers. To argue for such an equivalence is to commit a fallacy of composition, like arguing that because a house is composed of bricks, therefore it is a brick. Living things engage in computation. True enough, and we can identify some of the computational steps that they take. But that is a far cry from saying that the physical structure of an acorn encapsulates an algorithm that, when executed, issues in an oak tree. Unlike computer algorithms constructed by humans, we lack the broad outlines, to say nothing of a detailed articulation, of what such an "acorn-to-oak-tree algorithm" would look like and how it would operate.

external design. Thus, throughout this chapter, many references to design have been to external design. But design, as it appears in the term intelligent design, refers to patterns or distinguishing marks in things that give evidence of real teleology or intelligence (regardless of how those patterns got there). These two meanings, distinct as they are, however, hardly exhaust the semantic range of the word design. Design can also refer to any causal process that brings form to a thing, regardless of whether it is teleological or nonteleological and regardless of whether it acts internally or externally. For instance, Arizona State University offers a program in "biological design." On the program's homepage, one reads, "What is biological design? Biological design attempts to mimic or harness natural processes by understanding the rules by which nature designs highly adaptable and efficient systems."[33] Notice the non-Aristotelian juxtaposition of nature and design in this quote: nature is treated as the subject of the verb design.

Most importantly for this book's sequel, however, design needs also to be regarded as a generic term for signifying intelligence or teleology. Design is, in fact, a recognized synonym for teleology, or end-directedness, in general. For example, the teleological argument for God's existence is also called the design argument.[34] Some design arguments understand teleology as implemented through external design, others through internal nature. But design arguments are, in the first instance, concerned with teleology, construed quite broadly, and only secondarily concerned with the causal form that teleology must take. In any case, many references to design later in this book should be understood in this generic teleological sense. "Design explanations" are therefore explanations that explain by appealing to intelligence or teleology. "Products of design" are therefore things that result from intelligence or teleology. To say that something happened "by design" is to say that it happened for an end or on purpose. All such usage falls within recognized meanings of the word design. This is not to rule out that design may still mean external design, but when it does, I'll eliminate all doubt by referring explicitly to external design.

---

[33]   Quoted from http://www.biologicaldesign.asu.edu/home (last accessed October 4, 2013). Obviously, the biologists at Arizona State University are not suggesting that the designs they are examining are a consequence of a conscious intentional agent acting outside of ordinary biological processes to impose external design.

[34]   William A. Dembski, "The Design Argument," in *The History of Science and Religion in the Western Tradition: An Encyclopedia*, ed. G.B. Ferngren (New York: Garland, 2000).

Chapter 9

Natural Teleological Laws

It is by now no secret that I approach the discussion over information and materialism from the vantage of Christian theism. I therefore see nature as a created order endowed by its creator with certain powers, all of which may be regarded as teleological since they were intended by God. But Christianity goes further, holding to a supernatural deity, with God acting in ways that transcend nature's inherent powers. Although God has instituted these natural powers, they are not adequate to accomplish all that God intends for nature. We see this incompleteness of nature especially in the Christian doctrine of redemption, in which the salvation of humanity requires an act of divine grace that goes beyond what nature by itself is able to accomplish. Indeed, the very concept of grace is the giving of a gift that the recipient could not have conjured up on one's own.

Christian theism therefore regards nature as inherently incomplete, finding its completion in God. That said, Christian theism is compatible with God delegating to nature many of its powers (cf. the medieval distinction between primary and secondary causes, secondary causes operating under their own power, instituted by the primary cause, God). In fact, it's not clear that Christianity requires direct divine intervention in anything except for what pertains to the salvation of humanity (e.g., the Incarnation, Resurrection, sacraments, saving faith). All of natural history, insofar as it can be distinguished from salvation history, may thus result from natural powers implanted by God but which are free from direct divine control. Christian thinkers are far from united on this point, some preferring a hands-on interventionist deity even in natural history, others preferring a hands-off laissez-faire deity. In any case, theism, whether Christian or otherwise, allows a great deal of latitude to the nature of nature, not imposing a priori constraints on nature but letting inquiry and evidence dictate what nature is and what causal powers operate in it.

I raise this capacity of theism to accommodate a range of conceptions about nature because I want, as much as possible, to make common cause with naturalistic nonmaterialists, like Thomas Nagel. In his book *Mind & Cosmos*, Nagel recognizes the bankruptcy of materialism in its mechanistic understanding of nature, but at the same time he wants to find a naturalistic basis for the teleology that animates nature. I desire to make common cause with such naturalistic nonmaterialists not because it is politically expedient in the controversy with Darwinian materialism but because theistic and naturalistic nonmaterialists are both attempting, without the blinders of materialism, to understand how teleology operates in nature. Thus, it seems to me, both sides should be able to come to some basic, even if limited, agreement on how teleology operates in nature and, at those points of agreement, advance a common teleological understanding of nature.

Fruitful discussion between theistic and naturalistic nonmaterialists about teleology in nature often gets sidelined because the idioms we use tend to clash. For instance, as a theist, I assume that a personal intelligence is the ultimate source of information in nature, and that God is the best candidate for that intelligence. Naturalistic nonmaterialists, by contrast, agree that nature is more than matter but propose an impersonal and immanent naturalistic teleology in place of God as the source of that information. Accordingly, theistic nonmaterialists will tend to view a naturalistic teleology as logically downstream from, and thus as a poor metaphysical substitute for, divine action. Conversely, naturalistic nonmaterialists will tend to view divine action as an unnecessary addition to, and thus as a metaphysical distraction from, teleology as it actually operates in nature.

Although theistic and naturalistic nonmaterialists may thus appear to be at loggerheads, in fact there is a way forward for both sides to work together profitably to understand teleology in nature. Nagel himself opens the door to such a collaboration when he writes,

> Even though the theistic outlook, in some versions, is consistent with the available scientific evidence, I don't believe it, and am drawn instead to a naturalistic, though non-materialist, alternative. Mind, I suspect, is not an inexplicable accident or a divine and anomalous gift but a basic aspect of nature that we will not understand until we transcend the built-in limits of contemporary scientific orthodoxy. I would add that even some theists might find this acceptable; since they could maintain that God is ultimately responsible for such an expanded natural order, as they believe he is for the laws of physics.[1]

---

[1]   Quoted from Thomas Nagel's *New York Times* synopsis of his book *Mind & Cosmos*, titled "The Core of 'Mind & Cosmos,'" August 18, 2013, available online at http://opinionator.blogs.nytimes.com/2013/08/18/the-core-of-mind-and-cosmos/?_r=1 (last accessed September 25, 2013). In *Mind & Cosmos* (p. 95), Nagel expands on the point he makes in that synopsis: "My preference for an immanent natural explanation is congruent with my atheism. But even a theist who believes God is ultimately responsible for the appearance of conscious life could maintain that this happens as part of a natural

Practically speaking, how might these two parties make common cause, those who hold that teleology is an inherent property of nature (naturalistic nonmaterialists) and those who hold that teleology is a property of nature put there by God (certain, but not all, theistic nonmaterialists)? It seems, for starters, both parties can agree that certain items of information in nature are beyond the reach of purely material processes and should properly be traced to a nonmaterial source of information. Nagel, as we saw in the previous chapter, takes such an approach to the origin of life. Here are some further remarks from him on that topic:

> [N]o viable account, even a purely speculative one, seems to be available of how a system as staggeringly functionally complex and information-rich as a self-reproducing cell, controlled by DNA, RNA, or some predecessor, could have arisen by chemical evolution alone from a dead environment. Recognition of the problem is not limited to the defenders of intelligent design. Although scientists continue to seek a purely chemical explanation of the origin of life, there are also card-carrying scientific naturalists like Francis Crick who say that it seems almost like a miracle ... Some form of natural teleology ... would be an alternative to a miracle.[2]

Confronted with informational structures required for the origin of life, materialists, predictably, will search for a materialist explanation and continue that search even as careful analysis of the relevant material processes reveals that life's materialistic origin is vastly improbable.[3] Nagel is unwilling to ascribe the origin of life to such a probabilistic miracle (i.e., a vastly improbable event on the basis of material processes). At the same time, as a naturalist, he is unwilling to ascribe it to a divine miracle (i.e., God intervening supernaturally to bring about

---

order that is created by God, but that it does not require further divine intervention. A theist not committed to dualism in the philosophy of mind could suppose that the natural possibility of conscious organisms resides already in the character of the elements out of which those organisms are composed, perhaps supplemented by laws of psychophysical emergence. To make the possibility of conscious life a consequence of the natural order created by God while ascribing its actuality to subsequent divine intervention would then seem an arbitrary complication. Some form of teleological naturalism should for these reasons seem no less credible than an interventionist explanation, even to those who believe that God is ultimately responsible for everything."

[2] Nagel, *Mind & Cosmos*, 123–4.

[3] For the bankruptcy of materialistic origin-of-life scenarios, see William A. Dembski and Jonathan Wells, *How to Be an Intellectually Fulfilled Atheist (Or Not)* (Wilmington, Del.: ISI Books, 2008), which examines all the main proposals currently in vogue for how life might have originated by purely materialistic means, and shows all of them to fail badly.

life).[4] Instead, he desires a third way, that is, a natural teleology. Although the natural teleology that Nagel wants as an alternative to Darwinian materialism remains, for now, largely speculative,[5] he does nonetheless sketch a way to understand teleology in nature that teleologists, both naturalistic and theistic, can, it seems to me, get behind.

Specifically, Nagel proposes to understand teleology in terms of *natural teleological laws*. These laws would be radically different from the laws of physics and chemistry that currently are paradigmatic of the laws of nature. And yet, as we will see, such teleological laws fit quite naturally within an information-theoretic framework. The idea that teleology in nature, especially with regard to the origin of life, requires radically new laws or principles has been in circulation for several decades, and not just within the intelligent design community.[6] Often, however, such laws or principles are raised as sheer possibilities, without giving any sense of what they might actually look like; or else they are proposed in loose analogy to well-known self-organizational processes (drawn from

----

[4] Nagel explicitly rejects both these senses of miracle: "either in the sense of a wildly improbable fluke or in the sense of a divine intervention in the natural order." *Mind & Cosmos*, 124. Yet, unlike a probabilistic miracle, a divine miracle is at least on the side of teleology, even if it is a supernatural rather than a natural teleology of the sort that Nagel prefers. So why does Nagel prefer a natural teleology? Not on principled grounds but because of his allergy to theism: "My preference for an immanent natural explanation is congruent with my atheism." Elsewhere he'll refer to his "ungrounded intellectual preference" for such a view, holding up "the ideal of discovering a single natural order that unifies everything on the basis of a set of common elements or principles." Ibid., 95, 26, and 7, respectively.

[5] "These teleological speculations are offered merely as possibilities, without positive conviction." Ibid., 124.

[6] Paul Davies, for instance, in *The Fifth Miracle*, his book on the origin of life, writes: "[W]e have a good idea of the where and the when of life's origin, but we are a very long way from comprehending the how. This gulf in understanding is not merely ignorance about certain technical details, it is a major conceptual lacuna. I am not suggesting that life's origin was a supernatural event, only that we are missing something very fundamental about the whole business. If it is the case, as so many experts and commentators suggest, that life is bound to arise given the right conditions, then something truly amazing is happening in the universe, something with profound philosophical ramifications. My personal belief, for what it is worth, is that a fully satisfactory theory of the origin of life demands some radically new ideas." Quoted from Davies, *The Fifth Miracle*, 17. To this Davies adds that the key problem that needs to be resolved in understanding life's origin is the origin of biological information: "To comprehend fully how life arose from nonlife, we need to know not only how biological information was concentrated, but also how biologically useful information came to be *specified*, given that the milieu from which the first organism emerged was presumably just a random mix of molecular building blocks. In short, how did meaningful information emerge spontaneously from incoherent junk?" Ibid., 112–13.

physics, chemistry, or pure mathematics), yet without providing details for how the analogy actually elucidates the point in question, in this case, life's origin.[7]

Nagel, by contrast, sketches what a natural teleological law might look like. I quote his proposal, given in *Mind & Cosmos*, here in full because it connects, point for point, with the account of information given in this book. Indeed, Nagel's teleological laws are none other than the directed searches (or alternative searches) that are the basis of Conservation of Information treated in chapters 17 through 19 of this book. Here is Nagel's proposal:

> Natural teleology would require two things. First, that the nonteleological and timeless laws of physics—those governing the ultimate elements of the physical universe, whatever they are—are not fully deterministic. Given the physical state of the universe at any moment, the laws of physics would have to leave open a range of alternative successor states, presumably with a probability distribution over them.
>
> Second, among those possible futures there will be some that are more eligible than others as possible steps on the way to the formation of more complex systems, and ultimately of the kinds of replicating systems characteristic of life. The existence of teleology requires that successor states in this subset have a significantly higher probability than is entailed by the laws of physics alone—simply because they are on the path toward a certain outcome. Teleological laws would assign higher probability to steps on paths in state space that have a higher "velocity" toward certain outcomes [here Nagel cites an article by Hawthorne and Nolan titled "What Would Teleological Causation Be?"]. They would be laws of the self-organization of matter, essentially—or of whatever is more basic than matter.[8]

---

[7]   In the last note, for instance, I describe Paul Davies as raising all the right questions about life's origin. Yet nowhere in *The Fifth Miracle* does he even make a stab at answering them, that is, nowhere does he offer even a hint of the radically new ideas that he thinks will be needed to explain life's origin. In a similar vein, Stuart Kauffman will write *At Home in the Universe: The Search for the Laws of Self-Organization and Complexity* (New York: Oxford University Press, 1995). There he describes self-organizational processes from physics and chemistry (e.g., Belousov–Zhabotinsky reactions) as well as self-organizational models from pure mathematics (e.g., NK Boolean networks), yet he fails to show how any of these go beyond merely gesturing at the problem of biological information. The processes and models he considers are used as loose analogies at best and provide no substantive insight into life's origin (indeed, if they did, we would be hearing a lot more about them in current origin-of-life research).

[8]   Nagel, *Mind & Cosmos*, 92–3. The article by Hawthorne and Nolan is John Hawthorne and Daniel Nolan, "What Would Teleological Causation Be?" in John Hawthorne, *Metaphysical Essays* (Oxford: Oxford University Press, 2006), 265–83.

I must confess that when I first read this passage by Nagel, I dismissed his reference to teleological laws as more of the same handwaving on which I had surfeited over the years reading, and continually being disappointed in, the evolutionary and self-organizational literature. After years and years of reading about laws of nature that are supposed to generate biological information, but always finding that such laws, because modeled on the laws of physics and chemistry, were too informationally poor to explain the vast amounts of information required by biology, I was psychologically primed to dismiss Nagel's reference to teleological laws. Moreover, because of my continual past disappointments, I didn't, on that first reading, follow up his reference to Hawthorne and Nolan. Only in correspondence with Nagel, and at his urging to read the Hawthorne and Nolan paper, did it become clear to me what he was doing and that it matched up, precisely, with my own project as carried out in this book.

Let me therefore recast Nagel's idea of a natural teleological law within the information-theoretic framework that I have developed thus far in this book and as I will be developing it in later chapters. Nagel is a naturalist but not a materialist. Thus he sees nature as subject to physical constraints, which he calls the laws of physics. These laws are for him not deterministic. They allow plenty of freedom to nature. As it is, however, they allow so much freedom that for nature to exhibit teleology, it must produce events of exceeding improbability as gauged by the probability distributions that the laws of physics place over nature. Given the probability distributions compatible with these laws or physical constraints, for teleology to happen in nature requires a probabilistic miracle. Note that a probability distribution, in this context, is a way of assigning probabilities to different events or possibilities under consideration. Note also that Nagel's method of reasoning here with probabilities is an instance of the materialist-refuting logic outlined in the last chapter.

In terms of the information-theoretic framework developed so far in this book, all this is to say that when an aspect of nature is treated as a matrix of possibility, it comes with a probability distribution induced by ordinary physical constraints (Nagel's laws of physics). Moreover, such a distribution is spread out so diffusely over the matrix as to be unable to single out particular teleological ends, which we'll also call targets, with anything like a probability big enough for us to be justified in thinking that nature might reasonably be expected to attain these ends or targets. To anticipate chapters 17 through 19, which focus on search, when nature acts according to ordinary physical constraints as given by the laws of physics, it conducts a *blind search* that assigns very little probability to the ends or targets that nature, if teleological, would have. Ordinary physical constraints thus induce a blind search on nature, and blind search, which experience teaches cannot find a needle in a haystack, is effectively incapable of finding nature's ends or targets (except as a probabilistic miracle).

So how can nature break free of blind search, sidestepping the abysmally small probabilities that make it effectively impossible to attain nature's targets? Put differently, how is nature to amplify the probabilities of attaining these targets so that nature stands a realistic shot at actually attaining them? This is where Nagel's second requirement for a natural teleology comes in: teleological laws must exist that change the probabilities induced by ordinary physical constraints, assigning higher probabilities to nature's ends or targets so that these become realistically attainable. Or, as Nagel puts it, "teleological laws would assign higher probability to steps on paths in state space that have a higher 'velocity' toward certain outcomes."[9] The reference to "velocity" here comes from the Hawthorne and Nolan paper on teleological causation,[10] and concerns paths through state space that take an optimally quick or direct route to the end/target. Moreover, the reference to state space here is a standard multidimensional way of representing nature, with each point in state space representing one way nature as a whole can be, and a path through state space representing changes in nature over time.

The particulars of Hawthorne and Nolan's proposal for teleological laws need not detain us. In their paper, they specified two ways of representing teleological laws in terms of a (quasi) least action principle. While interesting and potentially useful for characterizing certain forms of teleology (embryological development comes to mind), I don't see their proposal as encompassing all that we might want to mean by teleological laws. Indeed, if the point of teleological laws is, as Nagel suggests, to change probabilities, so that targets exceedingly improbable under the laws of physics become sufficiently probable as to be realistically attainable, then it seems that teleological laws can be characterized, at least in the first instance, simply as probability distributions that assign higher probabilities to those ends/targets than are assigned by the laws of physics.

My identification of natural laws with probability distributions should not be cause for alarm. All the laws of physics specify what nature can and cannot do in terms of probabilities (for deterministic laws, the probabilities are all zero or one). If you will, any law can be redescribed in terms of a probability distribution that assigns higher probability according to what the law predicts as more likely. To be sure, probability theory is no substitute for the physical insight of a Newton or Einstein, but once their insights are in hand, their laws—Newtonian

---

9   Nagel, *Mind & Cosmos*, 93.
10   Hawthorne and Nolan, "What Would Teleological Causation Be?"

mechanics or Einstein's field equations—can be redescribed probabilistically. For instance, Newtonian mechanics may predict a particular trajectory for a cannonball. Correspondingly, a probability distribution may pick out that trajectory, in this case assigning it a probability of one, within a matrix of all possible cannonball trajectories.

If this identification between natural laws and probability distributions seems reasonable, the next one may seem a stretch. Stretch or not, however, this identification works. Specifically, I want to suggest that searches may also be identified with probability distributions, where success of the search in finding an end/target is gauged probabilistically, so that a search becomes more effective to the degree that the probability of finding the end/target, as assigned by the distribution, increases.[11] Given such a probabilistic redescription of search, the laws of physics then induce blind searches whereas teleological laws induce directed searches. Moreover, what distinguishes these two types of searches is that a directed search is able to locate an end/target not as a probabilistic miracle, as with a blind search, but as a reasonably probable event, one that we could expect to witness in real time.

I'm glossing over many details here. Yet I feel justified in doing so because all the issues just raised will be revisited and covered in detail later in this book as I explore the topic of search in depth (especially in chapters 17 through 19). A natural teleological law, *sensu* Nagel, is identical with a directed or alternative search as described later in this book. Moreover, all such searches are subject to a conservation law (Conservation of Information), which quantifies how much information these teleological laws can contain and express. This means that unlike classical teleologies, which are purely qualitative, natural teleological laws, when conceived as search, can, at least in principle, be quantified in precise information-theoretic terms.

For Nagel, natural teleological laws help to distinguish between, as he puts it, "an immanent natural teleology and a supernatural interventionist teleology":

> [An immanent natural teleology] could be accepted by a theist, as grounded
> ultimately in divine creation. But a natural teleology, whether free-standing
> or theistically explained, is a system of general teleological principles or laws.
> Supernatural teleology, by contrast, consists of individual events purposely brought

---

[11]   Characterizing search in terms of probability distributions is not new. Michael D. Vose did so in his article "Random Heuristic Search," *Theoretical Computer Science* 229(1) (1999): 103–42. Nonetheless, for a fully general treatment of search in terms of probability distributions, see chapters 17 and 18 and especially the references there to my work with the Evolutionary Informatics Lab.

about. With respect to the origin of life, for example, this would mean that a supernatural explanation of its occurrence on earth would imply nothing about the likelihood of its occurrence elsewhere in the universe. Whereas an immanent teleological explanation would imply that tendencies or principles were at work which make it much more likely to occur repeatedly than it would in a universe governed exclusively by the laws of physics and chemistry. This is a big difference, though at present I see no evidential grounds for choosing between the two. That is why I mention that my atheism is a conviction not based on evidence, though it leads me to seek a certain kind of solution to the evident inadequacy of materialism.[12]

Unlike Nagel, I'm not so convinced that natural teleological laws do in fact favor an immanent natural teleology over a supernatural interventionist teleology (or what in the last chapter I called divine external design). As Nagel admits, both forms of teleology are, at least for now, empirically indistinguishable. Indeed, insofar as they are incompatible with materialism, both will require probabilistic miracles (as gauged from the vantage of ordinary physical causality acceptable to materialism). Nagel suggests that once we start looking for patterns in the outcomes of nature, there would be a difference between these two forms of teleology. But it's not clear that advocating one form of teleology over the other in such cases would constitute anything more than a metaphysical preference. A supernatural interventionist teleology, if not capricious (and why should it be capricious?), could act consistently with certain policies, norms, or directives. In that case, a natural teleological law might as much characterize the behavior of a supernatural interventionist teleology as an immanent natural teleology.[13]

---

[12]   Thomas Nagel, personal email correspondence, September 26, 2013. I quote from this correspondence rather than from *Mind & Cosmos* because it provides a particularly clear statement of Nagel's view on the difference between immanent and supernatural teleology.

[13]   Paleobiologist Simon Conway Morris, in his book *Life's Solution: Inevitable Humans in a Lonely Universe* (Cambridge: Cambridge University Press, 2003), suggests that an immanent teleology more readily explains biological convergence than a supernatural teleology. But the case that he lays out, which is the best that I know for an immanent teleology, still seems to me to leave open a supernatural teleology (albeit, without ruling out teleological laws). "Convergence" here refers to a counterintuitive finding from evolutionary biology. When organisms share some feature, the first impulse of evolutionary biologists is to attribute it to evolution from a common ancestor. Similarity is thus explained as a common inheritance. Not every similar biological feature, however, can be attributed to descent from a common evolutionary ancestor. Indeed, biologists have shown that organisms can share a similar feature and yet have no common ancestor that exhibited that feature. This means that in the evolution of organisms sharing such a feature, the feature had to be *reinvented* (or *re-evolved*) separately on a number of occasions. This is biological convergence, and Conway

In closing this chapter, I want to revisit the role of matter in relation to natural teleological laws. Nagel, to argue that natural teleological laws are real and significant in nature, employs the materialist-refuting logic. The materialist-

---

Morris documents many fascinating examples of it. *Life's Solution* even includes a five-page, double-columned index cataloguing such convergences.

Biological convergence becomes downright astonishing when the similarity verges on identity. One of the best-known examples of a striking convergence is the camera eye in vertebrates and cephalopods (such as human and octopus eyes, respectively). These eyes are highly complex and almost point-for-point identical (the only obvious difference is the neural wiring—in vertebrates it is backwards, the nuclear layer being in front of the retina, thus resulting in a blind spot). Yet, evolutionary evidence, such as it is, suggests that humans and octopuses had separate evolutionary precursors of which neither possessed eyes at all. Thus, in the evolution of humans and octopuses, evolution required the reinvention of virtually identical camera eyes from scratch twice. This is remarkable. Nor is convergence an isolated, anomalous fact of biology. Rather, it is the norm. Virtually identical biological structures and functions keep getting reinvented, and in ways that cannot be attributed to a common inheritance from a common evolutionary ancestor.

For Conway Morris, biological convergence signifies that the evolutionary process is inherently teleological. In particular, biological convergence leads Conway Morris to reject Stephen Jay Gould's view that evolution is haphazard, riddled with contingencies, so that if we were to run the tape of life again, nothing would be the same—for Gould, not only might humans not exist, but neither organisms with our intelligence nor even organisms as we know them might exist. See Stephen Jay Gould, *Wonderful Life: The Burgess Shale and the Nature of History* (New York: Norton, 1989), 48, 50. In teleological language similar to Nagel's, but restricted to biology, Conway Morris writes (*Life's Solution*, p. 66): "Everything we know about biology argues that it is seeded with inevitabilities; in principle, there is an incomprehensibly enormous universe of possibilities, but in reality the number of destinations ... is a vestigially minuscule fraction of the theoretical possibilities that can never be visited not because the journey would never be made, but because the journey would never be possible in the Universe we happen to inhabit."

Such inevitabilities could be treated as a consequence of natural teleological laws. Such laws would sharply limit the number of trajectories that the evolutionary process may take, constraining it to converge on certain ends (e.g., camera eyes) and bypassing the vast majority of alternative trajectories, alternatives that would be compatible with material mechanisms like natural selection and genetic drift, but that would miss the ends or targets specified by natural teleological laws. Would such laws have to characterize an immanent natural teleology? Could they not equally characterize a supernatural intervening teleology that acts (according to certain policies, norms, or directives) to implement certain patterns consistently, such as a directive to bring about in animals a pair of eyes (camera or compound) for viewing light within a certain spectrum? Add engineering to a supernatural teleology, and we should expect to see past successful designs reused repeatedly. It's therefore far from evident that natural teleological laws clearly distinguish an immanent natural teleology from a supernatural interventionist teleology. Rather, it seems that such laws could characterize both forms of teleology.

refuting logic assumes, for the sake of argument, that nature is essentially material, only to show that matter is insufficient to account for all that happens in nature. But that raises a question: once the materialist-refuting logic has done its work in refuting materialism, how should nature be conceived? Nagel, in specifying his two requirements for natural teleological laws earlier in this chapter, hints that nature is more than matter. Thus he will muse about "the ultimate elements of the physical universe, whatever they are" and describe teleological laws as "laws of the self-organization of matter, essentially—or of whatever is more basic than matter." But if matter is not the most basic stuff of nature, what is? The short answer, as I've already indicated in earlier chapters, is information. I want therefore next to show how matter itself is a form of information.

Chapter 10
Getting Matter from Information

Materialism regards information as the ways matter can be structured. If it is structured in one way to the exclusion of others, then it conveys information. By itself, the ability of matter to convey information seems unproblematic: information can be embedded in matter and the existence of matter is compatible with information. But the big question for materialism is whether matter can, with no residual or remainder, provide an adequate account of information. And an even more daring question is whether matter itself might be a form of information. The last two generations have seen information slipping free from the grip of matter. Cybernetics founder Norbert Wiener, for instance, thought that information could not be subsumed under matter: "Information is information, not matter or energy. No materialism which does not admit this can survive at the present day."[1]

For materialism, when matter carries information, it does so accidentally in the sense that nonteleological rather than teleological forces of nature are thought ultimately to underlie the information. Think of a set of rocks arranged in a particular way at the fork in a road. If the rocks are arranged one way rather than another, it could be a signal from one traveler to another to "take a right." The arrangement of rocks would therefore convey information because one intelligence intends by it to communicate with another. Such information would have content, contain meaning, constitute semantic information—it would not just be information in the sense of brute arrangement, complexity, or contingency. Yet from the vantage of materialism, all such intention or semantics ultimately dissolves into the nonteleological interplay of matter. The arrangement of rocks as well as the arrangement of the brain responsible for arranging the rocks both result, in the end, from processes that are nonteleological—if, that is, materialism is true.

But why should we think materialism is true? Indeed, there is reason to think that materialism is false and that information (even information with an intentional or teleological underpinning) is more fundamental than matter. I remember once listening to a lecture in which the speaker pounded a desk to

---

[1] Norbert Wiener, *Cybernetics*, 2nd edn. (Cambridge, Mass.: MIT Press, 1961), 132.

make the point that matter is, of all things, most real. As theatrics go, it wasn't bad, but such displays hide that matter is in fact mysterious. Sure, we can pound on medium-sized objects composed of matter, such as desks, to make the point that matter is real. But what is matter, really? The beauty of materialism is that it casts the world as a giant billiard table on which all reality plays out as certain billiard balls (items of matter) interact mechanically with other billiard balls (other items of matter). Materialism offers a simple, easily conceptualized picture of what is supposed to constitute nuts-and-bolts reality. But such pictures give at best an illusion of understanding. In fact, they cloak vast ignorance about the true nature of reality.

To see why matter is not nearly as perspicuous a notion as materialists claim, it is instructive to see how materialism has played out in the philosophy of science from Newton to Einstein. I say philosophy of science rather than science per se, because science, with the rise of Newtonian mechanics, was quite happy with a materialist understanding of nature. In Newtonian mechanics, moving objects are treated as point masses located at their centers of mass (Democritus would have been pleased). But as philosophers tried to make sense of this materialist understanding of the world, they ran into difficulty. What made Newtonian mechanics so convincing was its success at matching observation. Indeed, without such observational support and the insight Newtonian mechanics thus seemed to provide in understanding nature, there would have been no point in preferring Newtonian mechanics to the old Aristotelian science. So the question arose, what were we, as empirically minded scientists, actually observing?

When philosopher John Locke, Newton's contemporary and a thorough-going empiricist, pondered this question, he encountered an impasse. Something—some substance—surely had to underlie our observations. But what was it? Perhaps the most famous quote from Locke's celebrated *Essay Concerning Human Understanding* is his answer, or I should say non-answer, to this question: "I know not what."[2] Consistent with Newtonian mechanics, Locke might have said

---

[2] The quote, which, in context, attempts to elucidate both spiritual and material substance, reads, "For putting together the ideas of thinking and willing, or the power of moving or quieting corporeal motion, joined to substance, of which we have no distinct idea, we have the idea of an immaterial spirit; and by putting together the ideas of coherent solid parts, and a power of being moved joined with substance, of which likewise we have no positive idea, we have the idea of matter. The one is as clear and distinct an idea as the other: the idea of thinking, and moving a body, being as clear and distinct ideas as the ideas of extension, solidity, and being moved. For our idea of substance is equally obscure, or none at all, in both: it is but a supposed *I know not what*, to support those ideas we call accidents. It is for want of reflection that we are apt to think that our senses show us nothing

that the ultimate substance, the thing undergirding our observation, was point particles of matter.[3] But the problem for Locke, as a good empiricist, was that we have no direct observational experience of such matter. And even if we did, why should we trust that observation gives us access to rock-bottom reality?[4] Indeed, we never observe matter as matter. George Berkeley, his idealism aside, made the point this way:

> I do not argue against the existence of any one thing that we can apprehend, either by sense or reflexion. That the things I see with mine eyes and touch with my hands do exist, really exist, I make not the least question. The only thing whose existence we deny, is that which philosophers call matter or corporeal substance. And in doing of this, there is no damage done to the rest of mankind, who, I dare say, will never miss it. The atheist indeed will want the colour of an empty name to support his impiety; and the philosophers may possibly find, they have lost a great handle for trifling and disputation.[5]

Matter is an abstraction drawn from the multitudinous array of objects we observe with our senses. This makes matter problematic as a basis for ontology. It is the old dilemma confronting Democritus, who, as we saw in chapter 1, regarded all reality as consisting of atoms in the void, but then could not justify such a materialist view given that all evidence for it would have to come from the senses, giving the senses logical priority over matter and thus making matter at

---

but material things. Every act of sensation, when duly considered, gives us an equal view of both parts of nature, the corporeal and spiritual." John Locke, *An Essay Concerning Human Understanding*, ed. Peter H. Nidditch (Oxford: Clarendon, 1975), 2.23.15, emphasis added. The quote by Newton in the next note makes essentially the same point.

[3]   Newton, as a theist, would have disagreed. God, for him, would have been the ultimate substance: "[God] is entirely void of all body and corporeal form, and therefore cannot be seen, nor heard, nor touched: nor ought he to be worshipped under the image of any corporeal object. We have ideas of its attributes, but we do not have the least knowledge of what the substance of any object is. We see only the shapes and colors of bodies, we hear only sounds, we touch only the external surfaces, we smell only odors, and taste flavors: we have no cognition of the inmost substances by any sense or act of reflection, and much less do we have an idea of the substance of God." Quoted from Dana Densemore, *Newton's Principia: The Central Argument*, 3rd edn., trans. W. H. Donahue (Santa Fe, N. Mex.: Green Lion Press, 2003), 487–8. The quote by Locke in the previous note makes essentially the same point.

[4]   "It is for want of reflection that we are apt to think that our senses show us nothing but material things." Locke, *Essay*, 2.23.15.

[5]   George Berkeley, *Principles of Human Knowledge*, in Howard Robinson, ed., *Principles of Human Knowledge and Three Dialogues* (Oxford: Oxford University Press, 1996), 38.

best an inference from sense data. Let's dwell on this point a bit longer because in our materialistic culture it is a point too easily passed over. If you want to be a materialist by simply making materialism an article of faith, you are welcome to it. Such *fideistic materialism*, however, is not the sort of materialism that we confront in our day. Rather, we confront a *scientific materialism* that attempts to justify materialism on the basis of science. And how does it use science to justify materialism? By arguing that the success of science flows directly from attempting to understand the world in materialist terms.[6]

Now I would grant that certain phenomena seem adequately explained on materialistic principles. The motions of planets, stars, and galaxies, for instance. But many things closer to home, such as consciousness, language, and intention, though having material correlates, are far from being given a full account in material terms, and that notwithstanding protestations by materialists like Daniel Dennett and Paul Churchland, who proclaim that a materialist resolution of all the deep problems of human nature is just around the corner and that anyone who bets against materialism ultimately winning the day is a fool.[7] But even if materialists were on stronger footing regarding these deep unresolved problems, the success of a materialist science is hardly the basis for a compelling argument about fundamental ontology.

Let us, for the sake of argument, grant that a materialist science has been overwhelmingly successful (and not, as it is now, an explanatory enterprise with vast gaping holes). Even in that case, why should we take matter as fundamental? The success of science, as a temporally conditioned fact, can at best tell us that science in its current practice has till now succeeded on materialist principles;

---

    6   See, for instance, Barbara Forrest's defense of methodological naturalism/materialism in "Methodological Naturalism and Philosophical Naturalism: Clarifying the Connection," *Philo* 3(2) (Fall–Winter 2000): 7–29. There she writes, "the philosophical naturalist justifies it [i.e., methodological naturalism/materialism] on the basis of the explanatory success of science and the lack of explanatory success of supernaturalism." Forrest's article is available online at http://www.infidels.org/library/modern/barbara_forrest/naturalism.html (last accessed June 5, 2013).

    7   See Paul Churchland, *Matter and Consciousness: A Contemporary Introduction to the Philosophy of Mind*, rev. edn. (Cambridge, Mass.: MIT Press, 1988) and Daniel C. Dennett, "'A Perfect and Beautiful Machine': What Darwin's Theory of Evolution Reveals About Artificial Intelligence," *The Atlantic* (June 22, 2012), posted online at http://www.theatlantic.com/technology/archive/2012/06/a-perfect-and-beautiful-machine-what-darwins-theory-of-evolution-reveals-about-artificial-intelligence/258829. I reply to Dennett here: "Dennett on Competence without Comprehension," *Evolution News and Views* (June 28, 2012), posted online at http://www.evolutionnews.org/2012/06/dennett_on_comp061451.html (both articles last accessed June 5, 2013).

it cannot tell us that in the future it will continue to succeed on materialist principles. Accordingly, materialism might be taken as a working hypothesis for investigating and understanding certain aspects of nature. But that's a far cry from dogmatically holding materialism as a first philosophy obligatory on all who would try to understand the true nature of nature.

Yet there is a still deeper problem with elevating materialism to a fundamental principle of science. Democritus glimpsed it. Locke and his fellow empiricists saw it more clearly, namely, that an empirical science never observes matter as such but rather must infer matter from observation. Observation, from the vantage of an empirical science, is logically prior to matter. Now it's interesting to trace where the philosophy of science went with this. Science, which tends not to be too self-reflective, at least as practiced by scientists (there are exceptions, such as Pierre Duhem[8]), has tended to embrace materialism, whether a stricter metaphysical sort that regards all reality as material or a milder methodological sort that regards science as a study properly limited to material categories. But philosophy, which puts a premium on consistency and coherence of a system of thought, found, especially when it reflected on scientific inquiry as actually practiced by scientists, that materialism is difficult, if not impossible, to justify, especially as a first philosophy.

What stands behind observation? This question admits no easy answer, in terms of matter or otherwise. The problem is that observation itself cannot tell us what stands behind observation—hence Locke's "I know not what." Observation may seem to tell us that matter stands behind observation. But observation trades in appearances, not necessarily in reality, and just because things appear material doesn't mean that they are or that that's all they are. There is no way to stand outside the observational act and verify that reality does in fact match up with observation (what would such verification be except further observation, which defeats the purpose of the exercise). So whence the confidence that observation is giving us true insight into the world?[9]

---

8   See Pierre Duhem, *The Aim and Structure of Physical Theory*, trans. P.P. Wiener (Princeton, N.J.: Princeton University Press, 1991 [1914]) and Pierre Duhem, *To Save the Phenomena: An Essay on the Idea of Physical Theory from Plato to Galileo*, trans. E. Dolan and C. Maschler (Chicago, Ill.: University of Chicago Press, 1969 [1908]).

9   G.K. Chesterton posed the problem more eloquently: "Reason is itself a matter of faith. It is an act of faith to assert that our thoughts have any relation to reality at all. If you are merely a sceptic, you must sooner or later ask yourself the question, 'Why should *anything* go right; even observation and deduction? Why should not good logic be as misleading as bad logic? They are both movements in the brain of a bewildered ape?' The young sceptic says, 'I have a right to think for myself.' But the old sceptic, the complete

To restore confidence, Descartes invoked a deity who would not deceive us.[10] Taking a more secular approach, Kant saw our reason as having an active role in structuring the appearances, the phenomena, given to us by observation.[11] This gave some objectivity to the phenomenal world. But the noumena, or "things in themselves," standing behind appearances were, for Kant, unknowable, which was in keeping with Locke's "I know not what."

Berkeley turned the problem on its head. For him there was no mind-independent world, material or otherwise, to be observed, but only minds that, in the act of observing, gave reality to things. Berkeley's idealism did not deny the reality of things but rather the ability of things to exist apart from minds. For him, to be was to be perceived, making material objects an expression of mind rather than vice versa, as it is for materialists.[12] Berkeley's move may seem like a step forward in understanding the connection between observation and the world. But then we need to inquire into the nature of observers and observation. What observation, at its most basic, seems to hand us is not full-fledged observers but sense experience. The skepticism of Hume can be seen as a response to Berkeley, in which a pure empiricism leads not to observers but to the sensory experiences that are constitutive of observation.[13]

---

sceptic, says, 'I have no right to think for myself. I have no right to think at all.'" Quoted from G.K. Chesterton, *Orthodoxy*, in *Collected Works of G.K. Chesterton*, vol. 1 (San Francisco, Calif.: Ignatius, 1986), 236, emphasis in original.

[10] "But once I perceived that there is a God, and also understood at the same time that everything else depends on him, and that he is not a deceiver, I then concluded that everything that I clearly and distinctly perceive is necessarily true." From the fifth meditation of René Descartes, *Meditations on First Philosophy*, in Donald A. Cress, trans., *Discourse on Method and Meditations on First Philosophy*, 4th edn. (Indianapolis, Ind.: Hackett, 1998), 91.

[11] Immanuel Kant, *Critique of Pure Reason*, trans. N.K. Smith (New York: St. Martin's, 1929 [1787]).

[12] "Some truths there are so near and obvious to the mind, that a man need only open his eyes to see them. Such I take this important one to be, to wit, that all the choir of heaven and furniture of the earth, in a word all those bodies which compose the mighty frame of the world, have not any subsistence without a mind, that their being is to be perceived or known; that consequently so long as they are not actually perceived by me, or do not exist in my mind or that of any other created spirit, they must either have no existence at all, or else subsist in the mind of some eternal spirit: it being perfectly unintelligible and involving all the absurdity of abstraction, to attribute to any single part of them an existence independent of a spirit. To be convinced of which, the reader need only reflect and try to separate in his own thoughts the being of a sensible thing from its being perceived." George Berkeley, *Principles of Human Knowledge*, 26.

[13] "And as the science of man is the only solid foundation for the other sciences, so the only solid foundation we can give to this science itself must be laid on experience and

The philosophy of science from Kant through Ernst Mach to the Vienna Circle of the 1920s and 30s attempts to synthesize sensory experience in a way that avoids skepticism and explains how science can count as knowledge (indeed, our best form of knowledge). Kant, for instance, saw the synthesis as requiring Euclidean (or flat) geometry, which for him helped to underwrite the science of Newton. Yet by the time of the Vienna Circle, Einstein had come along, and so the synthesis required non-Euclidean (or curved) geometry. The Vienna Circle focused especially on logic in synthesizing sensory experiences (hence the description of their movement as "logical positivism" or "logical empiricism"). This was not the logic of Aristotle but the powerful, and at the time new, logic developed at the hands of such philosopher–mathematicians as Gottlob Frege, Bertrand Russell, and Kurt Gödel.[14] Unfortunately, sense experience, even if articulated in a formal language and synthesized by the most powerful of logics, is incapable of getting very far beyond sense experience, and certainly not to the richness of reality that we appreciate in our less parsimonious moments (as, for instance, when we meditate on goodness, truth, and beauty).

In chapter 3 we considered what might be called the "Tang Problem" and applied it to materialism. Just as the breakfast drink Tang, consisting of orange juice solids, can never be reconstituted into fresh, full-fledged orange juice, so matter, at its most elemental and when reconstituted, has failed to yield the fullness of reality. Indeed, despite the promissory notes of many materialists, matter gives no evidence of having the wherewithal to complete this task of reconstitution. Materialists disagree with this pessimistic assessment of matter, and in doing so they defend a material reality that exists independently of us. Materialists are, and have always been, philosophical realists, embracing a metaphysics or first philosophy according to which a reality beyond appearance exists independently of us (the reality, in this case, being purely material).

---

observation ... For to me it seems evident, that the essence of the mind being equally unknown to us with that of external bodies, it must be equally impossible to form any notion of its powers and qualities otherwise than from careful and exact experiments, and the observation of those particular effects, which result from its different circumstances and situations. And though we must endeavour to render all our principles as universal as possible, by tracing up our experiments to the utmost, and explaining all effects from the simplest and fewest causes, it is still certain we cannot go beyond experience; and any hypothesis, that pretends to discover the ultimate original qualities of human nature, ought at first to be rejected as presumptuous and chimerical." David Hume, *A Treatise on Human Nature* (Oxford: Oxford University Press, 2007 [1739]), 4–5.

[14] See Jean van Heijenoort, *From Frege to Goedel: A Source Book in Mathematical Logic, 1879–1931* (Cambridge, Mass.: Harvard University Press, 2002).

The logical empiricists, by contrast, rejected metaphysics.[15] With sense experience, in its most immediate elemental form ("red here now"), as the basis for their philosophy, they were inherently incapable of looking beyond appearance (appearance being where sense experience resides) to any underlying reality (reality being the concern of first philosophy or metaphysics).[16] The logical empiricists were therefore anti-realists rather than realists. Even so, sense experience, as logical empiricists understood it, faced the same Tang Problem as materialism. The task of materialism is to show how the world can be reconstituted out of matter. The task of logical empiricism was to show how the world could be reconstituted out of sense experience. Though logical empiricism came crashing down in the 1940s and 50s as its verificationist understanding of meaning was shown to be either incoherent or irresolvable, its swan song was, in my view, sung in 1928 when Rudolf Carnap published *The Logical Structure of the World*.[17]

Carnap wrote in German, and so this title is a translation. The German title reads *Der logische Aufbau der Welt*. The German word "Aufbau" is a dynamic word suggesting action and hands-on construction. The English word "structure," which was used to translate "Aufbau," is a static word that really misses the point of the title and the book. Carnap's task in *Der logische Aufbau der Welt* was to sketch how all of human knowledge might be reconstituted through the ordering activity of logic on sense experience (or, more precisely, sense experience as articulated in a formal language). Alternatively, the book was an outline for the logico-empirical reconstruction of the whole of science. And yet even a cursory reading of *Der logische Aufbau* shows that logic and sense experience together are too meager to reconstitute the world, even if, as the logical empiricists held, it was a world of appearance (as opposed to an independently existing world

---

[15]   The anti-metaphysics and anti-realism of the logical positivists/empiricists is especially evident in A.J. Ayer, *Language, Truth, and Logic* (London: Penguin, 2001 [1936]) and A.J. Ayer, ed., *Logical Positivism* (New York: Free Press, 1959).

[16]   The history of the Vienna Circle and logical empiricism is more complicated than what I'm sketching here. The Vienna Circle included, inspired, and incited figures as diverse as Kurt Gödel (whose turn to logic can be credited to Moritz Schlick), Karl Popper, Ludwig Wittgenstein, and Otto Neurath. I mention Neurath because he is considered near the center of the Vienna Circle and yet reacted quite strongly against the phenomenalism of Carnap that I'm describing here and treating as representative of the Vienna Circle and logical empiricism. For Neurath's physicalist thesis in contrast to Carnap's phenomenalism, see his "Sociology in the Framework of Physicalism," in Otto Neurath, *Philosophical Papers 1913–1946*, eds. R.S. Cohen and M. Neurath (Dordrecht: Reidel, 1983 [1932]), 58–90.

[17]   Rudolf Carnap, *The Logical Structure of the World*, trans. R.A. George (Berkeley, Calif.: University of California Press, 1967 [1928]).

of matter, as held by materialists). In *Der logische Aufbau*, Carnap tried to make sense of science after science (even parapsychology![18]), but the details for a full logical construction in terms of sense experience were never given, and subsequent efforts by him and his fellow logical empiricists never filled them in.

This brief history in the philosophy of science is overly simple, to be sure, but it is nonetheless instructive. Not only does it show how materialism and empiricism, whether separately or in combination, have failed to supply the necessary resources for an adequate understanding of the world; but it also suggests a way forward. The problem for materialism and empiricism in reconstituting the world, whether in terms of elemental matter or elemental sensory experiences respectively, is ultimately informational. When we do science, we don't encounter matter in its raw state nor do we encounter sensory experiences in their raw state. Rather, we encounter certain patterns to the exclusion of others. In other words, we encounter information. The material and sensory features associated with these patterns are secondary. Indeed, those very features are themselves patterned and thus informational. The patterns, or equivalently the types of information conveyed, are primary.

To talk of patterns being primary might suggest that I'm advocating a form of Platonism, but I'm not. The patterns I'm talking about do not reside (or at least need not reside exclusively) in a Platonic heaven. Rather, the patterns I'm talking about are up close and personal. Think of recent work at the Large Hadron Collider to discover the Higgs boson. The Higgs boson is as fundamental a particle as contemporary physics is able to handle with current technology. Indeed, physics will need colliders operating at energy levels a trillion times that of the Large Hadron Collider (and thus with a diameter that of the entire solar system) to detect the X and Y bosons, the fundamental particles predicted by Grand Unified Theory, and the next step up in the particle zoo.[19] But what are

---

[18]   Ibid., 216. In his intellectual autobiography for the *Library of Living Philosophers*, Carnap describes an exchange with Ludwig Wittgenstein about parapsychology that captures Carnap's logical-empiricist spirit: "Another time [Wittgenstein and I] touched the topic of parapsychology, and he expressed himself strongly against it. The alleged messages produced in spiritualistic séances, he said, were extremely trivial and silly. I agreed with this, but I remarked that nevertheless the question of the existence and explanation of the alleged parapsychological phenomena [notice Carnap's insistence on phenomena as opposed to any underlying reality for them] was an important scientific problem. He was shocked that any reasonable man could have any interest in such rubbish." Quoted from Paul Arthur Schilpp, ed., *The Philosophy of Rudolf Carnap*, vol. 11 in *The Library of Living Philosophers* (Peru, Ill.: Open Court, 1963), 26.

[19]   David Lindley, *The End of Physics: The Myth of a Unified Theory* (New York: Basic Books, 1993), 173–4.

such particles and how do they present themselves to us? Fundamental particles are not objects of immediate intuition. They are not self-evident. Nor are they observable in any straightforward sense. Instead, physicists talk of "creating" such particles by carefully concentrating high energies in precise ways and then recording scatter plots of interactions involving these particles, with the detected particle exhibiting a characteristic "signature" predicted by physical theory.

My good friend and colleague Stephen Meyer has written a book titled *Signature in the Cell*, in which he argues that the cell's DNA contains information of a sort not reducible to purely material processes but instead requires intelligence.[20] Whether he is right or wrong about cells being the product of intelligence is not the issue here. What I want to call your attention to is that his book title rightly underscores that all of science trades in processes that leave signatures, that exhibit certain characteristic patterns to the exclusion of others—in other words, all of science trades, in the first instance, in information. In writing this, I'm not endorsing an instrumentalism or operationalism that defines particles as simply their patterns of activity or interaction. I'm happy to think of physical objects as real. But their reality is, I would argue, always inferred from the patterns, the information, they leave behind.

As a general rule, we know a thing by the patterns it leaves behind. A gravitational field, for instance, leads to certain patterns of motion among massive particles. Moreover, such particles exhibit their mass through certain patterns of interaction, with each other and with gravitational fields. Thus, we recognize that the balls in Newton's cradle have mass because of the pattern of motion they exhibit. There's a certain circularity here, but it's not vicious, nor is it avoidable, because patterns of interaction, once found, can be scrutinized only by looking for still further patterns of interaction (in the act of observation, a pattern of interaction needs itself to be interacted with). A God's eye view that sees things as they are without interacting with them seems not to exist, perhaps not even for God. The measurement problem in quantum mechanics is a special case of this general problem.[21]

What, then, is real according to this informational view of reality is the ability of a thing to produce a characteristic set of patterns. In other words, to say that an entity exists, and is therefore real, is to ascribe to it the ability to produce certain types of information to the exclusion of others. In Aristotelian terms, we might say that reality is gauged in terms of *potential* to produce information.

---

[20]   Meyer, *Signature in the Cell*, especially chs. 8 and 13.

[21]   See, for instance, Christopher G. Timpson, *Quantum Information Theory and the Foundations of Quantum Mechanics* (Oxford: Oxford University Press, 2013), 88–90.

Although I have sympathies with Plato and Aristotle, nothing of what I'm saying here entails a wholesale assimilation of their philosophies. I'm working at a completely commonplace level. We know things by the patterns they leave behind, and their ability to leave behind those patterns constitutes their identity and makes them real.

Where do these patterns reside? They reside in the world, the actual world, and we discover them as we identify matrices of possibility and then determine within those matrices which possibilities were realized to the exclusion of others (recall chapter 5). Thus, to determine whether the Higgs boson is real, one considers the different possible scatter plots that a certain preparation/configuration of the Large Hadron Collider might deliver (that's the matrix here) and then determines whether the actual scatter plot that was found matches the characteristic pattern predicted by the standard model of particle physics. Note that what I've described here is not an idealized reconstruction of what the physicists at CERN did—it's exactly what they did.[22] In general, this is exactly what scientists do, namely, identify a matrix of possibility and then determine the possibility that was realized. Robert Millikan's oil drop experiment, Charles Wilson's cloud chamber experiment, Gregor Mendel's pea experiment, Arthur Eddington's confirmation of general relativity from viewing a solar eclipse, and even Charles Darwin's use of biogeography to support evolution all follow this procedure.

Nothing in this informational approach to scientific inquiry violates empiricism, whether in spirit or in letter. Observation tells us whether a possibility has been realized within a matrix of possibility. Observation therefore retains its crucial role in science within this informational approach. But the informational approach to scientific inquiry dispenses with the pretense that observation can be independent of a context of inquiry, or, worse yet, that it can be built up from elemental sensory experiences.[23] Sensory experiences never

---

[22] When National Public Radio (NPR), for instance, announced the discovery of the Higgs boson, they published as key evidence for its existence the following (widely circulated) scatter diagram: http://media.npr.org/assets/img/2011/12/13/higgs-image_custom-23ab2 587699a4f8f99a51641f6dba8aed30fd806.jpeg (last accessed June 10, 2013).

[23] Recognition that observation is inherently theory laden was one of the key factors leading to the demise of logical empiricism. As Peter Kosso notes, "Observations in science are theory-laden. Accountable observation, the only kind that plays a contributing role in the acquisition and justification of knowledge about the world, bears an inseparable theoretical component. We are forced to give up the notion of pure, unaltered information from the world. Better to think of observational information not simply as given by nature but as actively taken by the observer in an activity that is guided by the theories, beliefs, and concepts in the mind of the actor. This dashes the [logical] empiricist's hope of a common ground of evidence agreeable to everyone regardless of his or her theoretical predisposition."

come to us in isolation but are always synthesized in full-blown perceptions, and perceptions do not happen against a blank slate but are always aligned by attention in light of background knowledge and interest. A matrix of possibility directs our attention and calls us to perceive certain patterns to the exclusion of others. The sense data of the logical empiricists are logically downstream from here (far and away downstream!) and of only incidental scientific interest. Indeed, many different combinations of sense data can yield isomorphic patterns having the same scientific significance (as evidenced by color-blind scientists finding their color-blindness an inconvenience but not a fundamental obstacle to scientific inquiry).

Where does this leave matter? Matter is fine as far as it goes, but it doesn't go nearly as far as materialists would like. Matter, as an abstraction from different types of material objects, leaves no characteristic pattern or signature. From the vantage of information, matter is therefore not real. To be sure, different types of matter are, or may be, real: massive particles such as protons and electrons, massless and almost massless particles such as photons and neutrinos, energetic fields, dark matter, dark energy, strings, superstrings, branes, etc. All of these can lay claim to being real. But to do so, each type of matter must display a characteristic signature in concrete circumstances (i.e., in relation to other things known to be real). Moreover, it makes its reality known by signing that signature within a matrix of possibility. Matter as such, however, is not real but merely an abstraction, just as the average American family, which has 2.3 children, is an abstraction. Such abstractions have some connection to reality, but they themselves are not real.

By adopting an informational approach to scientific inquiry, have I therefore eliminated materialism by definitional fiat? If so, that would be too easy. In fact, materialism remains a live option, but it must now establish itself by honest toil rather than by merely arrogating to itself privileges that it has not earned. It is not enough for the materialist to say, "Everything is material, prove me wrong." Rather, that everything is material must itself be established. And the way to establish it is to provide a complete catalogue of fundamental material objects (listing the different types of material objects along with their characteristic signatures) and then to show that all of reality as we know it can reasonably be reconstituted from them. Note that at this time we lack such a fundamental catalogue, to say nothing of how all such basic material entities (particles) would work together to reconstitute reality. Materialism is essentially a reductionist

Quoted from Peter Kosso, *Reading the Book of Nature: An Introduction to the Philosophy of Science* (Cambridge: Cambridge University Press, 1992), 119.

enterprise (a reduction to matter), and it must now flesh out the reduction to particular forms that matter takes rather than merely assert the reduction as an article of faith.

In making information primary, we take nothing of importance from matter. Matter is still permitted to prove itself. But it must prove itself not as an abstraction but in its particular forms. As matter takes on particular forms, it displays characteristic signatures. It is those, and only those, signatures to which we can attend. Any source behind those signatures will be inferred. Take an alpha or beta particle moving through a cloud chamber. The more massive alpha particle leaves a distinctive track (signature) that's different from the lighter beta particle. From these signatures, we infer that such particles exist and draw distinctions among them. In the case of material objects generally, such inferences are reliable and uncontroversial. But the reality of these material objects is mediated through the signatures, through the patterns, through the information that is characteristic of them.

The question therefore arises, what is more real, material objects or the information characteristic of material objects? I would say the information. The problem is that we can never get outside the information to embrace matter as such. It's not like the film *The Matrix*, in which the people inside the matrix can get out and then see that inside the matrix they had been brains in a vat. We live, move, and have our being inside a matrix of information. We have no way of getting outside that matrix. Moreover, according to the Judeo-Christian account of creation, there may be no outside. If creation is, as this religious tradition teaches, an effected word spoken by God,[24] then creation itself is a primal informational act. Moreover, the outworking of this creation in all its details will then be a series of echoes stemming from that primal act. Given such an account of creation, the search for a substratum of reality more basic than information would be futile. In any case, such a search will always be circular, never getting outside the circle of information.

---

[24] The expression "effected spoken word" (or some permutation of it) means this: an agent, in forming an intention, accomplishes it by first articulating the intention as a word, then transmitting that word through a speech act, and finally ensuring that this spoken word achieves its desired effect. When, for instance, a police officer intends for someone to stop, the officer speaks the word "stop," but that spoken word is effected (i.e., put into effect) only if the person who was told to stop obeys and does indeed stop. When the agent is God intent on creating a world, creation likewise becomes an effected spoken word. Compare Isaiah 55:11, God speaking: "So shall my word be that goeth forth out of my mouth: it shall not return unto me void, but it shall accomplish that which I please, and it shall prosper in the thing whereto I sent it."

Chapter 11
The Medium and the Message

If, up to this point, I have been successful at instilling doubts about the all-sufficiency of matter, some work remains in arguing for the all-sufficiency of information. Actually, I'm not arguing for the all-sufficiency of information as such because, in my view, information is, in the end, always the product of a creative intelligence. This would make intelligence rather than information the most basic metaphysical entity, placing all-sufficiency with intelligence rather than information. Indeed, as a theist, I regard an intelligent being, God, as the prime reality. The issue here, however, is not the primacy of intelligence or teleology for metaphysics. The issue, rather, is the primacy of information for science. I am arguing that information should properly be regarded as the prime entity and object of study in science, displacing matter from its current position of eminence.

Those who are not staunch materialists and think there could be more to nature than matter may find such a rising role for information intriguing. Even so, at this point in the argument, they may be unlikely to go the full distance in displacing matter with information. Accordingly, even though information may be indispensable to a proper understanding of the world, matter will, for many skeptics of materialism, still retain a high place and likewise seem indispensable. Materialists see the natural world as matter all the way down. Informational realists, like me, see the natural world as information all the way down. At this point in the argument, conceiving of the natural world as some mix of information and matter may seem the less radical and more reasonable course.

John Horgan defends this middle position, which leaves matter to exist alongside information:

> [W]hat's the problem with saying that everything comes down to information, bits, answers to our queries? ... [A]s the physicist Rolf Landauer liked to say, all information is physical—that is, all information is embodied in physical things or processes—but that doesn't mean that all things physical are reducible to information ... [T]he hard-headed part of me sees ideas like the "it from bit" [i.e.,

matter from information] as the kind of fuzzy-headed, narcissistic mysticism that science is supposed to help us overcome.[1]

Horgan, however, also admits to a soft-headed side that gives information primacy over matter. Thus, he "would love to believe" that information, consciousness, and mind are "not an accidental by-product of the physical realm but ... in some sense the primary purpose of reality."[2] In any case, he can't see how to get there, and so remains skeptical of information's ability to completely subsume matter, preferring instead a compromise between the two.

Such a compromise between matter and information has a long history. Aristotelian hylomorphism, for instance, conceived of substances as a combination of matter (Greek *hyle*) and (in)form(ation) (Greek *morphe*).[3] This same compromise comes up regularly in contemporary discussions of information. Thus one will read "information is real and tangible" but "it cannot exist without representation in a physical medium."[4] Or again, "information content is essentially massless, but the information medium has physical qualities. For example, a computer USB flash drive has the capacity to hold a certain quantity of data, but its weight doesn't measurably change by changing the data content."[5] Thus, even though information may transcend physicality, it must inevitably be embodied in a physical medium, and such a medium will presumably have to be material. This compromise between matter and information, as well as the distinction between the two, is often put in terms of the clichéd phrase "the medium and the message."

Now it's true that information always has a medium, but it's far from clear that this medium need be physical or material, where physicality or materiality is taken in some inherently non-informational sense. In fact, I would argue that the medium, like the message, is itself always inherently informational. To see how this might be the case, consider an example drawn from my own idiosyncratic experience with computers. Back in the early 1990s, I was a postdoctoral fellow in the philosophy of science at Northwestern University

---

[1]   Horgan, "Why Information Can't Be the Basis of Reality."

[2]   Ibid.

[3]   For a contemporary defense of hylomorphism, see James D. Madden, *Mind, Matter, and Nature: A Thomistic Proposal for the Philosophy of Mind* (Washington, D.C.: Catholic University Press of America, 2013).

[4]   Peter J. Denning and Tim Bell, "The Information Paradox," *American Scientist* 100(6) (2012): 470.

[5]   Donald E. Johnson, *Probability's Nature and Nature's Probability*, updated edn. (Charleston, S.C.: BookSurge, 2010), 28.

(under the direction of Arthur Fine and David Hull). There I came to use an email program called Eudora. It had the advantage of keeping all my email files in a convenient place on my computer's hard drive and organizing them in a way I liked. I kept using the program over the years. In 2006 the company making Eudora (Qualcomm) stopped producing it. Other programs that promised to do the same as Eudora were on the market, but I still preferred the final version of Eudora, which was released in 2006. For a while, this created no difficulties in that Microsoft's Windows XP operating system was still widely in use and ran Eudora without difficulties.

But as the years went by and Microsoft kept updating its operating system, my good friend Eudora stopped functioning very well (it was no longer fully compatible with the newer operating systems). I tried all sorts of workarounds to improve Eudora's performance on the newer operating systems (Windows Vista, Windows 7), but the one that finally worked was to run the old Windows XP operating system in simulation mode on a Windows 7 machine and then install the old Eudora program on the Windows XP simulation. I'm not recommending what I did to anyone, but here's the question this convoluted exercise raises: what was the medium for the message, the message here being the information in my Eudora program, the medium being the computational infrastructure supporting this program? As it is, the medium here was the Windows XP operating system. But this operating system was itself informational, so what was the medium for it? That would be the Windows 7 operating system that ran Windows XP as a simulation. And what was the medium for this Windows 7 operating system? In 2020, a decade after the release of Windows 7, it may no longer be possible to get Windows 7 to operate on any physical machine then readily available, but it may be possible to run it in simulation mode within, say, Windows 11 (or whatever the current version of Windows is at the time). Accordingly, one could have simulations running within simulations running within simulations.

Now it's true that in my case, the simulations end with Windows 7, which I have running on a Hewlett-Packard laptop, a physical machine. But what is this physical machine? Is it a material substrate inherently devoid of information until Windows 7 breathes computational life into it? Hardly. The physical device is itself an informationally intensive design with gigabytes of storage and processing power, all specifically adapted to running Windows operating systems. So let's analyze this device further into the minuscule items of silicon, plastic, and metal that compose it. At this level of analysis, we might be tempted to say that we've found an informationally free substrate. And true enough, at this level of analysis, we are not able to recover the computability of a Windows 7 operating system.

But these items of matter that compose my physical machine have characteristic signatures, exhibiting certain informational patterns to the exclusion of others, which, in fact, enable them, when suitably combined and configured, to run the Windows 7 operating system (by the way, Windows 7 is not the name we give to a set of physical states inside a computer; it is itself a program written almost entirely in some variant of the computer language C). In any case, the items of matter that compose my physical machine are themselves informationally rich entities. And given that we know matter only in concrete situations via characteristic signatures that particular forms of matter leave behind, I submit that even with the physical machines that provide the infrastructure for our daily computations, it's information all the way down.

An Aristotelian hylomorphist might at this point counter that it's not information alone but matter-plus-information all the way down, with matter and information combining at ever finer or coarser degrees of resolution. But in the example I just gave, there was no matter providing the computational infrastructure for Eudora and Windows XP. These were running as simulations within a Windows 7 programming environment. Hylomorphism's matter–information combination, though applicable in many everyday cases, therefore does not apply across the board. Information, as my example suggests, can run on information in the absence of matter. In fact, the inspiration for modern electronic computing comes from the Turing machine, invented by Alan Turing in the 1930s. A Turing machine (which consists of a read/write head, a set of states, and an infinitely long tape) is a purely mathematical construct. No materially embodied Turing machine exists (matter, as we know it, does not permit *infinitely* long tapes). All our actual materially embodied computers are finite approximations of these purely mathematical machines. These mathematical machines can in turn be represented as infinite sequences of 0s and 1s. They are thus a case of "information all the way down."

Likewise I would argue that the physical machines we use in practice (such as my Hewlett-Packard laptop) are also "information all the way down." The fact is, we don't know what matter is in itself. We know particular forms of matter as they leave behind characteristic signatures, that is, as they exhibit information. For all we know, the universe may itself be a giant computer simulation running not on an electronic machine composed of integrated circuits but on a purely mathematical device, such as a Turing machine. Some theorists take possibilities like this seriously.[6] The precise informational infrastructure that underlies the

---

[6]　See, for instance, Stephen Wolfram's attempt to understand the universe in terms of cellular automata in *A New Kind of Science* (Champaign, Ill.: Wolfram Media, 2002).

universe is, for now, an open problem. Yet even without this infrastructure's full articulation, the ubiquity and ineliminability of information in our study of the universe gives us good grounds to think that science need never look any further than information.

Matter, by contrast, when conceived as a non-informational substratum for information, seems entirely dispensable from science and even from metaphysics. Indeed, the evidence simply does not support that matter, as merely a passive receptacle for information, plays an indispensable role in our understanding of the world. Matter, to do useful scientific or metaphysical work, needs itself to be informational. I would go further, rephrasing a famous quote by economist Milton Friedman: *matter is always and everywhere an informational phenomenon.*[7] Indeed, everything we know about matter is, without remainder, informational.

Parsimony in reasoning therefore counsels dispensing with matter and putting the focus entirely on information. To be sure, we need not dispense with matter entirely since matter is a convenience to thought (much as Arabic numerals facilitate the thinking of mathematicians about numbers). Thus it is convenient to think of patterns that arise from sense experience as embedded in matter. Conveniences make life easier by keeping us from getting bogged down in details and drudgery. But conveniences are never necessities. We need necessities, we don't need conveniences.[8] We need information—we cannot do anything without it. Nonetheless, it is convenient to think of certain things as consisting of malleable material substrates that then get stamped with information. But

---

Nick Bostrom's "Are You Living in a Computer Simulation?" was cited earlier. There he presents a probabilistic argument for why it is reasonable to think we are living in a computer simulation. Edward Fredkin's digital view of physics, in which reality at its most fundamental is characterized in terms of computation or information processing, is discussed in Robert Wright, *Three Scientists and Their Gods: Looking for Meaning in an Age of Information* (New York: Harper & Row, 1988), part I.

[7] The original quote reads, "inflation is always and everywhere a monetary phenomenon." Milton Friedman, "The Counter-Revolution in Monetary Theory," IEA Occasional Paper, no. 33 (London: The Institute of Economic Affairs, 1970), 11, available online at http://0055d26.netsolhost.com/friedman/pdfs/other_academia/IEA.1970.pdf (last accessed June 14, 2013).

[8] I need to add a qualification here. If a form of inquiry stalls because it lacks a convenience, such a convenience can become necessary in the sense that without it no significant progress in the inquiry can be made. For instance, numbers exist and are what they are independently of the Arabic numerals. But without a convenient system of numerals like this, it's hard to imagine that the branch of mathematics known as number theory could have advanced appreciably (to say nothing of the rest of mathematics). That said, I know of no good argument for why matter, conceived abstractly in a perfectly general sense and without assuming some definite form, should be regarded as a "necessary convenience."

completely malleable matter simply awaiting information but itself devoid of it doesn't exist. Matter, if not an empty abstraction, always assumes definite forms. It is always informational. And however intently we study matter, we find not matter as such but further patterns of information.

Materialists, committed as they are to the primacy of matter, will certainly reject this subsumption of matter under information. But what about Aristotelians? An Aristotelian would urge compromise, arguing that what's real are substances and that these invariably consist of matter and information in combination, so that pure matter devoid of form is never an option. The Aristotelian would in this way continue to maintain a place for matter within metaphysics, yet without giving short shrift to information. But here I need again to raise the question of parsimony: why do we need matter at all? As a convenience, fine. But as a fundamental metaphysical entity, I see no reason for it. If, as I've argued, the reality of a thing is defined in terms of its potential to produce information (as identified through a matrix of possibility), then matter as such is a vague abstraction, particular material objects become significant through the characteristic signatures they are able to produce, and yet their very materiality dissolves on closer inspection into a regress of information, with patterns nested inside patterns nested inside patterns, and the only access to matter being informational. Moreover, given that information can reside in infrastructures that are themselves entirely informational (as my simulation example suggests and as the Turing machine reveals), I see no reason to take matter as anything other than a convenience to thought. With no disrespect for mythology, matter is a myth.[9]

---

[9] I mean that matter is a myth quite literally, namely, it is (or supplies) a narrative that helps us explain the world. It has fulfilled that role, especially with the rise of science in the seventeenth century, and done so admirably. But myths have a way of overstaying their welcome. Eventually newer, better, more insightful ways of thinking about the world arise. Like the ancient myths of old, the "matter myth" is outliving its usefulness. Compare Paul Davies and John Gribbin, *The Matter Myth: Dramatic Discoveries that Challenge Our Understanding of Physical Reality* (New York: Simon & Schuster, 1992).

Chapter 12

Embodiment and Transposition

If matter is a myth that does no real metaphysical work, matter, especially as conceived within a space–time–mass–energy continuum, is still a convenience to thought, especially to science. I'm not sure matter is quite as useful a convenience to thought for science as, say, the Arabic numerals are for mathematics, but let's give matter the benefit of the doubt. I therefore won't abolish matter, and I'll even be happy to talk of matter as a medium for information, albeit with the tacit understanding that matter in its concrete manifestations, rather than as a vague abstraction, is always a thoroughly informational entity. In fact, as a shorthand, we may define matter as *the medium for information*. Such a definition would, however, allow for physical matter, mathematical matter, and even spiritual matter (if the latter exists). Physical matter would thus refer directly or indirectly to sensible objects (i.e., objects inferred from their ability to impart patterns detectable by our senses). Mathematical matter would refer to mathematical objects such as the set of all infinite sequences of bits, a set capable of representing a Turing machine.

As for spiritual matter, if it exists, it would be stuff outside our space–time–mass–energy continuum that can nonetheless represent information and be a conduit for intelligence. Angels, within Christian theology, are thought to have spiritual bodies and would thus provide examples of the latter. Note that God, who in Christian theology is regarded as pure intelligence, has no body. God is therefore not a medium for information. And since information always exists in a medium (which, I'm claiming, is itself always informational), God is not information either. God creates information, but God in his being does not contain or exhibit information. Accordingly, it would not be possible to measure or otherwise investigate the "information content" inherent in God. Christian theism regards God as inherently beyond all human attempts to grasp him, though this theology also allows that God can act through embodied forms. Thus, in the liturgy of John Chrysostom, God is said to be "ineffable, inconceivable, invisible, incomprehensible, ever existing and eternally the same."[1] The apophatic tradition in Eastern Orthodox theology elaborates on this approach to God via negations.[2]

Although physical matter sounds reasonable enough to contemporary ears, talk of mathematical or spiritual matter will sound strange. Yet information (the message) always inheres in something else (the medium). That "something else" will, as I've argued, itself be informational, but the *informans* (what's doing the informing, i.e., the message) will nonetheless always be distinguishable from the *informandum* (what's being informed, i.e., the medium). Although defining matter as *informandum* makes good sense, matter is so tied in our thinking to physicality and sensory phenomena (i.e., to particular types of *informanda* that carry patterns impinging on our senses) that I'll also use another term. I'll therefore talk about the medium for information less in terms of matter and more in terms of embodiment. Information is always embodied, its embodiment is the medium for the message, and the embodiment, when analyzed in itself rather than as a carrier of information, will always itself be informational. In the metaphysics I'm developing, it's information "all the way down."

Even so, I want to reiterate that in talking about information going "all the way down," I don't mean to suggest that information is the only entity that exists. It's just that when there is an *informans–informandum* relationship, the *informandum* can itself be conceived as an *informans* or a set of *informantia* (plural of *informans*), and thus a chain of *informans–informandum* relationships can continue indefinitely in a regress. But such "information all the way down" chains are not, for me, ultimate. As a Christian theist, I regard intelligence (in the person of God) as the prime entity or ultimate fact. Accordingly, all information becomes a creative act either by this intelligence or by derived intelligences that in turn are created by this ultimate intelligence. To talk about information "all the way down" calls to mind those joke ontologies in which the world is said to rest on the back of a turtle, which in turn rests on a turtle, and so on, with turtles all the way down. My point about information all the way down is, by contrast, serious and straightforward. Information comes to us embodied. The embodiment itself, when taken on its own terms, is informational, exhibiting characteristic signatures or patterns. That embodiment, treated now as information, is itself embodied. And so on.

---

[1]   Widely available in books and online. This translation is available at http://www. orthodoxyork.org/liturgy.html (last accessed June 14, 2013).

[2]   For apophaticism, see Vladimir Lossky, *The Mystical Theology of the Eastern Church*, trans. by the Fellowship of St. Alban and St. Sergius (Crestwood, N.Y.: St. Vladimir's Seminary Press, 1976).

Where does this regress end? For physical matter in its known concrete forms, the regress has far from ended, with ever higher energies apparently eliciting ever novel material entities (this seems to be the lesson of particle physics). Moreover, since there is no limit to the amount of energy that may be concentrated and imparted to atomic and subatomic particles, there may be no end to this regress. For "mathematical matter," by contrast, if we go with standard set theory, everything ultimately seems to reduce to the empty set. Mathematician John von Neumann identified the empty set with the number 0, the set containing the empty set with the number 1, the set containing those two sets as 2, and so on, with the union of all these sets/numbers then identified as the natural numbers **N**. By considering function sets and power sets based on **N**, most of mathematics can be built up (there are some exceptions, such as classes and categories, but these need not detain us).[3]

At any rate, the empty set is unique in mathematics as an object in which embodiment and information coincide: the empty set embodies zeroness by containing exactly zero elements. Thus, in von Neumann's account of set theory, the information regress ends with the empty set. But is this where the information regress really ends? Is physical reality in the end just an expression of mathematical reality, with the empty set constituting the rock-bottom informational entity for all of physical reality as we know it?[4] Perhaps, but I question the value of speculating unduly about this information regress. As a Christian theist, who sees God's wisdom and power as unsearchable, I wouldn't be at all surprised if God allows an infinite regress of information and embodiment to mirror his own unsearchableness, at least in the realm of physical matter. In any case, my point about embodiment itself being thoroughly informational remains.

It's clear from experience that information always comes embodied. What's less clear is that information can always be re-embodied. When matter that embodies information disintegrates, we are likely to think that the information is

---

[3]   See Thomas Jech, *Set Theory*, 2nd edn. (Berlin: Springer, 1997), ch. 2 for the von Neumann number scheme. For category theory, see Steve Awodey, *Category Theory*, 2nd edn. (Oxford: Oxford University Press, 2010).

[4]   MIT physicist Max Tegmark takes such a view: "[N]ature is clearly giving us hints that the universe is mathematical. I've taken it to the extreme by proposing that our entire physical reality isn't just described by math, but that it is a mathematical structure, having no properties besides mathematical properties." Quoted from a discussion on the origins of mathematics at http://www.kavlifoundation.org/science-spotlights/kavli-origins-of-math (last accessed August 15, 2013). Tegmark's view, depending on its articulation, could be congenial with the informational view that I'm espousing. He promises to develop his view that physical reality is a mathematical structure at length in his forthcoming book *Our Mathematical Universe: My Quest for the Ultimate Nature of Reality* (New York: Knopf).

lost. And for the matter that did the embodying, it is. But this same information can, in principle, always be recovered and then realized in other embodiments. Information is *multiply realizable*. To say that information is multiply realizable is to say that the same information can be re-presented (that is, made present again) in numerous distinct embodiments. For instance, a musical composition can be realized as notes written in ink on paper, as an electronically scanned version of that document, as a live performance (provided it is without errors), or as an audio file on your computer, to name just a few possibilities. The material embodiment of information can always be destroyed. But information itself is transferrable to other embodiments. It is therefore indestructible and even eternal.

Information's multiple realizability may illuminate the Christian doctrine of bodily resurrection. In Scripture, Christ is seen as promising that once our present embodiment disintegrates at death, whatever constitutes our core identity will be freed from distortion and receive a new embodiment that God will preserve throughout eternity. Christ's resurrection is said not only to guarantee this promise but also to provide a model for our own resurrection. Thus, not only will who and what we are be realized again in a newly embodied form, but the new bodies that realize our core identity will be glorified, removing limitations (some, not all—we still won't be God) that kept us in check while we were still in bodies made of dust. Christ's resurrection and glorification are thus supposed to mirror our own.

How can this be? If what God creates is first and last information,[5] then our core identity is essentially informational. Thus, when we are resurrected, the information that defines us will be realized again (this is the information by which God created us, which was there at our first instant of life, and which over the course of our lives unfolded into our full-blown identity). But this information won't just be realized again. In addition, the information that defines our identity will, in resurrection, be *transposed* into a new medium that enriches and enhances who we are, thereby glorifying us.[6] We are all familiar with the transposition of information. Take Beethoven's Fifth Symphony. It is a magnificently rich orchestral work. And yet a four-year-old child can play the opening motif from the first movement with one finger on a piano. Here the transposition is from a richer to a poorer medium. Indeed, much is lost in transposing a full orchestral work to a piano version. But transposition need

---

[5]   Compare Genesis 1, in which God creates by an effected spoken word—and what is that except information?

[6]   My remarks on transposition draw heavily from C.S. Lewis, "Transposition," in *The Weight of Glory and Other Addresses* (New York: Collier, 1980), 54–73. I'm grateful to Jake Akins for drawing my attention to this essay.

not be in the direction of impoverishment. It can also be in the direction of enrichment. Arnold Schoenberg's orchestral arrangement of Brahms's G minor Piano Quartet would be an example.

Computer chess programs also illustrate transposition. When the same chess programs are played against each other, the version running on the more powerful computer tends to win. That's because, given the same program, the more powerful computer can examine more possible positions and thus perform a deeper analysis of what moves are likely to succeed. In consequence, even though I may write a chess program for my laptop computer, if I then run the program on the Cray XK7 supercomputer installed at Oak Ridge, presently the world's fastest computer running at close to 18 petaflops (i.e., almost eighteen thousand trillion floating point operations per second, which is orders of magnitude greater than the computing power of current laptops), I'll have transposed my program from a poorer to a richer medium. Provided the program is well designed and robust across different computing platforms, it will play far stronger chess in the richer than in the poorer medium.

For the ultimate computational transposition, consider what has been called the "super supercomputer," attributed to statistician David Blackwell.[7] This computer performs its first computational step in half a second, its next computational step a quarter of a second, its next in an eighth of a second, and so on. In general, the nth computational step takes 1 in 2^n seconds. Because the infinite mathematical series $\frac{1}{2} + \frac{1}{2^2} + \frac{1}{2^3} + \cdots$ sums to 1, such a computer would therefore perform any computation whatsoever in a single second. Because it would have infinite computational speed and memory, it could resolve any mathematical problem whatsoever. To an intellect endowed with such computational power, all mathematical truths would be immediately obvious, or, as Ludwig Wittgenstein would say, "surveyable" or "perspicuous."[8] Does God's mind have such computing power? Will humans, if bodily resurrected, be given minds with such computing power? Would having such computing power take the fun out of math for us? Who knows?

Many of the transpositions in this life take the form of damage. Consider the information in a book. Damage to the book can affect its readability. A page torn from a key passage may destroy the sense of the book. Or age may cause the pages to disintegrate and thus render them unreadable. In a similar vein,

---

[7] I've never been able to find a reference to Blackwell's super supercomputer. It may simply be an urban legend floating among mathematicians.

[8] Ludwig Wittgenstein, *Remarks on the Foundations of Mathematics*, rev. edn., eds. G.H. von Wright, R. Rhees, and G.E.M. Anscombe, trans. G.E.M. Anscombe (Cambridge, Mass.: MIT Press, 1983), 95, 143, 155.

our brains age, wear out, and get damaged (as in Alzheimer's disease). In such cases, a destructive transposition occurs that undermines a person's ability to think, feel, and act. Despite all the destructive transpositions that occur on this side of eternity, resurrection holds the promise of a transposition that is wholly positive and expansive. In the resurrection our embodied form is supposed not merely to be reconstituted but also to be transposed to a new reality in which wounds are healed, sorrows are comforted, limitations are overcome, and aspirations are fulfilled.

The promise of the final transposition is that anything of value will be preserved, enriched, and completed. This point is beautifully made in the film *Babette's Feast*, as in the short story by Isak Dinesen on which the film is based.[9] In the story, aspirations long thought to be dead are seen merely to have become dormant. The trigger to reawaken these aspirations, in this case, is the celebration of an extraordinary meal. The beauty and conviviality of the meal convinces the participants that nothing of value is ever really lost. As Philippa tells Babette in the very last lines of the short story, "'Yet this is not the end! I feel, Babette, that this is not the end. In Paradise you will be the great artist that God meant you to be! Ah!' she added, the tears streaming down her cheeks. 'Ah, how you will enchant the angels!'"[10] This is indeed the promise of resurrection, not to scotch the old and begin afresh, making all new things, but rather lovingly to embrace the old, making all things new.[11]

[9]   *Babette's Feast* by Isak Dinesen is widely available in book form and also available online at https://www2.bc.edu/~taylor/babette.html (last accessed September 21, 2013).
[10]   Ibid.
[11]   "Behold, I make all things new" (Revelation 21:5).

Chapter 13

Energy

In the dialectic between matter and information as described so far in this book, only information, and not matter, has proved itself indispensable to our understanding of the world. Indeed, matter, on closer inspection, always reveals itself either as an abstraction with no firm grip on reality or as itself an informational entity. Moreover, matter is a reductionistic concept in that items of matter are always to be understood in terms of smaller items of matter that jointly compose it.[1] Part–whole relations thus become intrinsic to matter, and any information that matter represents reduces to how those parts are structured into a whole. Materialism thus tends toward a static view of information in the sense that, once material constituents are suitably arranged and in no danger of rearrangement, matter will henceforth convey the information that's there and not lose it. The image of information associated with matter is that of a book in a hermetically sealed compartment: the ink arranged on paper to form a meaningful text will in this case constitute information that continues indefinitely.

Yet in most real-life situations, information is not static but dynamic—it is more verb than noun. Information is rarely if ever stored in a hermetic compartment.

---

[1]   In saying that matter is a reductionistic notion, I'm allowing that a material entity can exhibit properties that are unexampled in and unpredictable from the items of matter that compose it. Water, for instance, exhibits properties that arise only as multiple H_2O molecules band together. Emergent and supervenient properties are consistent with materialism. Such properties are sometimes thought to mitigate reductionism, but they do so by mystery-mongering, adding to matter an obscurantism that materialism was meant to avoid. Writing of supervenience, philosopher of language Stephen Schiffer elaborates: "'Supervenience' is a primitive metaphysical relation between properties that is distinct from causation and more like some primitive form of entailment ... I therefore find it more than a little ironic, and puzzling, that supervenience is nowadays being heralded as a way of making non-pleonastic, irreducibly non-natural mental properties cohere with an acceptably naturalistic solution to the mind–body problem ... The appeal to a special primitive relation of 'supervenience' ... is obscurantist. Supervenience is just epiphenomenalism without causation." From Stephen Schiffer, *The Remnants of Meaning* (Cambridge, Mass.: MIT Press, 1987), 153–4. For a defense of emergent properties within a materialistic framework that has a decidedly nonmaterialistic feel, see Harold J. Morowitz, *The Emergence of Everything: How the World Became Complex* (Oxford: Oxford University Press, 2002).

To be sure, information storage is an important aspect of information. But so is information processing. Information is in practice not something that sits by idly but something that happens and makes things happen. Information lives, moves, and works. Information changes dynamically, with information passing in, through, and out of matter. Even the book in a hermetic compartment was at one point in its history a collection of blank pages onto which ink had to be applied. Nothing in our experience preserves its information eternally. Anything that exhibits information needed at some point to be imparted with information. What causes information to undergo such dynamic transformations? The usual answer to this question is stated in one word: *energy*.

I want in this chapter to explore this answer. This answer is fine as far as it goes, but I will argue that it leaves untouched the primacy of information for science or for our understanding of the world generally. A nonreductionist might take the line that everything is fields of energy, that we ourselves are an energy field within the wider energy field of the universe, and that information, as something that emerges out of energy, is a subsidiary concept. According to such a view of energy, everything hangs together with everything else, so that the inherent bottom-up isolationism and reductionism of matter gives way to a top-down connectedness and holism of energy. Give this a New Age twist by invoking quantum theory and endowing the universe with an intrinsic teleology/intelligence, and there seems less reason to assign information the high importance I'm giving it.

Although I'm not ready to go the full New Age route in this way, I do see some merit to this energy holism. Indeed, I regard energy as a more important concept than matter. Even so, I will argue that energy is logically downstream from information in the sense that energy is always inferred from information, but not vice versa. Matter, as we've seen, is a myth, a convenience we can live without. Energy, by contrast, seems unavoidable in discussions about the dynamics of information. Information doesn't just sit there—it is dynamic, it happens. When information happens—and it happens all the time—what causes it to happen? Short of dismissing this question as unworthy of reply (if unworthy, on what grounds?), energy is as good an answer as exists. This answer makes energy the causal glue that connects diverse items of information in an informational universe.[2]

Language like this for describing energy will resonate with some and sound odd to others. The important point here, however, is the content we are able to

---

[2]   Compare John L. Mackie, *The Cement of the Universe: A Study of Causation* (Oxford: Oxford University Press, 1980).

give to the concept of energy as it relates causally to information. Let's therefore step back and consider how materialism makes sense of energy. Matter, from a materialist perspective, is endowed with energy, and changes in matter result from energy transfers among different items of matter. Indeed, contemporary physics regards matter and energy as flip sides of the same coin, as interconvertible with one another and thus different forms of the same material reality. Still, their interconvertibility aside, it is convenient to distinguish the two. Thus, within materialism, all of physical causality reduces to such energy transfers, where one material state (the cause) by a transfer of energy brings about another material state (the effect). Thus, for instance, a billiard ball with a certain momentum striking another billiard ball at a certain angle results in an energy transfer, causing the second ball to move at a certain speed and in a certain direction.

Physical causality as mediated by energy transfers can operate deterministically, as when the cause brings about exactly one effect. Or it can operate nondeterministically, as when the cause brings about one of several possible effects each of which is a live possibility. In nondeterministic physical causation, which of these possibilities occurs is governed by probabilities. A chunk of uranium falling to the ground in the Earth's gravitational field operates deterministically. That same chunk of uranium undergoing radioactive decay operates nondeterministically. All such physical causation, however, is understood in terms of energy transfers.

Now the big question before us is to what extent information depends on such energy transfers. How does information get into matter and where did it come from originally? When information is represented or embodied in matter (such as the information on the page that you are now reading, which is represented in ink on paper or pixels on a screen), it gets there by an energy transfer. Information in matter must first be transmitted to it, and the transmission of information must, given the presumption of materialism, be mediated by energy transfers that can be tracked in terms of physical causes acceptable to materialism. For instance, when a police officer holds up his hand for you to stop, information is transferred from him to you by light reflected from his hand to your retina.

Do information transfers invariably require such energy transfers? How we answer this question depends on how we define the term energy. If we define energy as whatever it is that transfers (or transforms or imparts) information, then any change or addition of information will, by definition, require energy. Such a definition of energy, however, opens the door to forms of energy unacceptable to materialism, for it says that energy is always involved whenever there is a transmission of information, even if the transmission has no material basis. Materialism, by contrast, would insist that any information transfer requires an energy transfer between material states where the energy in question has a clear material basis. Materialism therefore limits the concept of energy to what may be called *material energy*. Material energy is energy with a material basis. On the assumption of materialism, transfers of material energy constitute a necessary condition for any transfer of information: no material energy, no new information.

I am not a big fan of neologisms, but it seems that we do need a term to distinguish between two senses of energy: on the one hand, energy having a material basis, as mandated by materialism, in other words, what I'm calling material energy; and, on the other hand, energy as it could exist without the restriction of materialism. Given a broader construal of energy as anything that causes a transfer of information, material energy would be a particular form of energy but not (necessarily) coextensive with the whole of energy. Accordingly, given this general approach to energy as whatever causes information to transfer, it will help also to distinguish causation as such from causation as acceptable to materialism. We'll thus speak of causes/causation in general (which depend on energy of whatever sort that might be) versus material causes/causation (which depend on material energy). Note that by material causes, I don't mean Aristotle's material cause (as in his taxonomy of causation, which also includes efficient, formal, and final causes[3]), but any cause of information that depends solely on material energy, material energy being energy derivable from matter and thus acceptable to materialism.

What would energy that is not material energy look like? To answer this question, we first need to understand a fundamental distinction between information relationships and causal relationships. Whenever information is transmitted, an information relationship exists that takes the form of a correlation between two ends of a communication channel (I'm thinking of a communication channel here quite generally as anything that registers a transfer of information). Such a correlation can be understood on its own terms without reference to any intervening physical process that connects the two ends of the communication channel, and thus without reference to any relationships of material causes spanning that channel. In the absence of such an intervening physical process, information relationships can still hold. Fred Dretske explains the distinction:

---

[3]   For Aristotle's four causes see Georgios Anagnostopoulos, ed., *A Companion to Aristotle* (Oxford: Blackwell, 2009), ch. 13.

It may seem as though the transmission of information ... is a process that depends on the causal inter-relatedness of source and receiver. The way one gets a message from *s* [source] to *r* [receiver] is by initiating a sequence of events at *s* that culminates in a corresponding sequence at *r*. In abstract terms, the message is borne from *s* to *r* by a causal process which determines what happens at *r* in terms of what happens at *s*. The flow of information may, and in most familiar instances obviously does, depend on underlying causal processes. Nevertheless, the information relationships between *s* and *r* must be distinguished from the system of [material] causal relationships existing between these points.[4]

In distinguishing causal from information relationships, Dretske is here clearly thinking of causality in material terms: material energy, operating consecutively across a communication channel, takes information from one point to another through a series of energetic transfers, each acceptable to materialism. Now no one would deny that information can transfer in this way. The question is whether all information must transfer by material means and whether there are any counterexamples showing that it need not transfer thus. The materialist requirement that information relationships must supervene on material causal relationships (in the sense that any change in information relationships must be mediated through a change in underlying material causal relationships) can't be justified except by presupposing materialism. There is no independent evidence for this requirement. In fact, it's easy to construct thought experiments, and even find intriguing empirical evidence, for information relationships that transcend material causal relationships.

To understand just how different these two types of relationships are, consider the following thought experiment: Imagine that astronomers discover a star 600 million light years from Earth pulsing radio waves to us that we can detect. Looking over the pattern of pulses, astronomers find that the pulses come in two forms and that when these are interpreted as dots and dashes, the star is sending English messages in Morse code. More surprising still, the star begins a conversation with the astronomers, answering for them unknown but readily confirmed facts about astrophysics. But it doesn't stop there. Medical doctors learn how to cure diseases. Archeologists learn where to dig for lost civilizations. Mathematicians learn the solutions to many outstanding open problems. Better

---

[4] Dretske, *Knowledge and the Flow of Information*, 26. Carl Jung makes essentially the same point in developing his parallel notion of synchronicity, characterizing it as "an acausal connecting principle." See his *Synchronicity: An Acausal Connecting Principle*, trans. R.F.C. Hull (Princeton, N.J.: Princeton University Press, 1973).

than the oracle at Delphi, this star, by pulsing English messages in Morse code, answers our biggest questions precisely and in real time.

What are we to make of this star? Perhaps an alien civilization sent those messages a long long time ago. But how come the messages are in contemporary idiomatic English and in Morse code? Strange as it may seem, this thought experiment violates no physical law. Such a conclusion may seem counterintuitive because a physicist's first reaction is likely to be that it violates Einstein's theory of special relativity, according to which messages cannot be relayed at speeds faster than light. Indeed, since this star is 600 million light years from Earth, any signal we receive from the pulsar was sent millions of years ago. Yet the star seems to be responding to our questions instantaneously. The star's answers, if you will, precede our questions by millions of years.[5]

Material causality, in the sense of energy transfers acceptable to materialism, thus has no way of accounting for the correlation between events on Earth (i.e., questions we pose here on Earth) and radio transmissions from the star (i.e., answers arriving moments later). This thought experiment underscores Dretske's point about the fundamental difference between material causality and information transfer: "The information relationships between source and receiver must be distinguished from the system of [material] causal relationships existing between these points."[6] Precisely because there is no causal sequence of material energy transfers linking questions the astronomers are posing with answers arriving from the star moments later (but outputted by the star millions of years ago), there is no causal principle of physics to be violated. Yet there clearly is a transfer of information. Moreover, if energy is always required for a transfer of information, then this must be a nonmaterial form of energy.

Talking stars are the stuff of philosophical thought experiments and thus will seem far removed from ordinary experience and reality. Thought experiments like this do serve a purpose, however, in giving proof of concept, in this case showing that nonmaterial energy could, in principle, have compelling evidence.[7]

---

5   I've been playing with variants of this thought experiment for over twenty years. If memory serves, I first came up with it was in conversation with Charles Chastain. For an early version of this thought experiment, see my article "On the Very Possibility of Intelligent Design," in J.P. Moreland, ed., *The Creation Hypothesis: Scientific Evidence for an Intelligent Designer* (Downers Grove, Ill.: InterVarsity, 1994), ch. 3.

6   Dretske, *Knowledge and the Flow of Information*, 26. Note that in repeating the quote, I substituted "source" for *s* and "receiver" for *r*.

7   Of course, a hardcore materialist will always have alternative materialist explanations. Thus it might be argued that my amazing talking star is simply a statistical fluke across a vast ensemble of possible universes. Pure chance is bound to produce the talking star's pattern of

But is there any actual evidence of nonmaterial energy transferring information? If you reject materialism, you probably believe in miracles. Most miracles are not strict violations of physical law but informational miracles in the sense that patterns at two ends of a communication channel match even though no chain of material causality connects the two. Prophetic prediction, if precise enough, qualifies. Even Moses parting the Red Sea (Exodus 14:21–22), in which his prayer for deliverance and raising his rod are precisely correlated with a wind (natural force) that parts the sea, would qualify.

Miracles tend to be isolated rare events, vouchsafed to particular individuals in particular circumstances, often depending for their credibility on evidence that is intriguing and persuasive to those directly affected but far from bulletproof to independent investigators.[8] It can therefore be difficult to verify that a purported miracle exhibits an information relationship that cannot reasonably be accounted for in terms of a transfer of material energy. Yet without such a verification, there's no way to argue effectively, certainly not in a predominantly materialist climate, that a purported miracle constitutes a counterexample to the materialist maxim "no information transfer without a corresponding material energy transfer."

Still, some widely reported phenomena, if they indeed occur as reported, can be construed as evidence of information transfers induced by nonmaterial energy. Near death experiences (NDEs) come to mind. In some near death experiences, patients on the operating table are unconscious and yet afterward report out-of-the-body experiences in which they claim to have witnessed events going on in the hospital while they were unconscious.[9] Such reports get interesting when the events in question can be verified and are of a sort that could not have been guessed. Near death experiences therefore suggest that information can transfer from event to patient even though the patient was unconscious and in a location

---

Morse-coded messages in some possible world, and, by strange coincidence, it just happens to be ours. Consequently, there would be no intelligence behind the star's (apparent) messages. It would simply be the mimicking of intelligence by a chance event, vastly improbable in our universe but overwhelmingly probable across the ensemble of universes.

[8] See, for instance, the evidence for miracles provided in Craig Keener, *Miracles: The Credibility of the New Testament Accounts*, 2 vols. (Grand Rapids, Mich.: Baker, 2011). Such evidence is persuasive to those with no predisposition against miracles, but tends to leave materialists unconvinced.

[9] For such examples of NDEs, see Mario Beauregard and Denyse O'Leary, *The Spiritual Brain: A Neuroscientist's Case for the Existence of the Soul* (New York: HarperCollins, 2007), ch. 6. For a thorough review of NDEs, see Janice Miner Holden, Bruce Greyson, and Debbie James, eds., *The Handbook of Near-Death Experiences: Thirty Years of Investigation* (Santa Barbara, Calif.: ABC-CLIO, 2009). See also Pim van Lommel, *Consciousness Beyond Life: The Science of the Near-Death Experience*, trans. L. Vroomen (New York: HarperCollins, 2010).

that would, on materialistic grounds, have made it impossible for the patient to access that information.

Experiments for detecting psi phenomena likewise attempt to identify information transfers that cannot be accounted for in terms of material energy transfers. For example, suppose an experimental subject guesses significantly better than chance the identity of Zener cards, the cards being hidden from the subject's view.[10] Such an occurrence would suggest an information transfer lacking a corresponding material energy transfer. To really nail down such a conclusion, however, the experimental setup needs to rule out whatever material causes might be moving the information about shapes on the cards from experimenter to subject. Materialists don't think such experiments can ever decisively rule out that material energy is nonetheless causally responsible for such information transfers. Thus, in debunking supposedly successful psi experiments, materialists invariably try to uncover fraud or flaws in experimental design. Consequently, they look for evidence of (in)advertent signaling in which information is transmitted from experimenter to subject via causal processes acceptable to materialism.[11]

Now my point here is not to argue that near death experiences or psi phenomena demonstrate the existence of information flows that transcend material processes. Rather, what I want to underscore with such examples is the logic that relates information relationships and causal/energetic relationships. Information relationships are logically prior to causal/energetic relationships in the sense that information relationships must first be recognized before causal/energetic relationships can be inferred. With the talking star, for instance, we first had to see the connection between our questions and the answers that were arriving immediately afterward. That connection was an information relationship. Only then did we start looking for a material causal explanation of how this might happen. If it could be confirmed that there was no tampering with the signal from the star and that, given a fixed speed of light, the signals we are interpreting as answers were sent hundred of millions of years ago, any cause connecting questions to answers would likely have to be nonmaterial (barring

---

[10]   Zener cards are widely used in such experiments. There are five such cards, depicting either a circle, a square, a cross, a star, or three wavy lines.

[11]   This is the approach taken by debunkers like James Randi at the *Skeptical Inquirer* (http://www.csicop.com, last accessed September 9, 2013). See also Randi's book *Flim-Flam! Psychics, ESP, Unicorns, and Other Delusions* (Buffalo, N.Y.: Prometheus, 1982). For a defense of psi phenomena as a legitimate field of study backed by sound scientific evidence, see Dean Radin, *Entangled Minds: Extrasensory Experiences in a Quantum Reality* (New York: Simon & Schuster, 2006).

some hitherto undreamt capacities of matter incompatible with materialism as it is now conceived).[12]

More generally, in any inquiry, scientific or otherwise, if we are trying to understand an information transfer, the first thing we witness is an information relationship, and only then are we in a position to uncover how energy might have given rise to that relationship. Some form of energy must presumably be involved—we are supposing that information transfers require energy transfers (though not necessarily material energy transfers). Moreover, if the energy can't be material, then it must be nonmaterial. But the point I wish to repeat and emphasize is that, as with matter, energy is logically downstream from information. The first thing we always confront is information, and only then do we try to explain it in terms of energy. Energy is inferred from information, not vice versa.

---

[12] Anatole France captures perfectly the materialistic mindset in straining for materialistic explanations regardless of evidence. As the following passage by France makes clear, no evidence could ever convince him that something beyond the power of matter had acted:

> Happening to be at Lourdes, in August, I paid a visit to the grotto where innumerable crutches were hung up in token of a cure. My companion pointed to these trophies of the sick-room and hospital ward, and whispered in my ear: "One wooden leg would be more to the point." It was the word of a man of sense; but speaking philosophically, the wooden leg would be no whit more convincing than a crutch. If an observer of a genuinely scientific spirit were called upon to verify that a man's leg, after amputation, had suddenly grown again as before, whether in a miraculous pool or anywhere else, he would not cry: "Lo! a miracle." He would say this: "An observation, so far unique, points us to a presumption that under conditions still undetermined, the tissues of a human leg have the property of reorganizing themselves like a crab's or lobster's claws and a lizard's tail, but much more rapidly. Here we have a fact of nature in apparent contradiction with several other facts of the like sort. The contradiction arises from our ignorance, and clearly shows that the science of animal physiology must be reconstituted, or to speak more accurately, that it has never yet been properly constituted.

Quoted from France, *The Garden of Epicurus*, trans. Alfred Allinson (New York: John Lane, 1908), 176–7.

Chapter 14

An Informationally Porous Universe

I want next to consider how materialism, even on its own terms, has no way to block the flow of novel information into the universe from outside. Information, for materialism, is supposed to track physical causality. This means no information transfer without a corresponding transfer of material energy. Yet materialism doesn't merely make information transfers depend causally on transfers of material energy. Materialism regards the world as a closed nexus of material causes operating by unbroken natural laws (these laws are nonteleological).[1] The materialist universe is a causally closed universe. Causal closure, for the materialist, rules out not just information transfers unmediated by material energy transfers but also information entering this causal nexus from outside. For materialism, there is no outside. Materialism therefore urges not just causal closure but also informational closure. In other words, the world operates exclusively by material causes inherent in it, and any information in the world is likewise inherent in it or is manufactured from preexisting information by those material causes.[2]

---

[1] Consider the following quote by philosopher of biology Michael Ruse. Ruse is a Darwinian and a materialist, and so for him science is the enterprise that properly characterizes the world. And how does it do that? "Science," he writes, "attempts to understand this empirical world. What is the basis for this understanding? Surveying science and the history of science today, one thing stands out: science involves a search for order. More specifically, science looks for unbroken, blind, natural regularities (*laws*). Things in the world do not happen in just any old way. They follow set paths, and science tries to capture this fact." Quoted from Michael Ruse, "Creation-Science Is Not Science" (1982), available online at http://bertie.ccsu.edu/naturesci/Evolution/Unit16CreationSci/Ruse.html (last accessed June 19, 2013). This explains at least in part the appeal of Darwin's theory to Ruse and fellow materialists: "Darwinism," he writes, "is a theory committed to the ubiquity of law. In the language of the philosophers, it is a 'naturalistic' [read 'materialistic'] theory." Quoted from Michael Ruse, *Can a Darwinian Be a Christian? The Relationship between Science and Religion* (Cambridge: Cambridge University Press, 2001), 94.

[2] As in the last chapter, by material causes I don't mean Aristotle's material causes as distinguished from his formal, final, and efficient causes. I just mean physical causes acceptable to materialism.

Materialism infers informational closure from causal closure. In this chapter I show that materialism can't legitimately draw this conclusion. In particular, I show that the world can be informationally open even if it is causally closed in the sense demanded by materialism. Causal closure, if it could guarantee informational closure, would raise a specter for traditional theism, which regards the world as open to divine action. A world governed by unbroken natural laws seems to prohibit God from coherently interacting with it. Many theists find themselves attracted to causal closure, seeing in the material world a law-governed integrity that God, if he were a smart enough creator, would never need to violate.[3] But what sort of limitation does causal closure actually place on God? In fact, as we'll see, it does nothing to limit God's ability to get novel information into the world.

The challenge causal closure poses to traditional theism is how God, who is unembodied and therefore not composed of matter, could influence the material world, imparting information into it, and yet without imparting material energy. In other words, the challenge is to find a way for God to input novel information while at the same time respecting causal closure. Many theists regard causal closure as false and thus see divine action as in no way constrained by it. As a consequence, they do not feel the force of this challenge. Some theists, however, do feel the force of this challenge, seeing in the created order self-imposed constraints by God, up to and including causal closure. And certainly, many atheists think that causal closure effectively shuts God out of the world. But, as we'll see now, causal closure leaves the universe surprisingly porous, readily letting in novel information from outside. This is not to presume that there is an outside or that information is necessarily coming in from the outside. Rather, it is to point out that causal closure has no way of insulating the world from the outside (should an outside exist).

Models of the universe drawn from classical physics are supposed to be paradigmatic of informational closure. This is because classical physics is deterministic, and determinism precludes novel external information from

---

3   Howard Van Till's robust formational economy principle (RFEP) is a recent case in point. See Howard J. Van Till, "Naturalism and Divine Creativity, *or* Who Owns the Robust Formational Economy Principle?," in Gordon and Dembski, eds., *The Nature of Nature*, ch. 24. The theme that nature is self-contained and that any proper deity would never need to intervene in nature in the sense of adding to nature something that is not already inherent in it has a long history. A prime example is Baruch Spinoza, *Tractatus Theologico-Politicus*, trans. S. Shirley, intro. B.S. Gregory (1670; reprint, Leiden: Brill, 1989). Spinoza was certainly not a traditional theist, but it would not be fair to call him an atheist either. Spinoza's views have profoundly affected liberal Christianity, especially through Friedrich Schleiermacher.

getting into a system once it's up and running. A deterministic system does exactly what it was determined to do. If it is being interfered with from outside, then it is not deterministic. Deterministic systems therefore cannot exhibit information not already present, in some form, from the start. We'll return to deterministic models of the universe momentarily and show why even they cannot guarantee informational closure.

But first let us consider nondeterministic models of the universe. A nondeterministic universe, such as given by quantum mechanics, is readily seen to be informationally open. Such a universe will produce (seemingly) random events and can thus produce patterns of events that stand out against the backdrop of randomness (as a signal stands out from noise). Such patterns, if sufficiently salient (and, dare one suggest, intended by God), could reasonably be interpreted as constituting novel information inputted from outside the system. Accordingly, in a nondeterministic universe, divine action could impart information into matter without violating any physical laws by which matter operates.

At this point, materialists are apt to press theists for a precise account of how God introduces novel information into the world. On materialist principles, there must be some physical mechanism by which the information is imparted.[4] Moreover, thermodynamics will necessarily limit the information-processing power of matter and thus restrict the flow of information.[5] To be sure, thermodynamic limitations apply if we are dealing with a materially embodied information source that needs to output material energy to transmit information. But nothing prevents a nonmaterial deity from enlisting random processes, which, in virtue of their randomness, could turn out any number of ways, and then having these processes turn out one way rather than another.

A deity capable of co-opting randomness would impart information by arranging outcomes, but do so by channeling material energy in ways that violate

---

[4]   The physicist William Thomson (Lord Kelvin), though himself a Christian, embodied the materialist mindset when he stated, "I never satisfy myself until I can make a mechanical model of a thing. If I can make a mechanical model I can understand it. As long as I cannot make a mechanical model all the way through I cannot understand." Lord Kelvin, *Baltimore Lectures* (Baltimore, Md.: Publication Agency of Johns Hopkins University, 1904), 270. Of course, Thomson, as a Christian theist and therefore as a nonmaterialist, would have restricted this statement to the scientific questions that he, as a physicist, was interested in addressing. The point is that for materialism, there is in the end only matter and so Thomson's statement becomes not a gloss on physics but on the whole of reality.

[5]   For the computing power of the universe as a whole based on thermodynamics and quantum theory, see Seth Lloyd, "Computational Capacity of the Universe," *Physical Review Letters* 88(23) (2002): 7901–4. See also Anthony J.G. Hey, ed., *Feynman and Computation: Exploring the Limits of Computers* (Reading, Mass.: Perseus, 1999).

no principle governing matter. If divine action takes this form, the problem of finding the missing material energy by which God introduces novel information into the world simply does not arise. In that case, there is no missing material energy to be found—information is then being transferred without any transfer of material energy. To be sure, this means there would be no "mechanism" of divine action. But to ask for such a mechanism, if God is unembodied, is itself incoherent (because God has no parts, God is not a machine and therefore does not interact with the world mechanically). In any case, divine action that imparts information could be palpable even if it is not trackable in terms acceptable to materialism. Nondeterminism means that God can substantively affect the structure and dynamics of the physical world by imparting information, and yet without imparting material energy.

To say that the physical world is nondeterministic is not to reject the principle of sufficient reason. Often nondeterminism is taken to imply acausality, so that an event that is attributed to a random or nondeterministic process is regarded as having no cause, or at best an incomplete cause (i.e., whatever we are calling a cause does not provide a complete account of the event in question). If one views chance as fundamental and patterns in nature as anomalies of chance, then this view follows. But one can also view the patterns in nature as fundamental (indeed, God-given) and treat chance as derivative from those patterns. In my paper "Randomness by Design," I took this line of reasoning to its logical end, arguing that chance and randomness do not even make sense apart from underlying patterns and information.[6] We've seen this theme before in this book, where matter becomes an epiphenomenon of information.

The argument so far shows that a nondeterministic universe can be informationally porous and thus open to action by a deity able to impart information without imparting material energy. Quantum mechanics, when interpreted as a fundamentally probabilistic theory, offers such a picture of the universe, allowing God free play at the quantum level. I personally find this picture appealing, though I'm not completely convinced by it. Many scientists, however, find divine activity at quantum interstices unappealing. The materialism that dominates modern intellectual life conceives of the world as a closed causal nexus operating by unbroken natural laws. A deity who acts through quantum events (e.g., by collapsing wave functions), even though such

---

6   See my article "Randomness by Design," *Nous* 25(1) (1991): 75–106. There I argue that randomness is properly defined in relation to a given set of patterns. So long as no pattern in the set is matched, we ascribe randomness to the event in question. Randomness thus becomes a relativized notion—relativized, that is, to a set of patterns. Change the set of patterns, and what constitutes randomness changes as well.

a deity does not strictly speaking violate any physical law, is to many scientists unacceptable. For them, causal closure precludes any real-time divine interaction with the physical world. Moreover, if a probabilistic understanding of quantum mechanics is insufficient to guarantee such closure, then it may be time to reinstate determinism, even at the quantum level. The many-worlds approach to quantum mechanics does just that, viewing probabilities as a shorthand for the branching off of novel worlds at each quantum event, the branches themselves being fully determined.[7]

Yet surprisingly, causal closure, even if coupled with a deterministic universe, places *no restriction* on God's activity in the world. This may seem unexpected and even counterintuitive, but it is true nonetheless. To see this, consider again the talking star example of the previous chapter, only this time assume its behavior was determined from the moment of the Big Bang. Causal closure in a deterministic universe precludes what may be called *substitutional intervention*. In other words, it precludes God (or any other nonmaterial being) from overriding the causal structure of the world by bringing about effects that would otherwise not have happened (hence the reference to "substitutional"—God substitutes an effect for one that didn't happen but, given the world's causal structure, should have happened).

Nonetheless, a world barring substitutional intervention cannot preclude God from prearranging the initial structure of the world so that desired material effects are achieved even if they appear extraordinary and bespeak a deity active in the particulars of the moment. All that is required is that God build in the necessary information from the start so that it gets expressed at appropriate times and places. This is, in fact, an old idea. It comes up in Augustine's *Literal Commentary on Genesis*, where God is said to implant nature with seeds that come to fruition at appointed times and places.[8] It is implicit in Leibniz's ideas about concurrence and pre-established harmony, in which divine purposes and material effects precisely track one another.[9] Charles Babbage, the inventor of the modern digital computer, elaborated these ideas, arguing that God implanted nature with computational programs that activate at the right time

---

[7] For the debate about quantum many worlds, see Simon Saunders, Jonathan Barrett, Adrian Kent, and David Wallace, eds., *Many Worlds? Everett, Quantum Theory, & Reality* (Oxford: Oxford University Press, 2010).

[8] Augustine, *The Literal Meaning of Genesis*, trans. by J.H. Taylor, *Ancient Christian Writers*, 2 vols. (New York: Paulist Press, 1982), 1: 90, 141–2. Augustine writes here of "seminal principles" and "reason-principles" and "implanted causal reasons."

[9] Gottfried Wilhelm Leibniz, *Theodicy: Essays on the Goodness of God and the Freedom of Man and the Origin of Evil*, translated by E.M. Huggard (La Salle, Ill.: Open Court, 1985).

and place. Babbage put forward this view in his *Ninth Bridgewater Treatise*, which predated Darwin's *Origin of Species* by more than twenty years.[10]

Philosopher of science Michael Polanyi went even further in analyzing how the physical world is able to process information. According to Polanyi, the laws of nature assume certain general mathematical forms for which fundamental constants and free parameters need to be specifically calibrated. But, in addition, for any such laws to effectively describe nature, they must also take into account boundary conditions. For instance, Newton's law of gravity describes the behavior of objects in a gravitational field that employs a particular gravitational constant. But to specify the actual behavior of a ball released from a tower, we need to know the height of the tower. The height of the tower constitutes a boundary condition. All such boundary conditions allow unlimited degrees of freedom and, depending on the precise arrangement they take, can bring about vastly different effects—most of them ordinary, but some of them extraordinary. The information inherent in such effects reflects the information embedded in these boundary conditions.[11]

As an aside, the radical contingency and extreme variability of boundary conditions ensures that the physicists' search for a "theory of everything," even if attained, will explain virtually nothing. All of human technology, for instance, owes its existence to contingencies. Indeed, technology always and everywhere depends on precise arrangements of material parts to accomplish specific purposes. Such contingencies, while compatible with the theories of physics, are in no way determined by them (no more than written texts are determined by ink and paper). The completeness of physical theory can do nothing to alter this fact.

Accordingly, even in a world that is causally closed and fully deterministic, God, by carefully arranging the world from the start, could achieve all intended effects, up to and including acts of particular providence that appear to require direct, real-time intervention (though, in fact, they have been "front-loaded"). Note that even a full-throated physical determinism need not obviate libertarian free will: God could have arranged the physical world to reflect the freely made choices of free agents that have physical bodies.[12] The very structure of the

---

[10]   Charles Babbage, *The Ninth Bridgewater Treatise* (London: Murray, 1836).

[11]   See the following two articles by Michael Polanyi: "Life Transcending Physics and Chemistry," *Chemical and Engineering News* 45 (August 1967): 54–66 and "Life's Irreducible Structure," *Science* 113 (1968): 1308–12.

[12]   I'm assuming here a traditional theism that sees God as omniscient, where omniscience includes knowledge of future contingent events, and where such omniscience leaves a robust noncompatibilist human freedom intact. This view has been widely challenged but also ably defended. For such a defense, see William Lane Craig, "Divine Foreknowledge

physical world, which seemingly determines the movements of our bodies, would then itself be arranged by God to reflect our freely chosen actions as free agents linked to physical bodies.[13] In other words, our bodies do what they do because of the way in which the universe was constituted at the Big Bang, but God constitutes the universe at the Big Bang to ensure that our bodies do what we, as free agents, would have them to do. Accordingly, God would coordinate physical determinism with human freedom, making the former servant to the latter.

The lesson of causal closure is therefore counterintuitive: a world open to direct, real-time divine intervention could be empirically indistinguishable from a causally closed world that operates by unbroken natural laws (whether those laws be deterministic or nondeterministic), provided that God, from the start, is able to precisely arrange the unfolding of events. The Enlightenment view that we must choose between a world whose causal structure is ruled by unbroken natural laws or a God who supernaturally intervenes in the world is thus seen to be doubly mistaken. Divine concurrence, in which God acts through ordinary events, has always been a staple of Christian theology.[14] God is always able to work through natural laws, for they are his creation. More important, however,

---

and Newcomb's Paradox," *Philosophia* 17 (1987): 331–50, available online at http://www.reasonablefaith.org/divine-foreknowledge-and-newcombs-paradox (last accessed June 28, 2013).

[13] Note that in talking of a linkage between free agents and physical bodies, I'm not presupposing a mind–brain substance dualism. That's certainly an option, though from an informational perspective, this would take a slight twist, with mind, as customary in the substance-dualist tradition, constituting an intelligent cause but with brain then becoming an informational rather than reductionistically materialist entity. As long as there are appropriate correlations between the operations of mind and brain, the linkage I'm talking about could be said to obtain. Such a correlation could even take the form of an identity relation between the two, where, as in panpsychism, mind and brain end up being flip sides of the same reality. Given my informational perspective, this would make information inherently intelligent. Another possibility is to view the relation between mind and brain as one of brute dependency or interdependency, making minds a part of the nature of certain things (though not necessarily part of everything, as in panpsychism). Nonreductive physicalism allows for this possibility. The only possibility excluded from this discussion is reductive physicalism, in which mind reduces to the constitution and dynamics of matter, and where matter itself is viewed reductively in terms of particles interacting by purely mechanical principles.

[14] Joseph's brothers, after the death of their father Jacob, worry that Joseph will do them harm for selling him into slavery. Joseph's reply to his brothers provides a classic illustration of divine concurrence: "Even though you intended to do harm to me, God intended it for good, in order to preserve a numerous people, as he is doing today" (Genesis 50:20).

for this discussion is that what appears to be supernatural intervention could just be ordinary events suitably coordinated to achieve extraordinary results.[15]

In sum, the causal structure of the world has no way of barring God from getting novel information into the world to accomplish the divine purposes. God can, if he likes, get information into the world by performing miracles (the one who created the world and its laws is hardly bound by them). The more interesting lesson of this chapter, however, is that God can also get information into the world without performing miracles. In a world of irreducibly chance or random events, as some interpretations of quantum theory allow, God can channel such events toward preordained ends.[16] Yet even in a world whose material arrangement is entirely deterministic, God could so arrange its initial and boundary conditions that it unfolds precisely according to plan. Such a world would exhibit ongoing particular providence, with God moment by moment substantively influencing the world down to the finest details. Thus, regardless of one's view of the causal structure of the world, theism is always a live option and deism (the God who goes on vacation after creation) is never mandated. All our models of the universe given by science are informationally porous.

---

[15]   Compare Leibniz's idea of a "pre-established harmony" in his *Theodicy* as well as in "The Controversy between Leibniz and Clarke, 1715–16," in Gottfried Wilhelm Leibniz, *Philosophical Papers and Letters*, ed. L.E. Loemker, 2nd edn. (Dordrecht: Reidel, 1976), 710–15.

[16]   According to Proverbs 16:33, "The lot is cast into the lap but the whole disposing thereof is of the Lord." Compare this to the Fates of Greek mythology, who decided the destiny even of the gods. The Greek word for the Fates, *Moirai*, is also the word for lot, whose fundamental meaning is portion or share of something divided.

Chapter 15

Determinism

The world could be different in so many ways. What could be more obvious than this claim? And yet, reflection leads many to challenge it. Indeed, reflection suggests that things happen for a reason, and that when the reason is known, things could not have happened otherwise. Reflection therefore draws us to determinism. Contingency, the idea that mutually exclusive possibilities can all be live and that the occurrence of any one of these need not be inevitable, is incompatible with determinism. According to determinism, a state of affairs, call it B, is determined by a prior state of affairs, call it A, provided that if A obtains, then B must follow. Such an antecedent–consequent relation may be logical or causal. What makes it deterministic is that it admits no deviation.[1]

Determinism so characterized is a local affair in that it looks at any particular circumstance and asks what prior circumstance made it inevitable. Determinism, as an antecedent–consequent relation, attempts for each state of affairs to find an antecedent state of affairs that, with certainty, brings it about. Yet what's antecedent in one inquiry will be consequent in another, so determinism, as a grand metaphysical theory, is not about any one state of affairs being determined, but about every state of affairs being determined. And since determinism is defined in terms of antecedent–consequent relationships, what's needed for a full-blooded determinism is that all states of affairs be interlocked in this way, with every state of affairs determined by a prior state of affairs.

Determinism thus entails a regress in which one asks for a given state of affairs what determined it, and then what determined what determined it, and so on. Where does this regress end? If one is a theist and a determinist (as in the Augustinian–Calvinist tradition), the regress ends with an act of creation by God. Materialism, by contrast, has no place to go beyond a material nature, and so the regress must ever reside in material nature. The regress and the

---

[1]   The rationalist tradition in philosophy collapsed the two, assimilating causal necessity to logical necessity. Thus F.R. Tennant writes of Spinoza that he "assumed the order and connexion of pure ideas to be identical with the order and connexion of things, and *causa* to be identical with *ratio*. Hence it was natural for representatives of the rationalistic school to assert that laws concerning actuality were characterised by logical necessity." F.R. Tennant, *Miracle and Its Philosophical Presuppositions* (Cambridge: Cambridge University Press, 1925), 10.

material nature in which it resides thus become a brute fact. If, as Carl Sagan claimed, the cosmos is all there ever was, is, or will be,[2] and if that cosmos is deterministic, then there is nothing to explain why this regress took the particular form it did. Any such explanation would presuppose a vantage outside nature, which materialism disallows. Indeed, materialism delivers a world entirely bent in on itself.

Determinism assures us that in the unfolding of the universe, each state of affairs was inevitable given the states of affairs leading up to it. But why did we end up with these states of affairs taken as a whole and not others? We may live in a universe that, in the 2012 United States presidential election, made Obama's victory over Romney inevitable. But why did we end up in such a universe at all? What made the universe such that it would guarantee victory to Obama and defeat to Romney? Such questions, even when asked within the perspective of a metaphysical determinism, suggest that the question of contingency never fully goes away. Contingencies that are eliminated locally because states of affairs are determined by prior states of affairs reemerge globally as soon as one asks about the world as a whole and why the totality of states of affairs, as interlocked in antecedent–consequent relations, assumes one form rather than another. Once this question is raised, it admits three responses: One can simply refuse to answer it, taking a locally determined world as a brute fact. Alternatively, accepting local determinism, one can nonetheless admit that global contingency is real and try to understand it. Or one can deny that any contingency is real and attempt to justify why the world is determined not just locally but also globally.

The first of these options is not very satisfying, inviting those who hold the other two options to make their best case and argue for either real contingency or comprehensive determinism. Materialism, historically, has been more comfortable with a comprehensive determinism. Typically, materialism has justified a comprehensive determinism by making the universe much bigger than it appears. Epicurean materialism, for instance, posited a universe of infinite time and infinite matter. In such a universe everything that's possible becomes inevitable because all combinations of matter get tried out somewhere in the

---

[2]   The opening line on page 1 of Carl Sagan, *Cosmos* reads, "The Cosmos is all that is or ever was or ever will be."

universe, and not just once but infinitely often.[3] Eternal recurrence is a theme in such cosmologies. In them, everything possible becomes actual and necessary.[4]

We see this impulse also in modern cosmology where the actual universe is taken to be much much bigger than the known physical universe. The piece of the universe that we know may seem quite small and contingent, but when factored in with all the other pieces of the universe, our story becomes inevitable. Inflationary cosmologies tend in this direction with their bubble universes, according to which the known universe is but one bubble. Yet the starkest contemporary example of this impulse occurs with quantum many worlds, in which anything physically possible is realized in the multiworld, which constitutes the actual universe. Within the many-worlds interpretation of quantum mechanics, the known universe is just one of infinitely many branches, all of which together exhaust the full range of physical possibilities and form the multiworld.[5]

The main materialist retort to contingency, both in antiquity and through to the present, has been to eliminate contingency by making all possibilities equally real (whether by expanding the universe beyond all ascertainable bounds or by positing eternal recurrence of a universe that cycles through all possibilities or some combination of the two).[6] Declaring all possibilities real as a matter of metaphysical fiat, however, is not very impressive. The appeal of materialism these days is supposed to be its overwhelming support by science. Materialists don't want materialism to be an object of faith but of cold, sober calculation. And yet a metaphysical fiat that declares all physical possibilities equally real seems not to admit any compelling justification except that it provides a more comfortable setting for materialism.

---

[3] Strictly speaking, Epicurean materialism, insofar as it looks to Epicurus himself as its fountainhead, allowed for contingency since his atoms were endowed with *swerve* that would allow them to act spontaneously in multiple, mutually exclusive ways. Epicurus introduced his now infamous swerve in order to preserve free will. Epicurus's followers, however, who were committed to his program of systematically eliminating any supernatural influences from nature, were happy to let the swerve go by the board. For a helpful history of Epicurean materialism that addresses these points, see Wiker, *Moral Darwinism*, chs. 1 and 2.

[4] For an interesting history of the doctrine of eternal recurrence (also known as eternal return), see Ned Lukacher, *Time-Fetishes: The Secret History of Eternal Recurrence* (Durham, N.C.: Duke University Press, 1998).

[5] For quantum multiworlds, see David Deutsch, *The Fabric of Reality: The Science of Parallel Universes—and Its Implications* (New York: Penguin, 1997). For how inflationary cosmology vastly expands on the known physical universe, see Alan Guth, *The Inflationary Universe: The Quest for a New Theory of Cosmic Origins* (Reading, Mass.: Addison-Wesley, 1997).

[6] See John Leslie, *Universes* (London: Routledge, 1989), ch. 4.

Even for a world presumed to consist only of matter, questions such as the following inevitably arise: Why does our universe have the form it does? Why do the laws governing that universe exhibit a fine-tuning suggestive of intelligence? Why does life seem to bear the hallmarks of intelligence? Declaring all physical possibilities equally real means that all such questions can be dismissed by simply noting that anything that could happen does in fact happen, and it just happens to be happening to us, so here we are, end of story. Yet where is the independent evidence that other possibilities are as real as the possibilities we actually observe? In our experience, when one thing happens it closes the door to other things happening. The materialism of our day is supposed to be a scientific materialism, looking to science to justify materialism. Yet science is a thoroughly empirical enterprise. Thus, when the pointer points here, suggesting such and such a conclusion, it is not pointing there, which would suggest a different conclusion. Science, as an empirical enterprise, depends fundamentally on observation, and observation delivers one possibility to the exclusion of others. In other words, observation presupposes contingency and delivers information.

A thorough-going determinism that denies all contingency, by contrast, keeps all doors eternally open, not as a matter of practical reason but as a matter of metaphysical principle (whether atheistic or theistic). Just as solipsism can avoid logical contradiction, so can denying contingency via the plenitude of realized possibilities. But absence of logical contradiction is a very limited guide to truth when it comes to such far-flung metaphysical options. Witness: "I saw the defendant with a smoking gun." Attorney: "No, you saw a cleverly disguised space alien with a smoking gun." The contradiction in such cases would be palpable even if not logical. In any case, we feel in our bones that the universe we inhabit could have been different. And in many practical circumstances we desperately want to know why it wasn't different (e.g., a businessman facing bankruptcy, an athlete suffering a career-ending injury, or even a professor of metaphysics denied tenure). Global determinism, in eliminating all contingency, contradicts this very deep intuition, trivializing our role in the world as agents who would make a difference.

Chapter 16

Contingency and Chance

Leaving aside determinism, which denies that anything could be different, we now face the problem of trying to understand its opposite, contingency, which asserts that things could well have been different. Broadly speaking, contingency can take two forms: (1) contingency of the world as a whole and (2) contingency within the world. Thus one can look for contingency in the very structure of the universe with respect to its basic laws, constants, and boundary conditions. Alternatively, one can look for contingency in the subsequent unfolding of the universe. In that case, even if the underlying structure of the universe is determined, what happens in it might be contingent. On the other hand, even if the local functioning of the universe is determined, its global structure might be contingent. These two ways of understanding contingency, however, are not mutually exclusive. Thus the world's global structure as well as its local functioning might both be contingent.

Materialism resists contingency of the world taken as a whole. If the very structure of the world is contingent, then why did it assume that structure to the exclusion of others? The theistic answer, that God, in an informational act, actualized one world by ruling out others and thus freely intended our world to be as it is, won't fly with the materialist. Yet the materialistic answer, that chance, operating without intelligent input, actualized our world to the exclusion of others has its own problems. Take an appeal to chance such as the following: The world assumed the structure that it has because of a quantum fluctuation. Presumably this means that the quantum vacuum (which a moment's reflection reveals is not a true nothing) fluctuated in one way rather than another.[1]

Yet if we take this explanation seriously, are we, in addition, to believe that there was just one quantum fluctuation and that we are living in it? If a quantum fluctuation can give rise to the universe as we know it, why can't it give rise to

---

[1]   For the absurd materialist logic by which, as a matter of sheer wordplay, the language of physics, rather than physics itself, transforms nothing into something, see Lawrence M. Krauss, *A Universe from Nothing: Why There Is Something Rather than Nothing* (New York: Free Press, 2012) as well as Stephen Hawking and Leonard Mlodinow's mistitled *The Grand Design* (New York: Bantam, 2010). Krauss equivocates on what he means by "nothing" and Hawking does not mean by design the product of intelligence.

others? Once chance is invoked as responsible for the structure of our universe, it's hard to deny that chance could produce other universes. And if others, why not all of them? But in that case, everything that's possible becomes actual, which takes us full circle to the determinism of the previous chapter. Indeed, a world in which all possibilities are actualized is fully deterministic.

In any case, invoking chance to account for the universe as a whole can't help but commit an argument from ignorance. The problem is that without some non-arbitrary way of assigning probabilities to whatever we are calling chance, and thus without some knowledge of the underlying processes that give rise to those probabilities, chance becomes an empty word. *Why did the bridge over there collapse? Hey, stuff happens. The bridge's collapse is just one of those things. It was chance.* Such an explanation is no explanation at all. It is vacuous. A legitimate appeal to chance in this case would be based on knowledge of, say, weaknesses in the bridge's cables along with the probability that these would snap given their wear and tear. Now the problem with the universe taken as a whole is that we *cannot* have knowledge of such probabilities. Let me state this point less delicately: it's not that we are ignorant of the underlying probabilities; it's that we cannot but be ignorant of the underlying probabilities.

To be sure, we can make up probabilities—numbers are obedient servants and we can do what we like with them. A given model of universe formation might assign a high probability to the formation of our particular universe, and this could be viewed as indirect evidence for that model.[2] Alternatively, theology, by suggesting that God is inclined to create certain types of universes, might assign a high probability to creating one like ours. All such probabilities, however, are speculative in the extreme. The problem here is that the preconditions for the universe's existence cannot be inferred from the conditions by which the universe operates. C.S. Lewis, to make this very point, distinguished "probabilities inside a given frame" from "how probable it is that the frame itself" takes the form that it does. The frame, in this case, is the universe, and this frame gives rise to certain probabilities, some of which are ascertainable. But how the universe

---

[2]   For the underlying logic of this probabilistic approach to evidence, see Richard M. Royall, *Statistical Evidence: A Likelihood Paradigm* (London: Chapman & Hall, 1997). For why this approach doesn't work, see Dembski, *Design Revolution*, ch. 33, titled "Design by Elimination Versus Design by Comparison." For an application of this logic to cosmology, see Lee Smolin, *The Life of the Cosmos* (New York: Oxford University Press, 1997). Smolin argues that universes are formed through a quasi-Darwinian process in which black holes form universes that in turn form black holes, with universes that are better than others at forming black holes having a selective advantage. Smolin then takes any evidence for our own universe being good at generating black holes as evidence for his theory.

itself arose is outside our experience, implying that we have no empirical basis for ascertaining the probability of this frame. Lewis illustrated this point with the following analogy:

> Granted a school timetable with French on Tuesday morning at ten o'clock, it is really probable that Jones, who always skimps his French preparation, will be in trouble next Tuesday, and that he was in trouble on any previous Tuesday. But what does this tell us about the probability of the timetable's being altered? To find that out you must eavesdrop in the masters' common-room. It is no use studying the timetable.[3]

Likewise, studying the processes and probabilities by which the known physical universe operates (which is all science can do) does nothing, and indeed can do nothing, to elucidate the probabilities by which the universe came into existence in the first place. Probabilities for universe formation, by their very nature, are independent of known processes operating within the known universe. Indeed, such probabilities assume a God's eye view ("the masters' common-room"). A God's eye view could stand outside the universe and assess how it came to exist and what accounts for its structure. But, as humans, we have no such view. We are, instead, thoroughly part of the universe, and whatever probabilities we can reasonably assign must be based on those processes of which we are a part. In answering why there is something rather than nothing and why it takes the form that it does, materialism thus offers no advantage over theism. In particular, a materialism that takes the world as a whole to be contingent cannot but explain that contingency by invoking a form of chance whose probabilities are conjured out of thin air (indeed, no air at all). No evidence, in this case, could confirm chance. God, by contrast, might at least have some evidence in his favor.[4]

---

[3] C.S. Lewis, *Miracles: A Preliminary Study*, rev. edn. (1960; reprinted New York: HarperCollins, 1996), 164–5.

[4] Consider the following evidence that would have convinced atheist philosopher Norwood Russell Hanson to become a theist: "Suppose, however, next Tuesday morning, just after breakfast, all of us in this one world are knocked to our knees by a percussive and ear-shattering thunderclap. Snow swirls, leaves drop from trees, the earth heaves and buckles, buildings topple and towers tumble. The sky is ablaze with an eerie silvery light, and just then, as all of the people of this world look up, the heavens open, and the clouds pull apart, revealing an unbelievably radiant and immense Zeus-like figure towering over us like a hundred Everests. He frowns darkly as lightning plays over the features of his Michelangeloid face, and then he points down, *at me*, and explains for every man, woman and child to hear: 'I've had quite enough of your too-clever logic chopping and word-watching in matters of theology. Be assured N.R. Hanson, that I do most certainly exist!'" Quoted from Norwood

It's worth pondering here what these difficulties of assigning probabilities to the entire universe mean for fine-tuning arguments. A fine-tuning argument looks at a feature of the universe that could be continuously varied along some dimension, notes that for the universe to be life-permitting this feature could take values within only a very narrow band among its possible values, and concludes that an intelligence is therefore responsible for the fine-tuning because it would be too improbable for that feature to fall within that very narrow band by chance. The usual response by materialists to fine-tuning arguments is to invoke multiple universes, which wash out the improbability here by giving chance as many opportunities as it needs to achieve the fine-tuning with high probability (the rationale being that any event, however improbable when taken individually, if given enough opportunities, can attain any level of high probability).[5]

But since we are talking about features of the universe that need to be in place *before*[6] the universe can be said to exist and operate, it's not clear where those probabilities that are applied to the universe as a whole are coming from or how they can be coherently grounded. Certainly, a fine-tuning argument identifies an instance of information in that values within a very narrow band along some dimension are realized to the exclusion of others (thus exemplifying the standard reduction of possibilities that is characteristic of information). But measuring that information is problematic. Even referring to a "very narrow band" along some dimension may be nothing more than an artifact of how we human beings represent numbers.[7] For all the universe

Russell Hanson, *What I Do Not Believe and Other Essays*, eds. S. Toulmin and H. Woolf (New York: Springer, 1971), 313–14.

[5]   See John Leslie, *Universes*, 6–8. See also Bernard Carr, ed., *Universe or Multiverse?* (Cambridge: Cambridge University Press, 2007), which has articles by many of the leading physicists who speculate about multiple universes, including Stephen Weinberg, Leonard Susskind, and Martin Rees.

[6]   The sense of "before" here is not temporal but logical, as in logical priority.

[7]   For a similar argument, see Timothy McGrew, Lydia McGrew, and Eric Vestrup, "Probabilities and the Fine-Tuning Argument: A Skeptical View," *Mind* 110(440) (2001): 1027–37. The abstract of this paper is short and reads, "Proponents of the Fine-Tuning Argument frequently assume that the narrowness of the life-friendly range of fundamental physical constants implies a low probability for the origin of the universe 'by chance'. We cast this argument in a more rigorous form than is customary and conclude that the narrow intervals do not yield a probability at all because the resulting measure function is non-normalizable. We then consider various attempts to circumvent this problem and argue that they fail."

By normalizability the authors mean that the range of possible values for an instance of fine-tuning does not admit a uniform probability distribution. In the absence of any observational evidence for probabilities, uniform probabilities are often introduced because, by apportioning probabilities as evenly as possible (which is what uniform probabilities do),

knows, the band may be wide. Thus, without some compelling way of assigning a probability distribution to that dimension, there is no way to say whether the fine-tuning is probable or improbable, and thus no way to evaluate the amount of information associated with it. I personally regard fine-tuning arguments as suggestive, as pointers to an underlying intelligent or teleological cause. But I see no way to develop them into rigorous statistical inferences precisely because their probabilities cannot be grounded in any observed processes (indeed, observation itself presupposes fine-tuning).

We have been considering contingency of the world as a whole. Let us now turn to contingency within the world. Here probabilities can be assigned non-arbitrarily, and so invoking chance need no longer be a placeholder for ignorance. Since contingency always involves one possibility happening to the exclusion of others, the probabilities now range over possibilities capable of happening in the world. What, then, causes one possibility to be realized from such a matrix of possibilities? In fact, when some theorists discuss this aspect of chance, they will refer to chance as an acausal notion. On this view, nothing causes what happens to happen.[8] Others will argue that the probabilistic setup causes what happens

---

they are thought to introduce no bias and thus satisfy the principle of indifference (also known as the principle of insufficient reason). This justification is not without difficulties. For instance, there can be different ways to assign uniform probabilities that come up with different answers, as with Bertrand's paradox—see P.E. Tissler, "Bertrand's Paradox," *The Mathematical Gazette* 68(443) (1984): 15–19. For the principle of indifference/insufficient reason, see William A. Dembski and Robert J. Marks II, "Bernoulli's Principle of Insufficient Reason and Conservation of Information in Computer Search," *Proceedings of the 2009 IEEE International Conference on Systems, Man, and Cybernetics*, San Antonio, Texas (October 2009): 2647–52. For a general account of uniform probabilities, see William A. Dembski, "Uniform Probability," *Journal of Theoretical Probability* 3(4) (1990): 611–26.

[8]   Philosopher Bradley Monton, for instance, takes this approach to chance. Questioning whether an intelligent cause might reasonably explain a quantum event such as the decay of a radioactive atom, he remarks, "Even though an appeal to an intelligent cause is (let's suppose) the best explanation of the decay, does that mean that we should believe that that explanation is the true one? The answer is *no*. It could be that *all* the explanations of the decay are false; it could be that the right account of the decay is that there's no explanation for why the atom decayed when it did: the decay was just a spontaneous event, with no cause. Thus, we can believe that an intelligent cause is the best explanation for the decay, while also believing that an intelligent cause had nothing to do with the decay." Quoted from Bradley Monton, *Seeking God in Science: An Atheist Defends Intelligent Design* (Peterborough, Ont.: Broadview, 2009), 36. This conception of chance is sometimes referred to as *absolute chance* or *spontaneity* or *tychism*, the latter term introduced by Charles Peirce. For Peirce's view, see Andrew Reynolds, *Peirce's Scientific Metaphysics: The Philosophy of Chance, Law, and Evolution* (Nashville, Tenn.: Vanderbilt University Press, 2002).

to happen, but could equally well have caused other things to happen. On this view, causation can be nondeterministic, taking the form of chance operating according to probabilities. Such *probabilistic causation* is a well-developed area of study in the philosophy of science.[9]

Before getting into the metaphysics underlying chance, however, I need a minimal working definition of chance. I'll use the following: the realization of one possibility to the exclusion of others according to a probability distribution.[10] This definition makes sense regardless of what's ultimately behind this realization–exclusion, whether it's acausal, nondeterministically causal, or agent causal (as would be the case if, contrary to materialism, intelligence is the fundamental mode of causality, thus making chance a veiled mode of agent causation—more on this momentarily). This definition of chance is, to be sure, saying that there is something to chance that cannot be reduced to physical necessity, that is, to things happening because other physical things are forcing them to happen that way, and only that way (we are, by this point in the argument, setting aside determinism and taking contingency seriously). Moreover, this definition insists that chance needs to be disciplined by probabilities if it is to perform any useful work.

But even with so innocuous an understanding of chance, chance remains a problematic notion. Probability admits uncertainty at the level of individual chance events but brings order when these events are considered aggregately. Thus, even though the outcome of a single coin toss may be totally uncertain, multiple coin tosses tend to yield stable patterns. For instance, as a coin is tossed repeatedly, the proportion of heads will tend to ½. This stable pattern to coin tossing is justified both theoretically (various probabilistic laws of "large

---

[9] A seminal figure in this area is Patrick Suppes. See his *Probabilistic Metaphysics* (London: Blackwell, 1984). See also Ellery Eells, *Probabilistic Causality* (Cambridge: Cambridge University Press, 1991) and Nancy Cartwright, *Hunting Causes and Using Them: Approaches in Philosophy and Economics* (Cambridge: Cambridge University Press, 2007).

[10] By a probability distribution, I mean a model from the mathematical theory of probability used to describe the probabilistic behavior under consideration. For instance, the probability distribution for coin tossing is given by a probability measure $\mathbf{P}$ on the (Borel) subsets of $\{0,1\}^{\mathbf{N}}$, which is the infinite Cartesian product of the dyadic set $\{0,1\}$, indexed by the natural numbers $\mathbf{N}$, with each member of this Cartesian product denoting an infinitely long sequence of coin tosses (0 for tails, 1 for heads). Finite runs of coin tosses can then be represented as subsets of $\{0,1\}^{\mathbf{N}}$, and the probability measure $\mathbf{P}$ will assign a given finite run of length m the probability $(\frac{1}{2})^{m}$. For a more detailed discussion of this way of thinking about probability distributions, see any measure-theoretic treatment of probability, such as Patrick Billingsley, *Probability and Measure*, 3rd edn. (New York: Wiley, 1995).

numbers" confirm it) and practically (when people flip coins a large number of times, they tend to see roughly the same proportion of heads and tails).[11]

It is a remarkable and mysterious thing that chance events, when viewed aggregately, exhibit stable and expected patterns. Indeed, on materialist grounds, there is no known independent "fact of the matter" to suggest why this should be so. Why should coins (or, if coins seem too deterministic, consider instead quanta of light passing through a polarizing filter) exhibit predictable probabilistic behavior? What is it about a rigid homogeneous disk with distinguishable sides that, when flipped repeatedly by a nonlinear dynamical system such as you or me, should lead to heads roughly half the time and tails the other half? Geometric symmetry of the coin doesn't begin to address the deep conceptual problem that underlies this question.

The problem is that chance, as characterized probabilistically, can and will violate all expected patterns. Flip a fair coin, and the long-run proportion of heads will tend to ½. Several theorems from probability theory guarantee this result.[12] But we don't live in the long run—our entire lives and even the life of the universe occur in the short run. Moreover, we have no independent means to verify that the probabilities we are observing in the short run are representative of the true underlying long-run probabilities (if such even exist). Flip a coin in the long run, and you'll encounter short runs consisting of any finite sequence of coin tosses whatsoever. A fundamental theorem of probability theory called the Strong Law of Large Numbers guarantees this result.[13] Thus, if you flip a coin long enough, you'll see a sequence of coin tosses that, if interpreted in the universal character set UTF-8 (0 for tails, 1 for heads), will spell out the entire works of Shakespeare. There will also come an occasion when you witness a trillion trillion trillion heads in a row, and that with a fair coin!

Probabilities therefore raise a deep epistemic problem: how do we know that, with the chance events we are witnessing in this life, we are not coming in, as it were, on coin tosses that are completely uncharacteristic or nonrepresentative

[11] This combination of theory and practice comes up especially in gambling. See Richard A. Epstein, *The Theory of Gambling and Statistical Logic*, 2nd edn. (Oxford: Academic Press, 2013).

[12] These theorems fall under what are called "laws of large numbers" and also "large deviations." See respectively T.K. Chandra, *Laws of Large Numbers* (Oxford: Alpha Science International, 2012) and S.R.S. Varadhan, "Large Deviations," *The Annals of Probability* 36(2) (2008): 397–419, the latter being a survey article available online at http://arxiv.org/pdf/0804.2330v1.pdf (last accessed July 3, 2013).

[13] See Heinz Bauer, *Probability Theory and Elements of Measure Theory*, trans. R.B. Burckel, 2nd English edn. (New York: Academic Press, 1981), 172.

of their "normal" chance behavior? Probability theory is happy to treat coins as having a certain propensity to behave probabilistically in certain ways.[14] Yet probability theory also insists that coins with that propensity, when flipped long enough, will, over arbitrarily long finite runs (these are nonetheless still "short runs"), behave in ways totally at odds with that propensity. So how can we tell the difference between probabilistic behavior that is characteristic of an underlying probability distribution and probabilistic behavior that is uncharacteristic?

This question cuts to the core of the scientific enterprise. Indeed, when we look at nature, how do we know that we aren't seeing the equivalent of a trillion trillion trillion heads in a row when chance would "ordinarily" present a roughly equal proportion of heads and tails? To say that an equal proportion is "expected" or will happen "normally" or is "likely on average" begs the question, for why should we expect chance to behave that way *for us*? If we had independent evidence that chance was, in a given short run, behaving representatively of the underlying probability distribution, there would be no problem. But we have no independent access to such underlying probability distributions. All we have access to are chance processes acting in short runs giving us data that we would like to use as evidence of the underlying probability distribution (if such even exists). But we have no way of knowing if that evidence is representative of the underlying probability distribution or radically at odds with it.

To invoke the improbability of representative samples that deviate too much from underlying probability distributions is no help here. It begs the question to say that radical deviation from expectation is too improbable and therefore we should expect short-run probabilities to match up (roughly) with long-run probabilities. Such an argument presupposes that we have reliably ascertained a baseline probability distribution characteristic of long-run behavior and that short-run behaviors, if they deviate from it sufficiently, are so unlikely as to be best ascribed to some other probability distribution. But it's the very ascertainability of the baseline that's at issue here since the baseline distribution

---

[14]   This is not to endorse the propensity interpretation of probability but simply to note that even this interpretation, which takes as realist an approach to probability as exists, allows probabilistic processes to do things that are completely unrepresentative of their probabilistic underpinnings. And if this is true of the propensity interpretation, it is even more true of other interpretations, whose probabilities purport to have even less of a hold on reality. The argument here is a fortiori, from propensity to other interpretations. For the propensity interpretation of probability as originally propounded, see Karl R. Popper, "The Propensity Interpretation of Probability," *British Journal for the Philosophy of Science* 10 (1959): 25–42. For its more recent discussion among philosophers of science, see Donald Gillies, *Philosophical Theories of Probability* (London: Routledge, 2000), chs. 6 and 7.

will have had to be inferred from short-run data, and these by themselves can never guarantee that they derived from the presumed baseline or even an approximation to it. If you will, probability theory guarantees that probabilities will with small probability misrepresent themselves, but that small probability of misrepresentation is no grounds for confidence that probabilities have not misrepresented themselves because the very use of probabilities presupposes that they have not misrepresented themselves.

Let's give this problem a name: *the problem of probabilistic induction*. This problem is a variant of the classic problem of induction, but with a twist. In the classic problem of induction, the problem was how to generalize from past instances of some regular occurrence to its future occurrence. Given Hume's empiricism and the skepticism of causality that it engendered (i.e., how could we know that anything causes anything else if all we observe are constant conjunctions of events and not the underlying causal linkages that constrain one to proceed from the other?), there was no way to underwrite the reliability of induction as a tool for inquiry.[15] Now for Hume, at least, accurate observation of past regularities was something that could be taken for granted. The validity of projecting those regularities into the future could not be justified on Humean grounds, but the very regularities themselves, as observed in the past, were unquestioned.

With the problem of probabilistic induction, past observations lack this sort of solidity. In this case, past observations form a sample and yield statistics that we want to take as representative of an underlying probability distribution responsible for the sample. In addition, we will want to project this sample and its associated statistics into the future to give us insight into future samples. In the classic problem of induction, if there were an underlying cause, it could at least in part justify the induction, suggesting that the future ought to resemble the past because the same causes that were operating in the past should also be operating in the future. Moreover, there could be independent evidence

---

[15]   "The conclusion that Hume has pretty well established about causal inferences—that the inference from an observed event to another event as its cause or effect is never deductively valid, even if we include in the premises the fact that a great many similar sequences have occurred—is not a surprising one; it may not have been clearly realized before Hume pointed it out, but it would now be accepted by most philosophers without dispute. The more sweeping conclusions about such inferences which he suggests but fails to establish—that these inferences are not even reasonable or probable, that they are to be ascribed to imagination, custom, and habit rather than to reason, that it is out of the question to try to justify them on any ground except that they are natural, instinctive, and unavoidable—are interesting and important. They raise those problems about induction, probable inference, and the confirmation of hypotheses which are still a major area of dispute and investigation." Mackie, *Cement of the Universe*, 18–19.

for certain causal processes being responsible for the past regularities (e.g., the induction from all observed ravens being black to all ravens being black would receive a causal justification if genetic data could be shown to confirm the raven's black color). But with probabilistic induction, the underlying cause would be a probability distribution, and there is no independent way to determine whether an observed sample matches expectation with that probability distribution. Indeed, it's in the nature of probability distributions that they not only permit deviations but also guarantee violent deviations—in the long run, any finite run, however bizarre or atypical of the underlying probability distribution, is sure to happen.

In my book *No Free Lunch*, I provided a non-question-begging approach to this problem of probabilistic induction.[16] There I characterized the activity of intelligence as making a choice, that is, actualizing one possibility to the exclusion of another in order to advance a purpose or intention (note that the very word *intelligence* derives etymologically from the Latin and means to *choose between*, thus presupposing genuine contingency). Moreover, I noted that when intelligence acts, it has probabilistic side-effects. Accordingly, chance is no longer *sui generis* but becomes *a probabilistic side-effect of intelligence*. For instance, because the English language follows certain conventions, when we write, we find that letters and combinations of letters occur with certain relative frequencies (e.g., the letter "e" appears 13 percent of the time; the letter "u" always follows "q" except for a few transliterated foreign words[17]). Such relative frequencies are probabilistic. Yet they occur reliably even though the texts to which they apply are fully intended (writing, as I'm verifying at this moment, is an intentional activity). Moreover, any significant deviation from these probabilistic expectations will itself result from an intentional act.

To see how deviations from probabilistic expectations can themselves be intentional, consider Ernest Vincent Wright's 50,000-word novel *Gadsby*.[18] This novel completely omitted the letter "e." Here is the opening paragraph:

> If youth, throughout all history, had had a champion to stand up for it; to show
> a doubting world that a child can think; and, possibly, do it practically; you

---

[16]   Dembski, *No Free Lunch*, ch. 6.

[17]   For the frequency distributions of Latin letters in different languages, see http://wiki. stat.ucla.edu/socr/index.php/SOCR_LetterFrequencyData (last accessed July 11, 2013).

[18]   Ernest Vincent Wright, *Gadsby* (Los Angeles, Calif.: Wetzel, 1939). The same idea, with respect to the same letter of the alphabet, was also put into practice by the celebrated French novelist Georges Perec in his novel, *La disparition* (Paris: Editions Denoel, 1969), translated as *A Void* (London: Harvill Press, 1994).

wouldn't constantly run across folks today who claim that "a child don't know anything." A child's brain starts functioning at birth; and has, amongst its many infant convolutions, thousands of dormant atoms, into which God has put a mystic possibility for noticing an adult's act, and figuring out its purport.[19]

Now it is quite certain that after completing his novel, Wright didn't wake up one morning and discover—to his surprise—that it nowhere contained the letter "e." The omission was clearly by design. In fact, as he cheerfully admits in his introduction, "The entire manuscript of this story was written with the E type-bar of the typewriter tied down; thus making it impossible for that letter to be printed. This was done so that none of that vowel might slip in, accidentally; and many did try to do so!"[20] Design, accordingly, explains such violations of probabilistic expectations.

Yet design can also explain matches with probabilistic expectations, though in this case it will not be as a direct intended product of design but as a byproduct. We saw this with letter distributions of English texts. We see it more generally in the aggregate behavior of intelligent agents, a point underscored by actuaries as they calculate probabilities associated with human behaviors (e.g., accident statistics) and thereby provide the rigorous risk assessments used to set our home, auto, and life insurance rates. Actuarial data provide plenty of empirical evidence that byproducts of design can exhibit random behavior that matches up precisely with expected long-run probabilistic outcomes.[21]

But one doesn't have to be an actuary to confirm this point. It's easy to see the match between byproducts of design and probability from the comfort of one's laptop computer. To get letters of the alphabet that look completely random (i.e., the letters appear drawn from a probability distribution that renders them equiprobable and each probabilistically independent of the rest), simply take English texts written by different authors and "convolve" them, that is, align the texts (omitting spaces and punctuation) and then, letter by corresponding letter, add them together cyclically so that A+B=C, B+B=D, A+B+C=F, A+Z=A, B+Y=A, D+E+Y=H, etc.[22] Simply

[19] Quoted from http://spinelessbooks.com/gadsby/01.html (last accessed February 6, 2013), which has the entire book online.

[20] Quoted from http://spinelessbooks.com/gadsby/ (last accessed February 6, 2013).

[21] For the underlying mathematics, see Vladimir I. Rotar, *Actuarial Models: The Mathematics of Insurance* (Boca Raton, Fl.: CRC Press, 2007).

[22] Convolution in this sense is a group action and has the effect of mixing things up. For the underlying mathematics, see Walter Rudin, *Fourier Analysis on Groups* (New York: Wiley, 1962). For its application specifically to randomness, see Persi Diaconis, *Group*

convolving two independent English texts in this way will yield something that looks pretty random (a fact that is the basis for the Vigenère, running key, and one-time pad cryptosystems[23]), but convolving ten or more will be indistinguishable from chance for any randomness checker. And yet such convolutions of texts are fully intentional—each text is intended and the convolution itself is intended.

Materialism is willing to allow that byproducts of intelligence can follow well-defined probability distributions provided that intelligence itself is conceived as ultimately reducible to purely material processes. On the other hand, materialism is unwilling to allow that chance is in every case the byproduct of intelligence. Within materialism, intelligence or design must, in the final analysis, be the unintended product of material processes, and in a material world with genuine contingency, such processes must be ascribed to accidental forces in nature, and thus to chance (not necessarily to pure chance, in the sense of maximally entropic, uniform probability distributions, but to stochastic processes that can combine deterministic and nondeterministic elements[24]). Consequently, within a materialism that admits contingency, design must be viewed as a byproduct of chance (bearing in mind that chance will here need to include necessity as a special case, in which probabilities collapse to zero and one).[25] Byproducts of design or intelligence can and do follow well-defined probability distributions, but within materialism design or intelligence is itself the byproduct of chance.

Why do byproducts of intelligence, such as letter frequencies of English texts, follow well-defined probability distributions, exhibiting probabilistic behavior

---

Representations in Probability and Statistics (Hayward, Calif.: Institute of Mathematical Statistics, 1988). Yoram Sagher, a mathematics professor of mine when I was a graduate student, remarked in one of the analysis courses that I took with him that convolution was the most important operator in mathematics. I suspect he was a bit biased because his field was analysis. Nonetheless, to this day I think that he was on to something.

[23] See Simon Singh, *The Code Book: The Evolution of Secrecy from Mary, Queen of Scots to Quantum Cryptography* (New York: Doubleday, 1999), ch. 2.

[24] Often when people think of chance, they think of pure chance in the sense of an arrangement that's as random or mixed up as possible. Uniform probability measures that distribute probability weights as widely and diffusely as possible and thus maximize entropy are prototypical of chance in this sense. But chance need not be taken in so narrow a sense. A process that's highly predictable but allows some small random deviations is still a chance process, as for instance the voting behavior of certain regions that are inveterately Democratic or Republican. Stochastic processes that incorporate even the smallest element of chance will thus still exemplify chance. For stochastic processes and how they go well beyond pure chance, see Richard F. Bass, *Stochastic Processes* (Cambridge: Cambridge University Press, 2011).

[25] We've seen this competition between chance and design before, or at least a variant of it. In chapter 8, we saw how nature could be used to subsume design, and likewise how design could be used to subsume nature.

that's reliable and predictable? Although it's enough for my argument to treat this phenomenon as a brute fact (i.e., it's simply a fact that intelligences, when they act, induce reliable probabilistic side effects), a rationale for it can be given. Intelligences, when they act, tend to operate in accord with certain standards, policies, and conventions. These, in virtue of their consistent application (that's why they are standards, policies, and conventions), induce regular patterns. The very regularity of these patterns in turn induces stable probabilistic behavior. Take again letter frequencies of English texts. These would not yield well-established probabilities unless English orthography were fixed and in widespread use, as is the case. Or consider auto accidents. Their probabilistic distribution depends on people driving on the same side of the road, obeying certain speed limits, being aware that drunk driving entails serious penalties, and many other conventions. Change these, and the statistics for auto accidents will change as well. Intelligences use standards, policies, and conventions to facilitate their designs and purposes. Yet those same standards, policies, and conventions have (often unintended) probabilistic consequences.

How much of chance should be conceived as a probabilistic byproduct of intelligence? All of it? Only some of it? Perhaps chance is a dual notion, with byproducts of intelligence being one aspect of chance and probabilistic behavior of unintelligent mechanistic processes (e.g., quantum mechanical systems) being another aspect of it. Such a compromise position, however, seems unsustainable. From the vantage of materialism, matter invariably swallows up intelligence, reducing it to the motions and modifications of matter. On the other hand, from the vantage of even the most generic theism (and I include here deism, process theism, panentheism, and pantheism in addition to ethical monotheism), intelligence becomes a fundamental and irreducible feature of reality that has a say in everything. As a consequence, intelligence becomes interwoven throughout the fabric of reality, making it impossible to sever chance from intelligence or rule out that chance is the byproduct of intelligence. So the logic of one's ultimate metaphysics pushes toward one view or the other, toward chance as devoid of intelligence or toward chance as an expression, albeit indirect, of intelligence. Thus, I would say, the generic theist may regard chance as, in every case, a byproduct of intelligence.[26]

---

[26] The use of letters in English texts, the incidence of auto accidents, the flipping of fair coins, and the outcomes from quantum mechanical devices would therefore all exhibit chance behaviors that are byproducts of intelligence. A theism that holds to a doctrine of creation will have no trouble accepting this unified conception of chance. Creation is always about the source of being of the world, asserting that it is intelligent. Since in a created world

Earlier, I gave a minimal working definition of chance as the realization of possibilities according to a probability distribution. I then argued that this definition, by itself, gives no basis for confidence that short-run probabilistic behavior (which is all we can ever observe) ought to be representative of an underlying probability distribution. The question therefore arises, how, if at all, does treating chance as a byproduct of intelligence improve on the rational foundations of probability by justifying that short-run probabilistic behavior may rightly be regarded as representative of an underlying probability distribution. Although this question seems reasonable enough, I want to suggest that it slips in an unwarranted assumption, and once this assumption is exposed, no matching of observed short-run probabilities with putative underlying long-run probabilities is required.

The unwarranted assumption is that intelligent agents are *governed* by probabilities in the sense of being *constrained to obey* underlying probability distributions. This assumption assigns primacy to underlying probability distributions and makes intelligent agents their servant. The problem here is that it gets the logical dependence of intelligence to probability backward, and it does so by wrongly looking to materialism for inspiration. Within a materialism that takes contingency seriously (contingency being the focus of this chapter), probability distributions become the prime organizing principle of reality—they become the "laws" that characterize the behavior of matter (which for the materialist is all that reality consists of). Matter thus becomes the servant of underlying probability distributions, albeit with occasional short-run disobedience because probability distributions only guarantee obedience in the long run. Moreover, within materialism, intelligence is the servant of matter. Thus, by transitivity of servanthood, intelligence becomes the servant of probability.

But once intelligent agents are no longer viewed as purely material, there is no underlying probability distribution that they are ineluctably constrained to obey. Intelligent agents are, in that case, free agents. They thus act freely, and any probabilities connected to them are logically downstream from their free choices. Probabilities, on this view, become descriptive rather than prescriptive. They simply take whatever form intelligent agents give them at a given time, and they are highly subject to change over time as intelligences vary their purposes, goals, desires, aversions, standards, policies, conventions, etc. Thus worlds identical up to a given time that differ radically in their probabilistic behavior afterward are not being untrue to some common underlying probability distribution but

---

all causal chains lead back to an intelligent creator God, nothing in a created world will be devoid of intelligence, chance included.

are simply seeing the expression of their intrinsic intelligence change. As these expressions of intelligence change, so do the probabilities.

I have been arguing that materialism is unable to give a coherent account of chance as contingency governed by probability and that it makes better sense to think of chance as a byproduct of intelligence. Materialism does, however, have another option for making sense of chance, and that is to try to understand it deterministically. This option therefore picks up on the last chapter, which focused on determinism. Determinism has found a place for chance, historically, by treating it not as brute contingency operating in nature but as a measure of ignorance of underlying deterministic processes. Accordingly, chance arises because we just don't know enough about the precise configuration and dynamics of matter. A perfect intelligence with perfect knowledge can dispense with chance (recall the Laplacean demon, who by knowing the precise positions and momenta of all particles in the world at a given moment can predict and retrodict the entire course of the universe down to the finest details[27]). But since we are finite rational agents with a very approximate knowledge of nature, chance becomes indispensable to our understanding of the world.

This view of chance, as occurring against a deterministic backdrop and constituting a measure of ignorance, is bolstered in our day with results from random number generation and nonlinear dynamics (chaos). Random number generation, if we set aside sampling from quantum mechanical systems, consists of deterministic computer programs that generate sequences of

---

[27] The Laplacean demon appears in Pierre Simon de Laplace, *A Philosophical Essay on Probabilities*, trans. F.W. Truscott and F.L. Emory (New York: Dover, 1996), 4. Note that Laplace himself did not refer to the demon as a demon but as an "intelligence which could comprehend all the forces by which nature is animated and the respective situation of the beings who compose it." This intelligence, he continued, "would embrace in the same formula the movements of the greatest bodies of the universe and those of the lightest atom; for it, nothing would be uncertain and the future, as the past, would be present to its eyes. The human mind offers, in the perfection which it has been able to give to astronomy, a feeble idea of this intelligence." An interesting question that follows from Laplace's ruminations is whether matter is capable of embodying an intelligence for which "nothing would be uncertain and the future, as the past, would be present to its eyes." There is a problem of self-reference here since any such intelligence, as materially embodied, would have to know itself completely, including its entire past and future. Stephen Wolfram, in *A New Kind of Science*, is happy to treat reality as a computer simulation, and yet that simulation knows itself only by sequentially performing computations, not in one grand intuitive grasp of the sort that Laplace attributes to his intelligence/demon.

digits approximating certain probability distributions.[28] Moreover, nonlinear dynamics or chaos provides deterministic ways of generating points in space that are extremely sensitive to initial and boundary conditions, and thus whose distribution can appear random.[29]

Such a deterministic approach to chance, however, always betrays itself. John von Neumann said it this way: "Any one who considers arithmetical methods of producing random digits is, of course, in a state of sin. For, as has been pointed out several times, there is no such thing as a random number—there are only methods to produce random numbers, and a strict arithmetic procedure of course is not such a method."[30] Von Neumann's insight applies equally to random trajectories of points generated by nonlinear dynamical systems (which are likewise deterministic). It's not that, for various practical purposes, we can't treat such numbers or trajectories as the chance product of a probability distribution (as in Monte Carlo simulations). Indeed, we can and do. Yet by their very nature such outputs will exhibit patterns totally at odds with the chance processes supposedly responsible for them.

All such deterministic approaches to chance depend on methods that, as von Neumann noted, are inherently incapable of producing random outcomes. Typically, some (usually simple) deterministic algorithm or function generates a sequence of numbers or points in space to be attributed to chance. But such methods, once identified, exhibit behaviors that would not be expected from sampling a probability distribution. Consider, for instance, coin tossing, denoting tails by 0 and heads by 1. There is a sequence of 0s and 1s known as the Champernowne number that lists binary numbers in increasing lexicographic order: 0 1 00 01 10 11 000 001 010 011 100 101 110 111 etc. (I've inserted spaces for ease of viewing, but these need to be removed in defining the actual

---

[28]   James E. Gentle, *Random Number Generation and Monte Carlo Methods* (New York: Springer, 2010).

[29]   James Gleick, *Chaos: Making a New Science* (New York: Penguin, 1987). This book, dated as it is, gives the sense of excitement that existed almost thirty years ago when nonlinear dynamical systems were starting to be understood, applied, and simulated computationally. Although much of the promise of this "new science" was never realized, its core insights about how and why nonlinear systems differ radically from linear ones remain valid.

[30]   John von Neumann, "Various Techniques Used in Connection with Random Digits," in Institute for Numerical Analysis (U.S.), *Monte Carlo Method: Proceedings of a Symposium Held June 29, 30, And July, 1, 1949, In Los Angeles, California, Under the Sponsorship of the Rand Corporation, And the National Bureau of Standards, With the Cooperation of the Oak Ridge National Laboratory*, eds. A.S. Householder, G.E. Forsythe, and H.H. Germond (Washington, D.C.: U.S. Govt. Print. Off., 1951).

number).[31] The Champernowne number has many properties that we would expect to see from actual coin tossing, and people who don't see this lexicographic pattern are apt to think that it resulted from actual coin tossing.

Actual coin tossing, however, does not match such simple patterns. Moreover, once we see the pattern, we know it's not random. Actual coin tossing would, for von Neumann, constitute a proper method for generating random numbers (presumably even better would be sampling from a quantum mechanical system[32]). But deterministic systems, once they are identified as such and their behavior is understood, exhibit patterns that betray their deterministic origin and thus demonstrate that they are not the result of chance (chance being conceived as contingency characterized by probability). The Champernowne number has roughly the same number of 0s and 1s in any finite initial segment and the number of alternations between 0s and 1s occurs roughly 50 percent of the time. Both these facts are consistent with what we would expect from genuine coin tossing. And yet, we don't expect from genuine coin tossing a precisely predictable lexicographic sequence. The sequence is therefore clearly nonrandom.

In conclusion, the upshot of this chapter is that chance is better understood as a byproduct of intelligence than as a probabilistic phenomenon intrinsic to matter. As I've argued, treating chance as a byproduct of intelligence dissolves a key problem at the foundations of probability, namely, the problem of probabilistic induction, or how short-run probabilistic data can be reliably matched with underlying probability distributions and their long-run expectations. This problem simply disappears if one takes chance to be the byproduct of intelligence. In that case, there is no underlying probability distribution whose expectations must be matched. There is simply the intelligence whose actions lead to side-effects that can be characterized probabilistically (and whose probabilistic characterization is subject to change as the intelligence changes its standards, policies, and conventions). In any case, we have good examples of chance as the byproduct of intelligence.

---

[31] The Champernowne sequence lists the 1-digit binary numbers first, namely, 0 and 1, and lists them in that order because 0 is counted before 1. Next it lists the 2-digit binary numbers, namely, 00, 01, 10, and 11, and lists them in that order because, if 0 precedes 1, then this is their lexicographic order. And so on for triplets, quadruplets, etc. of binary numbers. For more on the Champernowne sequence, see G.H. Hardy and E.M. Wright, *An Introduction to the Theory of Numbers*, 5th edn. (Oxford: Clarendon Press, 1979), 128.

[32] Such "genuine" random numbers are available online from a radioactive decay process: https://www.fourmilab.ch/hotbits (last accessed March 27, 2014).

By contrast, I just argued that determinism offers no adequate representation of chance, invariably revealing patterns that could never reasonably be ascribed to chance (cf. the Champernowne number). In addition, I've argued that making chance a *sui generis* probabilistic notion of the sort required by materialism renders the reliability of short-run probabilistic data unjustifiable, thus exacerbating the problem of probabilistic induction. Indeed, it becomes an act of faith for the materialist that short-run probabilities do not misrepresent themselves. A Cartesian deity capable of guaranteeing human knowledge is, unfortunately, unavailable to the materialist to ensure that probabilities won't deceive us.[33]

Before moving to the next chapter, I want to add two postscripts. First, some materialists bristle at understanding contingency in terms of chance. The materialism of our day is a scientific materialism that looks for its justification to science, and science tends to be wary of chance as an explanation. The problem is that invoking chance in scientific explanations can seem trivializing, as in invoking mere luck. Richard Dawkins puts it this way: "We can accept a certain amount of luck in our explanations, but not too much."[34] This is why Dawkins is so quick to dismiss the charge that evolutionary explanations are chance explanations: "This belief, that Darwinian evolution is 'random,' is not merely false. It is the exact opposite of the truth. Chance is a minor ingredient in the Darwinian recipe, but the most important ingredient is cumulative selection, which is quintessentially *non*random."[35]

Dawkins's attempt to minimize the role of chance in evolution is misleading. The fact remains that the creative potential for Darwinian processes comes from variations: "Unless profitable variations do occur," noted Darwin, "natural selection can do nothing."[36] But, within Darwinism, any such profitable variations are random (for instance, within neo-Darwinism, variations result from genetic copying errors). Moreover, given Dawkins's materialism, these variations must be sifted through a selection process that itself is the result of accidental forces of nature. To say that selection is nonrandom is therefore like saying that once a die is cast and has landed, the face that appears is nonrandom. True enough, but getting there certainly involved a good deal of randomness, and the same holds for natural selection if materialism is true.

The late philosopher Richard Rorty was therefore more forthright than Dawkins in admitting the towering role that chance plays in Darwinian

---

[33] Compare Descartes, *Meditations on First Philosophy*, fifth meditation.

[34] Dawkins, *Blind Watchmaker*, 139.

[35] Ibid., 49.

[36] Darwin, *On the Origin of Species*, 82.

evolutionary theory. "Keeping faith with Darwin," wrote Rorty, means realizing that "our species, its faculties and its current scientific and moral languages, are as much products of chance as are tectonic plates and mutated viruses."[37] So chance, when conceived broadly as chance and necessity (with necessity being a special case of chance where probabilities go to zero and one), underlies the materialist understanding of contingency even if some materialists, like Dawkins, don't care for the term.

The second postscript is this. Insofar as materialism is ready to explain contingency as chance governed by probability, contingencies associated with the choices of intelligent agents will, in the end, have to be reduced to chance (albeit, the probabilities characterizing chance will, in this case, be richer than the "pure chance" of maximally entropic, uniform probabilities). By contrast, a nonmaterialism that takes intelligence as fundamental is, I've argued, within its rights to take chance as derivative from intelligence. Materialism finds this last option, to be sure, unacceptable, though, as I've shown, there is good evidence for seeing chance processes as the byproduct of intelligence. In any case, as we've seen, in trying to block a reduction of chance to intelligence, materialism rejects intelligence as a fundamental entity or mode of explanation, making it entirely derivative of matter.

Such a reductive view of intelligence is perfectly understandable. On materialist grounds, intelligence will seem far downstream from the nuts and bolts of reality. Nuts-and-bolts reality, for the materialist, is matter jostling with no purpose and, through a blind evolutionary process, giving rise to organisms whose intelligence is an accident of natural history, with intelligence itself being entirely in the service of survival and reproduction. This is as it must be if materialism is true. I want to stress, however, that the nonmaterialist is under no obligation to buy into this world picture, nor is the nonmaterialist, having explained chance in terms of intelligence, now required to explain intelligence

---

[37]   Richard Rorty, "Untruth and Consequences," a review of *Killing Time* by Paul Feyerabend, in *The New Republic* (July 31, 1995): 32–6. As a neo-pragmatist, Rorty took his prime inspiration from the American pragmatist John Dewey. Dewey recognized that in the late eighteenth century the design argument was still "approved by the sciences of organic life" and "the central point of theistic and idealistic philosophy." But, as far as Dewey was concerned, the Darwinian revolution in biology changed all that: "The Darwinian principle of natural selection cut straight under this philosophy. If all organic adaptations are due simply to constant variation and the elimination of those variations which are harmful in the struggle for existence that is brought about by excessive reproduction, there is no call for a prior intelligent causal force to plan and preordain them." Quoted from John Dewey, *The Influence of Darwin on Philosophy and Other Essays* (New York: Henry Holt, 1910), 11–12.

in terms of some other causal power. Nonmaterialists, in making intelligence the most basic part of reality (whether as a part of nature or over and above nature), are within their rights to explain chance in terms of intelligence—full stop.

Chapter 17

Search

Materialists take the things close to our hearts, such as consciousness, intelligence, and beauty, and make them byproducts or epiphenomena of our material constitutions. And how could they do otherwise given their assumption that materialism is true? Yet materialism's truth is itself in question. Consequently, a leitmotif throughout this book has been that epiphenomena are reciprocal in the sense that if one thing is epiphenomenal on (or a byproduct of) another, then the other can just as well be epiphenomenal on it. Materialism makes nonmaterial things material. But nonmaterialism can likewise make material things nonmaterial. The logic of epiphenomena works in both directions. Thus, earlier, we saw that matter could just as well be a byproduct of information, in contrast to the conventional materialist approach, which treats information as a byproduct of matter.

Likewise, in the previous chapter, we saw that chance could be epiphenomenal on intelligence instead of, as materialists require, that intelligence be epiphenomenal on chance. In fact, I argued in that chapter that the stronger case is for chance being epiphenomenal on intelligence in that we have good evidence of chance processes being byproducts of intelligent agency. Conversely, I argued that treating chance as an irreducible contingency governed by probabilities always entails a circularity in which probabilities observed from short runs had to be assumed, without justification, to be representative of underlying probability distributions characterizing the long run.

Since this argument was just presented in the previous chapter, I won't rehearse it further. But a point to appreciate is that most materialists won't concede the problem here—they just don't see it. What's the big deal, they would contend, if we can't justify projecting short-run probabilities into the long run? If this is a circularity, it is virtuous rather than vicious. Our use of probabilities is at least self-consistent. And, in any case, even if (probabilistic) induction is a problem, it's still the best we can do. Practical reason urges that we use the past to understand the future, and short-run probabilities to understand expected long-run probabilities. Moreover, given that reality is fundamentally material and nonteleological, chance cannot be an epiphenomenon of intelligence.

Intelligence must instead be an epiphenomenon of chance. Materialism is compelled to draw such conclusions.

In this and the next two chapters, I'm going to argue that chance is no help to materialism even if one takes a more pragmatic line and removes the requirement that chance be given a proper theoretical underpinning. The previous chapter examined chance for its logical coherence and justification, and concluded that it makes better sense not as an irreducible probabilistic phenomenon but as a byproduct of intelligence. In what follows, we leave aside such questions of coherence and justification and ask whether chance, regardless of its theoretical underpinning, when simply treated as contingency governed by probability, provides a mode of explanation that effectively supports materialism. In particular, is intelligence something that can be effectively explained away in terms of some underlying chance process? Contrary to materialism, I'm going to argue that chance has no way to keep the world safe from teleology and intelligence.

To see how materialists try to subsume teleology and intelligence under chance (broadly construed so that chance also includes necessity, for which probabilities collapse to zero and one), consider evolutionary biologist David Sloan Wilson's response to a challenge I posed at an MIT conference back in 1999.[1] Questioning the power and ubiquity of Darwinian processes, I asked him to imagine a supergenius molecular biologist who invented some hitherto unknown molecular machine, inserted the genes for it into a bacterium, and then set this genetically modified organism free, allowing it to reproduce in the wild. Suppose, for instance, the machine is a nano-engineered syringe that uses carbon dioxide to overinflate other bacteria, causing them to explode and thereby allowing their contents to be consumed (no such molecular machine, as far as I know, exists in the wild). Finally, let us assume the biologist destroyed all evidence of having created this molecular machine.

So my challenge to Wilson was this: If a Darwinian biologist found this bacterium with the novel molecular machine in the wild, would that machine be attributed to design or to natural selection? This molecular machine clearly was designed (even in an external design or engineering sense). Yet by reflexively attributing such machines to blind material processes (such as the Darwinian mechanism of natural selection acting on random variations), one will miss the truth about its origin. With this thought experiment, I was trying to get Wilson

---

[1]   The conference in question was titled *Empathy, Altruism and Agape: Perspectives on Love in Science and Religion* and occurred October 1–3, 1999 at a hotel just off the MIT campus. A website dedicated to the conference remains online to this day: http://www.altruisticlove.org (last accessed July 8, 2013).

to admit that design explanations could, at least in principle, be legitimate in biology. Yet when I presented this scenario to him, he shrugged it off, remarking that natural selection created us and so, by extension, would also have created my novel molecular machine.[2]

Wilson's response is too easy and does nothing to answer whether design explanations may legitimately be employed in the natural sciences. Indeed, even if natural selection created us, as Wilson believes, it remains an open question whether life could exhibit features accountable only in terms of the premeditated action of intelligent agents. Human genome researcher Craig Venter, for instance, has a project in synthetic genomics in which he has written his name and that of his cohorts into the genome of a *Mycoplasma* bacterium.[3] He did this as a watermark to secure his intellectual property rights to a particular *Mycoplasma* lineage. Such design, clearly, could not be confused with the direct action of natural selection or other natural forces.

One way to counter Wilson's response is to cite intelligent design's critique of Darwinian evolution. This critique argues that the evidence of biology disconfirms natural selection as the primary engine for creating organisms like us. The arguments here are, in my view, strong, a point acknowledged even by some naturalists, who are not reductive materialists but who also reject supernaturalism. They see intelligent design as having raised legitimate concerns about Darwinian evolution even if they are not ready to accept its conclusion that intelligence is responsible for life.[4] As for intelligent design's critique of Darwinian evolution, it is well known, so I won't review it here.[5] In any case, nothing in what I'm about to write hinges on the success of intelligent design in challenging Darwinian and other (seemingly) unguided forms of evolution.

---

[2]   Although Wilson did not cite Dawkins in his reply to me, he might well have had him in mind: Richard Dawkins, *The Extended Phenotype: The Long Reach of the Gene* (Oxford: Oxford University Press, 1982). In this book, Dawkins argues that an organism's phenotype extends beyond its embodiment to all its effects on its environment, which would therefore include any of its products of design. The extended phenotype thus subsumes design under biology.

[3]   See Alexis Madrigal, "Wired Science Reveals Secret Codes in Craig Venter's Artificial Genome," *Wired*, posted January 28, 2008 at http://www.wired.com/wiredscience/2008/01/venter-institut (last accessed July 8, 2013).

[4]   For critiques of conventional evolutionary theory by thinkers who see intelligent design as raising some interesting questions even if in the end they disagree with it, see Thomas Nagel, *Mind & Cosmos* and Shapiro, *Evolution: A View from the 21st Century*.

[5]   For intelligent design's critique of conventional evolutionary theory, see Dembski and Wells, *The Design of Life* as well as Stephen C. Meyer, *Darwin's Doubt: The Explosive Origin of Animal Life and the Case for Intelligent Design* (San Francisco, Calif.: HarperOne, 2013).

The far more interesting question that Wilson's response raises is whether tracing the origin of intelligent agents like us to natural selection does indeed eliminate the need for teleology and intelligence from the nuts-and-bolts level of reality. Once evolution has done its work, concepts like teleology and intelligence are presumably indispensable for describing the action of (evolved) beings like us. But what of teleology and intelligence before creatures exhibiting these have evolved? Wilson is an atheistic materialist, and he clearly thought that by invoking natural selection he had dispensed with teleology and intelligence at the more basic levels of material being. But, in fact, natural selection does nothing to eliminate teleology and intelligence or even to contract their scope. Natural selection, far from being a true replacement for design (construed broadly, and not as external design), merely kicks the design problem down the road.

A precise theoretical justification for the claim that natural selection is inherently teleological comes from certain recent mathematical results known as Conservation of Information (CoI) theorems. These will be summarized and their significance explained in this and the next two chapters. They have emerged over the last decade from the field of computational intelligence, a field that comprises neural networks, fuzzy sets, and, most significantly for this discussion, evolutionary computing.[6] Starting in the mid-1990s, No Free Lunch (NFL) theorems were proved showing that for any given search strategy, its average performance was no better than blind search (i.e., random guessing).[7] These theorems were startling at the time because it had been thought that some search strategies would necessarily be better across the board than others.[8]

---

[6]   See Andries P. Engelbrecht, *Computational Intelligence: An Introduction* (Hoboken, N.J.: Wiley, 2007).

[7]   David Wolpert and William Macready are the names most prominently associated with NFL. For a summary of their work see David Wolpert and William Macready, "No Free Lunch Theorems for Optimization," *IEEE Transactions on Evolutionary Computation* 1(1), 1997: 67–82; and Joseph Culberson, "On the Futility of Blind Search: An Algorithmic View of 'No Free Lunch'," *Evolutionary Computation* 6(2), 1998: 109–27.

[8]   Regarding the stir surrounding NFL when it was first mooted, a colleague tells the following personal anecdote: "I was present when Bill Macready gave an early version of the NFL paper at ICGA 95 in Pittsburgh. The attack from some quarters was ferocious. Many EA people really did believe John Holland when he said 'the GA is all but immune to some of the difficulties—false peaks, discontinuities, high dimensionality, etc.—that commonly attend complex problems'. And since Holland's GA was popularly thought of as 'Nature's algorithm', they were worried Macready was attacking Darwin himself!" Notes: (1) Bill Macready is, with David Wolpert, the main originator of NFL (see previous note); (2) ICGA is International Conference on Genetic Algorithms; (3) EA refers to evolutionary algorithms; (4) GA refers to genetic algorithms; (5) John Holland is regarded as the father

NFL thus became a great equalizer, showing that whatever strengths a search strategy displays for certain types of searches are counterbalanced by weaknesses it displays for other types of searches.[9]

Whereas NFL focused on average performance of search, Conservation of Information or CoI raised the next logical question, namely, what allows particular search strategies to be successful for particular searches.[10] For instance, for a fitness landscape that ascends everywhere to a single peak, a hill-climbing strategy will work very well at finding the global optimum (i.e., the highest peak). Yet for a fitness landscape with many local optima, hill climbing will do poorly, confusing local optima with the global optimum (i.e., confusing lower peaks with the highest peak). The details of such searches are unimportant for this discussion. The point to realize is that those whose job it is to find the right optimization procedure for a given problem (e.g., operations research people) must, for a given search, try to choose one search strategy that works well to the exclusion of other search strategies that work less well. Such a choice of strategy identifies one possibility to the exclusion of others within a matrix of possibility (the matrix, in this instance, consisting of search strategies, or classes of different

---

of genetic algorithms; (6) the comment ascribed to John Holland is accurate and very widely quoted, coming from his book *Machine Learning: An Artificial Intelligence Approach, 2* (San Mateo, Calif.: Morgan Kaufman Publishers, 1986), 105.

[9]   Kevin Murphy underscores and expands on this same point (note that he uses the term "models" where I used "strategies"): "Much of machine learning is concerned with devising different models, and different algorithms to fit them. We can use the methods such as cross validation to empirically choose the best method for our particular problem. However, there is no universally best model—that is sometimes called the no free lunch theorem [here Murphy cites the work of David Wolpert]. The reason for this is that a set of assumptions that works well in one domain may work poorly in another. As a consequence of the no free lunch theorem, we need to develop many different types of models, to cover the wide variety of data that occur in the real world. And for each model, there may be many different algorithms we can use to train the model, which make different speed–accuracy–complexity tradeoffs." Quoted from Kevin P. Murphy, *Machine Learning: A Probabilistic Perspective* (Cambridge, Mass.: MIT Press, 2012), 24–5. Although Murphy refers to the No Free Lunch or NFL theorem (singular), in fact there are several different NFL theorems, which make different mathematical assumptions, such as whether a fitness function is fixed or can vary with time. All such NFL theorems share the conclusion that no search strategy (or model), on average, outperforms a purely random or blind search. For a helpful review article about the NFL theorems, see Y.-C. Ho, Q.-C. Zhao, and D.L. Pepyne, "The No Free Lunch Theorems: Complexity and Security," *IEEE Transactions on Automatic Control* 48(5) (2003): 783–93.

[10]   For a review article on Conservation of Information, see William A. Dembski and Robert J. Marks II, "Life's Conservation Law: Why Darwinian Evolution Cannot Create Biological Information," in B. Gordon and W.A. Dembski, eds., *The Nature of Nature: Examining the Role of Naturalism in Science* (Wilmington, Del.: ISI Books, 2011), 360–99.

types of searches). It follows that such a choice of search strategy entails an input of information into the search in the exact actualize–exclude informational sense emphasized throughout this book.

Conservation of Information begins with the insight that searches ordinarily achieve success not by accident or good fortune but by incorporating into themselves target-specific information that raises the probability of successfully locating the target. On this view, searches that locate a target even though the objective probability of successfully doing so is extremely low do so by sheer dumb luck and are not truly successful searches. Rather, successfulness of a search is gauged in terms of objective probabilities for finding the target. The more successful searches are those with the higher probability of success, not those that simply get lucky. That higher probability of success, however, is purchased at the price of information incorporated into the search. Accordingly, searches are not blank slates whose success at locating targets comes despite not knowing anything about them. Searches are successful not because of what they do but because of what was done to them before they do what they do, that is, because they were from the start provided with the information needed to be successful.

Conservation of Information, however, goes further than simply noting that searches attain success by utilizing prior information. As a collection of precise mathematical results (the Conservation of Information theorems), CoI shows that successful search (i.e., one that locates a target) requires at least as much input of information as the search by its success outputs. Conservation of Information therefore quantifies input and output of information in successful search, and states that there is a precise mathematical relation between the two, with input at best equaling, and otherwise exceeding, output. Moreover, since evolution can itself be conceived as a form of search,[11] CoI shows that evolutionary processes do not create novel information but merely shuffle around existing information. So where did this information come from originally? CoI shows with mathematical precision why chance is inherently incapable of providing an adequate answer to this question, in turn suggesting that teleology and intelligence provide a better answer.

---

[11]   Some evolutionists dispute that evolution is a search, but I'll show momentarily that it is. In any case, the term "evolutionary search" has wide currency and was invented not by the intelligent design community but by the evolutionary computing and evolutionary biology communities. Titles like the following are common in the evolutionary search literature: R. Deaton, R.C. Murphy, J.A. Rose, M. Garzon, D.R. Franceschetti, and S.E. Stevens Jr., "A DNA Based Implementation of an Evolutionary Search for Good Encodings for DNA Computation," in *Proceedings of the 1997 IEEE International Conference on Evolutionary Computation, Indianapolis, April 13 – 16* (Washington, D.C.: IEEE, 1997), 267–72.

I've gotten ahead of my story, so let's back up. The term "Conservation of Information" has a short history. Nobel prize-winning biologist Peter Medawar used it in the 1980s to describe mathematical and computational systems that are limited to producing logical consequences from a given set of axioms or starting points, and thus can create no novel information (everything in the consequences is already implicit in the starting points). His use of the term is the first that I know, though the idea he captured with it is much older, namely, that axiomatic and algorithmic systems contain all their logical consequences implicitly. Note that he called this the "Law of Conservation of Information."[12]

Computer scientist Thomas English, in a 1996 paper, also used the term "Conservation of Information," though synonymously with the then recently proved results by Wolpert and Macready about No Free Lunch (NFL).[13] In English's version of NFL, "the information an optimizer gains about unobserved values is ultimately due to its prior information of value distributions." To understand what English here means, think of yourself searching for a target by observing candidate solutions one after another (e.g., suppose 52 playing cards are laid out on a table and you're turning up cards one after another looking for the ace of clubs, which is your target). The possible solutions you've observed so far will help in the search only if you have prior information about how earlier observations assist in locating the target (e.g., previous cards turned over will help you locate the ace of clubs only if you have prior information about how those turned-over cards can help in locating your target, such as knowing that a club is always to the right of a heart). Without such prior information, the search is no better than random. As with Medawar's version of Conservation of Information, in English's version information is not created from scratch but redistributed from existing sources.

Baylor engineer Robert Marks and I have since extended these ideas about Conservation of Information.[14] As he, I, and some of his students have developed it, CoI applies to search, showing that searches must employ existing information to successfully locate targets, and that locating targets through

---

[12] Peter Medawar, *The Limits of Science* (New York: Harper & Row, 1984), 78–82.
[13] Thomas M. English, "Evaluation of Evolutionary and Genetic Optimizers: No Free Lunch," in L.J. Fogel, P.. Angeline, and T. Bäck, eds., *Evolutionary Programming V: Proceedings of the Fifth Annual Conference on Evolutionary Programming* (Cambridge, Mass.: MIT Press, 1996), 163–9, available online at http://boundedtheoretics.com/EP96.pdf (last accessed July 11, 2013).
[14] For a complete account of our work, visit the publications page of the Evolutionary Informatics Lab at http://evoinfo.org/publications (last accessed July 11, 2013). Marks founded and directs this lab.

search never outputs more information than was inputted into the search initially. Simply put, searches, in finding targets, output information. At the same time, to find targets, searches need to input information. CoI, as we have developed it, shows that the output cannot exceed the input. Just how this works will be described shortly.

Now search may seem like a fairly restricted topic. Unlike energy conservation, which applies at all scales and dimensions of the universe, Conservation of Information, in focusing on search, may seem to have only limited physical significance. But in fact, Conservation of Information is deeply embedded in the fabric of nature. Search is a very general phenomenon. The reason we typically don't think of search in broad terms applicable to nature generally is that we tend to think of it as finding a particular predefined object. Thus our stock example of search is losing one's keys, with search then being the attempt to recover them. But we can also search for things that are not pre-given in this way. Sixteenth-century explorers were looking for new, uncharted lands. They knew when they found them that their search had been successful, but they didn't know exactly what they were looking for. Often we know that we've found what we're looking for even though it's nothing like what we expected, and sometimes even violates our expectations.

Another problem with extending search to nature in general is that we tend to think of search as confined to human contexts. Humans search for keys, and humans search for uncharted lands. But, as it turns out, nature is also quite capable of search. Do a Google search on the term "evolutionary search," and you'll find quite a few hits. Evolution, according to some theoretical biologists, such as Stuart Kauffman, may properly be conceived of as a search.[15] Kauffman is not an intelligent design proponent, so there's no human or human-like intelligence behind evolutionary search as far as he's concerned. Nonetheless, for Kauffman, nature, in powering the evolutionary process, is engaged in a search through biological configuration space,[16] searching for and finding ever-increasing orders of biological complexity and diversity.

---

[15]   In fact, Kauffman will refer to Darwinian and other evolutionary mechanisms as "search strategies": "Ways of making a living, natural games, that are well searched out and well mastered by the *evolutionary search strategies* of organisms, namely, mutation and recombination, will be precisely the niches, or ways of making a living, that a diversifying and speciating population of organisms will manage to master." Quoted from Stuart Kauffman, *Investigations* (New York: Oxford University Press, 2000), 20, emphasis added.

[16]   Think of biological configuration space as comprising the different ways matter can be organized to be either biologically functional or biologically useless. Biological configuration space will therefore include full organisms, tissues, cellular machineries,

Evolutionary search is not confined solely to biology (wetware) but also takes place inside computers (hardware). The field of evolutionary computing (which includes genetic algorithms) intersects that area of mathematics and engineering known as operations research, whose principal focus is on optimization.[17] Optimization is about finding solutions to problems where the possible solutions admit varying and measurable degrees of goodness (optimality), with actual solutions attaining a certain minimal level of goodness and, ideally, achieving the very highest level of goodness that, in the given circumstance, is possible. Evolutionary computing fits this mold, seeking items in a search space that achieve a certain fitness level or acceptability threshold. For many purposes it is fine to think of these as the "optimal solutions," though if one thinks of optimality in the stricter sense of literally best, then these solutions are better referred to as *satisficing* solutions (i.e., solutions that suffice to satisfy a certain minimum level of acceptability).[18]

Incidentally, the irony of doing a Google "search" on the target phrase "evolutionary search," as described two paragraphs back, did not escape me. Google's entire business is predicated on performing optimal computational searches, where optimality is gauged in terms of the link structure of the web. As pages are linked to from other pages on the web, they take on increasing

---

strands of DNA, etc. as well as chemical and structural arrangements that serve no biological function. In combinatorial terms, most arrangements of matter are going to be biologically useless. That's because life resides on a razor's edge, with arrangements of matter that are dead far outnumbering those that are alive.

[17] The operations research people I've talked to, who do optimization for a living, tend to be unimpressed with evolutionary computing, seeing it as one among many methods for resolving the optimization problems they encounter in industry and business, and often preferring other methods over it. Thus, at the annual conference of the professional society for operations research (INFORMS—Institute for Operations Research and the Management Sciences, www.informs.org), one will find only a handful of papers focusing on evolutionary methods in optimization problems. The number will not be zero, but it's not as though evolutionary ideas are sweeping the field of operations research. Operations research journals will therefore publish a modicum of titles such as Su Nguyen, Mengjie Zhang, Mark Johnston, and Kay Chen Tan, "Hybrid Evolutionary Computation Methods for Quay Crane Scheduling Problems," *Computers & Operations Research* 40(8) (2013): 2083–93. Though evolutionary computing, strictly speaking, is concerned with optimization and targeted search, and thus falls under operations research, its natural research community tends to be the theoretical computer scientists, especially those taken with the presumed power of evolution processes in biology. See, for instance, Kenneth A. De Jong, *Evolutionary Computation: A Unified Approach* (Cambridge, Mass.: MIT Press, 2006).

[18] See Melanie Mitchell, *An Introduction to Genetic Algorithms* (Cambridge, Mass.: MIT Press, 1996), 124.

importance, that is, they rank more highly with Google. All pages on the web can thus be seen as comprising a matrix of possibility that undergirds a fitness landscape, where fitness is gauged in terms of the number and quality of links going to a particular page (Google especially rewards .edu and .gov links). This fitness landscape is dynamic, depending on how links change as well as Google's current algorithm for evaluating the quality of links. Thus, when Google changes its algorithm, as with its Panda and Penguin updates,[19] its fitness landscape changes as well. For a Google keyword search, the first ten entries that one sees are for those pages presently ranking highest for the keyword (i.e., having the highest Google fitness value for the keyword).

We live in an age of search. We now realize that search extends well beyond the direct activity of humans to include biology, computers, and the web. Still, search may seem limited in that nuts-and-bolts physical reality gives no obvious evidence of it. Where, for instance, in the daily operations of nature, as characterized by the laws of physics and chemistry, do we see search? Search, it seems, makes few, if any, appearances in the physical sciences. But is that true? If overt appearances are few, search nonetheless seems presupposed throughout the physical sciences. The physical world is life permitting—its structure and laws allow (though they do not necessitate) the existence of not just cellular life but also intelligent multicellular life. For the physical world to be life permitting in this way, its laws and fundamental constants need to be configured in very precise ways.[20] Moreover, it seems far from mandatory that those laws and constants had to take the precise form that they do. The universe itself, therefore, can be viewed as the solution to the problem of making life possible. Now problem-solving is itself a form of search, namely, finding the solution (among a range of candidates, which is to say a matrix of possibility) to a problem.

Still, for many scientists, search fits uneasily into the physical and biological sciences. Something unavoidably subjective and teleological seems involved in search. Search always involves a goal or objective, as well as criteria of success and failure (as judged by what or whom?) depending on whether and to what degree the objective has been met. Where does that objective, which we are calling a

---

[19]   Online businesses that depend on the search engines, and especially Google, for their profitability can be negatively impacted when the search engines change/update their search algorithm. See, for instance, Nick Stamoulis's blog post about the Google Panda and Google Penguin updates at http://www.brickmarketing.com/blog/panda-penguin-updates.htm (last accessed July 16, 2013).

[20]   Such an argument is made in great detail in Guillermo Gonzalez and Jay W. Richards, *The Privileged Planet: How Our Place in the Cosmos Is Designed for Discovery* (Washington, D.C.: Regnery, 2004).

target, come from other than from the minds of human inquirers? Are we, as pattern-seeking and pattern-inventing animals, simply imposing these targets/patterns on nature even though they have no independent, objective status? Such concerns have merit, but they need not to be overblown.[21] If we don't merely presuppose a materialist metaphysics that makes mind, intelligence, and agency a property of suitably organized matter, then it is an open question whether search and any teleology inherent in it are mere human constructions (and thus illegitimately foisted on nature), or, instead, realities embedded in nature (and thus, in principle, objectively ascertainable from nature). What if nature itself is the product of mind and the patterns it exhibits are solutions to search problems formulated by such a mind?

Scientific inquiry that's free of prejudice and narrowly held metaphysical assumptions should, it seems, leave open both these possibilities, able to consider patterns that are mere human constructions and patterns that are objectively real. After all, the patterns we're talking about are not like finding Santa Claus's beard in a cloud formation—who, if they look hard enough, won't see Santa's beard? The fine-tuning of nature's laws and constants that permits life to exist at all is not like this. It is a remarkable pattern and may reasonably be regarded as the solution to a search problem as well as a fundamental feature of nature, or what philosophers would call a natural kind, and not merely a human construct.[22] Whether an intelligence is responsible for the success of this search is a separate question. The standard materialist line in response to such cosmological fine-

---

[21]   I'm thinking here especially of skeptic Michael Shermer, who writes, "Perceiving the world as well designed and thus the product of a designer ... may be the product of a brain adapted to finding patterns in nature. We are pattern-seeking as well as pattern-finding animals ... Finding patterns in nature may have an evolutionary explanation: There is a survival payoff for finding order instead of chaos in the world ... We are the descendants of the most successful pattern-seeking members of our species. In other words, we were designed by evolution to perceive design." Quoted from Shermer, *Why Darwin Matters*, 38–9. The problem with this quote is that it gives too wide a scope to self-deception. Clearly, not all patterns are self-deceiving. Even Shermer will grant that some patterns, such as the scent of a predator, are not merely foisted by organisms onto the environment but objectively ascertainable and indeed necessary for the organisms' survival. Proponents of intelligent design argue that patterns in biology and cosmology that signal intelligent activity are of this sort, that is, objective and real. For a catalogue of such objectively real patterns in nature, see Gonzalez and Richards, *The Privileged Planet* as well as Dembski and Wells, *The Design of Life*.
[22]   For natural kinds and the debate surrounding this topic, see Joseph Keim Campbell, Michael O'Rourke, and Matthew H. Slater, eds., *Carving Nature at Its Joints: Natural Kinds in Metaphysics and Science* (Cambridge, Mass.: MIT Press, 2011).

tuning is to invoke multiple universes and view the success of this search as a selection effect: most searches ended without a life-permitting universe, but we happened to get lucky and live in a universe hospitable to life.[23]

In any case, it is possible to characterize search in a way that leaves the role of teleology and intelligence open without either presupposing them or deciding against them in advance. Mathematically speaking, search always occurs within a matrix of possibilities (the *search space*), with the search being for a subset of this matrix (known as the *target*). Success and failure of search are then characterized in terms of a probability distribution over this matrix of possibilities, the probability of success increasing to the degree that the probability of locating the target increases.

To illustrate this conception of search, consider protein synthesis. Proteins are made of L-amino acids joined in sequence by peptide bonds. Not all such sequences, however, are biologically functional. Proteins are, by definition, those amino-acid sequences that fold into functional shapes or conformations. Consider now all possible L-amino acid sequences joined by peptide bonds of length 100. Let's take this as our matrix of possibilities—our search space. Within this matrix, consider those sequences that fold into a stable three-dimensional structure and thus could serve a biological function. Let's take this as the target. This target is not a mere human construct. Nature itself has identified this target as a precondition for life—no living thing that we know can exist without proteins. Moreover, this target admits rigorous probabilistic estimates. Beginning with the work of Robert Sauer, cassette mutagenesis and other experiments of this sort performed over the last several decades suggest that the target has probability no more than 1 in 10^{60} (assuming a uniform probability distribution over all amino acid sequences in the reference class).[24]

The mathematics used to characterize search in connection with Conservation of Information is straightforward and general. Whether in specific

[23] We've seen this theme of positing many worlds to keep the known actual world safe from teleology and God before, namely, in chapter 15. For a critique of many worlds or multiple universes, see William A. Dembski, "The Chance of the Gaps," in Neil Manson, ed., *God and Design: The Teleological Argument and Modern Science* (London: Routledge, 2002), 251–74.

[24] J. Bowie and R. Sauer, "Identifying Determinants of Folding and Activity for a Protein of Unknown Sequences: Tolerance to Amino Acid Substitution," *Proceedings of the National Academy of Sciences* 86 (1989): 2152–6. J. Bowie, J. Reidhaar-Olson, W. Lim, and R. Sauer, "Deciphering the Message in Protein Sequences: Tolerance to Amino Acid Substitution," *Science* 247 (1990): 1306–10. J. Reidhaar-Olson and R. Sauer, "Functionally Acceptable Solutions in Two Alpha-Helical Regions of Lambda Repressor," *Proteins, Structure, Function, and Genetics* 7 (1990): 306–10.

circumstances search so characterized also involves unavoidably subjective human elements or reflects objectively given realities embedded in nature can be argued independently of the mathematics. Such an argument speaks to the interpretation of the search, not to the search itself. Such an argument parallels controversies surrounding the interpretation of quantum mechanics: whether quantum mechanics is inherently a mind-based, observer-dependent theory; whether it can be developed independently of observers; whether it is properly construed as reflecting a deterministic mind-independent multiuniverse, etc. Quantum mechanics itself is a single, well-defined theory, albeit one that admits several interpretations.[25] Likewise, search as described here has a single, straightforward theoretical characterization, even if it can be given diverse metaphysical interpretations.

One clarification, already touched on, is worth underscoring here while we're still setting the stage for Conservation of Information. For most people, when it comes to search, the important thing is the outcome of the search. Take an Easter egg hunt. The children looking for Easter eggs are concerned with whether they find the eggs. From the scientific vantage, however, the important thing about search is not the particular outcomes but the probability distribution over the full range of possible outcomes in the search space. The problem with just looking at particular outcomes is that a search might get lucky and find the target even if the probabilities are against it. The important thing for a search is that it have a high probability of success, and not that, as an outside shot, it happens on a particular occasion to yield success. This preference for probability distributions over individual outcomes parallels communication theory, in which what's of interest is not particular messages sent across a communication channel but the range of possible messages and their probability distribution.[26]

To see what's at stake here, consider an Easter egg hunt again. Suppose there's just one egg carefully hidden somewhere in a vast area. This is the target and blind search is highly unlikely to find it because the search space is so vast. But

---

[25] "An interpretation of quantum mechanics is essentially an answer to the question 'What is the state vector?' Different interpretations cannot be distinguished on scientific grounds—they do not have different experimental consequences; if they did they would constitute different *theories*." Anthony Sudbery, *Quantum Mechanics and the Particles of Nature* (Cambridge: Cambridge University Press, 1984), 212.

[26] "[A communication engineer's] preoccupation with averages is perfectly understandable. What the engineer wants is a concept that characterizes the whole statistical nature of the information source. He is not concerned with individual messages. A communication system must face the problem of handling any message that the source can produce." Dretske, *Knowledge and the Flow of Information*, 11.

there's still a positive probability of finding the egg even with blind search, and if the egg is discovered, then that's just how it is. Now it may be, because the egg's discovery is so improbable, that we might question whether the search was truly blind and therefore reject this (null) hypothesis. Maybe it was a guided search in which someone, with knowledge of the egg's whereabouts, told the seeker, "warm, warmer, no—colder, warmer, warmer, hot, hotter, you're burning up." Such guidance gives the seeker added information that, if the information is accurate, will help locate the egg with much higher probability than mere blind search. This added information therefore changes the probability distribution characterizing success of the search.

But again, the important point, from a scientific vantage, is not how the search ended but the probability distribution under which the search was conducted. One doesn't have to be a scientist to appreciate this point. Suppose someone has a serious medical condition that requires treatment. Let's say there are two treatment options. Which option should one go with? Leaving aside cost and discomfort, one will want the treatment with the better chance of success (i.e., the treatment that historically has demonstrated the larger proportion of patients exhibiting significant improvement and thus the treatment that gives the higher probability of recovery). This is the more effective treatment, effectiveness being gauged in terms of probability of outcome rather than actual outcome. Now, in particular circumstances, it may happen that the less effective treatment leads to a good outcome (in which case the patient got lucky). Or it may happen that the more effective treatment leads to a bad outcome (in which case the patient got unlucky). But all such considerations are after the fact. In deciding which treatment to take, one will take the prudent course and go with the one that has the higher probability of success.

The Easter egg hunt example provides a preview of Conservation of Information. Blind search, if the search space is too large and the number of Easter eggs is too small, is highly unlikely to succeed in locating the eggs. A guided search, in which the seeker is given feedback about one's search by being told when one is closer or farther from the egg, by contrast, promises to dramatically raise the probability of successfully locating the eggs. The seeker, in this case, is being given vital information bearing on the success of the search. But where did this information that gauges proximity of seeker to egg come from? Conservation of Information claims that this information is itself as difficult to find as locating the egg by blind search, implying that guided search is no better at finding the eggs than blind search once this information must be accounted for. Let's now turn to Conservation of Information in earnest.

Chapter 18

Conservation of Information

Having set the stage for Conservation of Information, I need now to fill in some details. As a backdrop for explaining Conservation of Information, I will focus on evolutionary biology (and by extension on evolutionary computing), trusting that as Conservation of Information's relevance to biology becomes clear, its scope and applicability for the rest of the natural sciences will be that much more readily accepted and acceptable. As it is, most biological configuration spaces for evolution are so large and the targets they present are so small that *blind search* is highly unlikely to succeed (blind search, on materialist principles, ultimately reduces to the jostling of life's molecular constituents through forces of attraction and repulsion; genetic mutation would be a consequence of such jostling).

Given this weakness of blind search in locating small targets, an *alternative search* is required if the target is to stand a reasonable chance of being found. Evolutionary processes driven by natural selection constitute such alternative searches. Indeed, they do a much better job than blind search. Yet there is a cost—an information cost—which these processes incur, but which they cannot, as we will see, earn on their own. Note that when the probability of successfully locating the target is significantly greater than blind search, so that locating the target with such an alternative search would no longer constitute a "probabilistic miracle," as it would under blind search, we also refer to an alternative search as a *directed search*. This usage connects with our discussion of natural teleological laws in chapter 9. For this chapter, however, so as not to prejudge how teleology connects with search, I'll stick with the more neutral language of alternative search.

Conservation of information is concerned with information costs. What, then, is an information cost? As we saw in chapter 6, information, as a numerical measure, is usually defined as the negative logarithm to the base two of a probability (or some logarithmic average of probabilities, often referred to as entropy). This has the effect of transforming probabilities into bits and of allowing them to be added (like money) rather than multiplied (like probabilities). Thus, a probability of one-eighth, which is the probability of tossing three heads in a row with a fair coin, corresponds to three bits, which is the negative logarithm to the base two of one-eighth. Such a logarithmic transformation of probabilities is useful in communication theory, where what gets moved across communication channels is bits rather than probabilities and the drain on bandwidth is determined additively in terms of number of bits. Yet, for simplicity, we can characterize information, as it relates to search, solely in terms of probabilities, thus cashing out Conservation of Information, along with its information costs, purely probabilistically. Since this is a book on the metaphysics rather than the science of information, let's make that simplification here.

Let's therefore think of probabilities in financial terms as a cost—an information cost—that measures the information required to make a search successful. To see how probabilities might measure cost, suppose there's some event you want to have happen. If it's certain to happen (i.e., has probability 1), then you own that event—it costs you nothing to make it happen. But suppose instead its probability of occurring is less than 1, let's say some probability p. This probability then measures a cost to you of making the event happen. The more improbable the event (i.e., the smaller p), the greater the cost. Sometimes you can't increase the probability of making the event occur all the way to 1, which would make it certain. Instead, you may have to settle for increasing the probability to q, where q is less than 1 but greater than p. That increase, however, must also be paid for. And in fact, we often pay real money to raise probabilities. For instance, students pay tuition costs in hopes of a degree that will improve their prospects (i.e., probabilities) of landing a good, high-paying job.

For an example closer to the heart of Conservation of Information, yet one in which actual money is paid to raise probabilities, imagine you are about to play a lottery. Suppose it's fair, so the government doesn't skim anything off the top (i.e., everything paid into the lottery gets paid out to the winner). Moreover, one ticket is sure to be the winner. Let's say a million lottery tickets have been purchased so far at one dollar apiece, exactly one of which is yours. Each lottery ticket therefore has the same probability of winning, so your lottery ticket has a one in a million chance of coming out on top (which is your present p value), entailing a loss of one dollar if you lose and a gain of nearly a million dollars if you win ($999,999 to be exact). Now, let's say you really want to win this lottery—for whatever reason you earnestly desire to hold the winning ticket in your hand. In that case, you can purchase additional tickets. By purchasing these, you increase your chance of winning the lottery. Let's say you purchase an additional million tickets at one dollar apiece. Doing so boosts your probability of winning the lottery from .000001 to .500001, or to about one-half.

Increasing the probability of winning the lottery has therefore incurred a cost. With a probability of roughly .5 of winning the lottery, you are now much more likely to gain approximately one million dollars. But it also cost you a million dollars to increase your probability of winning. As a result, your expected winnings, computed in standard statistical terms as the probability of losing multiplied by what you would lose subtracted from the probability of winning multiplied by what you would win, equals zero. Moreover, because this is a fair lottery (i.e., fair in the statistical sense of not being biased in favor of lottery organizers or players), it equals zero when you only had one ticket purchased, and it equals zero when you had an additional million tickets purchased. Thus, in statistical terms, investing more in this lottery has gained you nothing.[1]

Conservation of Information is like this. It is not exactly like this because Conservation of Information focuses on search whereas the previous example focused on betting strategies. But just as increasing your chances of winning a lottery by buying more tickets offers no real gain (it is not a long-term strategy for increasing the money in your pocket), so Conservation of Information says that increasing the probability of successfully locating a target by modifying a search requires additional informational resources that, once their cost is factored in, do nothing to make the modified search any more effective than the original search. To make the same point slightly differently, when we try to increase the probability of success of a search, the task of locating the target, instead of becoming easier, remains as difficult as before or may even (and often does) become more difficult once additional underlying information costs are factored in.

In referring to ease and difficulty of search, I'm not being mathematically imprecise. Ease and difficulty, characterized mathematically, are always complexity-theoretic notions, presupposing an underlying complexity measure.[2] In this case, complexity is cashed out probabilistically, so the complexity measure is a probability measure,[3] with searches becoming easier to the degree that success in locating targets becomes more probable, and searches becoming more difficult to the degree that success in locating targets becomes more improbable. Accordingly, since we are thinking of probability as a cost, with cost going up the smaller the probability, it also makes sense to talk about the cost of a search, with the cost going up the more difficult the search, and the cost going down the easier the search.

---

[1] For the probability theory that is the basis of this example, see chapter 1 of Sheldon M. Ross, *An Elementary Introduction to Mathematical Finance*, 3rd edn. (New York: Cambridge University Press, 2011).

[2] For an overview of complexity theory, see Dembski, *Design Inference*, ch. 4.

[3] Technically speaking, a probability measure becomes a complexity measure when it is logarithmically transformed into an information measure. Ibid.

The reason we speak of "Conservation" of Information is that the best we can do, whenever we try to raise the probability of successfully locating a target, is *break even*, rendering a search no more difficult than it was at the start. In that case, information is actually conserved. Yet it can also happen that in trying to improve a search's probability of success, the probabilistic costs exceed the probabilistic benefits. Thus, we may introduce an alternative search that, when taken by itself, improves on the original search by raising the probability of locating the target, but that, once the costs of obtaining this alternative search are themselves factored in, exacerbates the original search problem.[4] Accordingly, the combined probability cost of finding such an alternative search and then, with it, finding the target can actually be greater than the probability cost of simply finding the target with the original search.

Some technical mathematics underlies CoI's main claim that all attempts to improve a search's probability of success incur probabilistic costs that always equal or exceed the probabilistic benefits.[5] Nonetheless, here's a simple example that illustrates how CoI works.[6] Suppose you are appearing on Monty Hall's program *Let's Make a Deal*. Behind one of three curtains is a prize. For definiteness, let's say the prize is behind curtain 1, but you don't know that. Suppose you know nothing about which curtain the prize is likely to be behind. The probability of finding the prize simply by guessing is therefore 1/3.[7] Suppose now someone hands you a ticket of the form $<x,y>$ where x and y range over the numbers 1, 2,

---

[4]   Specific cases of this phenomenon are known and documented, such as epistasis, when the fitness of a phenotype cannot be decomposed additively. See Colin R. Reeves and Jonathan E. Rowe, *Genetic Algorithms: Principles and Perspectives* (Norwell, Mass.: Kluwer, 2003), ch. 8.

[5]   For three key theoretical papers on Conservation of Information, which together lay out the mathematical apparatus undergirding CoI as well as how CoI may reasonably be interpreted and applied in the sciences, see William A. Dembski and Robert J. Marks II, "Conservation of Information in Search: Measuring the Cost of Success," *IEEE Transactions on Systems, Man and Cybernetics A, Systems & Humans*, 5(5) (September 2009): 1051–61; William A. Dembski and Robert J. Marks II, "The Search for a Search: Measuring the Information Cost of Higher-Level Search," *Journal of Advanced Computational Intelligence and Intelligent Informatics* 14(5) (2010): 475–86; William A. Dembski, Winston Ewert, and Robert J. Marks II, "A General Theory of Information Cost Incurred by Successful Search," in R.J. Marks II, M.J. Behe, W.A. Dembski, B.L. Gordon, and J.C. Sanford, eds., *Biological Information: New Perspectives* (Singapore: World Scientific, 2013), 26–63.

[6]   I'm indebted to John Camp for this example.

[7]   We're assuming uniform probabilities throughout this example. CoI can also be formulated without this assumption of a uniform probability baseline. For CoI without the uniform probability assumption, see Dembski, Ewert, and Marks, "A General Theory of Information Cost."

and 3. Think of "1" as referring to curtain 1, "2" to curtain 2, and "3" to curtain 3. There are nine such tickets:

$$<1,1>, <1,2>, <1,3>$$
$$<2,1>, <2,2>, <2,3>$$
$$<3,1>, <3,2>, <3,3>$$

Suppose the ticket that was in fact handed to you was <2,1>. You interpret this ticket as narrowing down the possible curtains behind which the prize resides. Accordingly, you now know that the prize is behind either curtain 1 or 2. Assuming you know nothing about which of these two curtains is more likely to have the prize behind it, your probability of finding the prize with this ticket, given that the prize is in fact behind curtain 1, is 1/2.

Having this ticket therefore increases your probability of successfully finding the prize from 1/3 to 1/2. But now the question arises, how did someone know to hand you the ticket marked <2,1>? You might just as well have been handed ticket <2,3>, in which case your probability of finding the prize would have gone down to 0. Or you might have been handed ticket <1,1>, in which case your probability of finding the prize would have gone up to 1. As it is, absent any knowledge of which tickets are more or less helpful in locating the prize, the probability of being handed ticket <2,1> (i.e., the ticket you were actually handed) would be 1/9. And so, even though the probability of finding the prize given that you were handed ticket <2,1> is 1/2, the probability of finding the prize once the probability of being handed that ticket is also factored in becomes the product $1/2 \times 1/9$.

The probability of finding the prize with a particular search (in this case, by using a particular ticket) is the conditional probability of finding the prize given the particular search multiplied by the probability of having the particular search in hand. In symbols: $\mathbf{P}(\text{find prize with search}) = \mathbf{P}(\text{find prize} \mid \text{search}) \times \mathbf{P}(\text{search})$. In general, $\mathbf{P}(A|B)$, the conditional probability of A given B, may be thought of as the probability of A once B is folded into one's background knowledge, skill set, or working resources. A, in the context of CoI, denotes locating a target (in the present example, finding a prize) and B denotes the search that makes this possible. But B itself has a probability, namely, $\mathbf{P}(B)$. Hence, if the probability of obtaining the search itself is extremely low, so is the probability of finding the prize with it. To be sure, if the search can be presupposed, the conditional probability of finding the prize given the search may be quite high. But that's not the probability of interest. The availability of the search needs itself to be factored in, and that availability is assessed probabilistically.

To make the underlying logic here clearer, imagine someone tells you that he's going to be a millionaire (he's not right now). You're skeptical. But this person then tells you that he's sure to win the lottery and that if he does in fact win it, he'll be a millionaire. Granted, the probability of becoming a millionaire is high if one wins the lottery (this probability corresponds to the conditional probability $\mathbf{P}(\text{find prize} \mid \text{search})$). But appealing to the lottery for riches merely shifts the improbability of becoming a millionaire to the improbability of winning the lottery. If winning the lottery is highly improbable, then it is futile to invoke winning the lottery to boost one's probability of becoming a millionaire. Likewise, with search, the improbability of securing the search needs itself to be factored into assessing how likely it is that the target can be found with the search (the target, in this case, being the prize behind curtain 1).

Hence the probability of finding the prize behind curtain 1 with ticket <2,1>, once the probability of being handed that ticket is also factored in, is 1/2 × 1/9. This same probability calculation applies also to tickets <1,2>, <1,3>, and <3,1>. Moreover, for ticket <1,1> the probability of finding the prize is 1 × 1/9 (since the probability of finding the prize with ticket <1,1> is 1). For the remaining tickets, the probability of finding the prize is zero. Thus, adding all these probabilities together yields

$$(1/2 + 1/2 + 1/2 + 1/2 + 1) \times 1/9 = 1/3.$$

This is the probability of finding the curtain with the prize behind it by using a ticket that has probability 1/2 or better of locating the prize, but also factoring in the probability of having such a ticket in the first place. Thus we see that once the probability of having such a ticket is factored in, the probability of locating the curtain with the prize hasn't increased at all. In fact, it's just stayed the same. It was 1/3 before, and it remains at 1/3. This is what Conservation of Information says, that the probability stays the same or even gets worse once we factor in the probability cost of getting a search that improves on the probability of the original search.

A variant of this example shows how use of these tickets can also cause the probability of finding the prize to go down (which, according to CoI, is what happens with searches if information is not conserved). Suppose instead of boosting our probability of successful search to at least 1/2 by using these tickets, we want to boost it all the way to 1. There's only one ticket that does that, namely, <1,1> (assuming, again, that the prize is behind curtain 1). In that case, the probability of finding the prize given ticket <1,1> is 1, but the probability of getting that ticket in the first place is 1/9. So the probability of obtaining the prize with a search that guarantees success (i.e., with ticket <1,1>), once the probability of obtaining that search is itself factored in, is $1 \times 1/9 = 1/9$. Thus, in this case, the probability of locating the prize has actually diminished from 1/3 to 1/9. In a sense, trying to purchase too much probability by "turbocharging" the search has proved counterproductive, substantially reducing the original probability of successful search.

With Conservation of Information, there's always a more difficult search that gets displaced by an easier search. Yet once the difficulty of finding the easier search (difficulty being understood probabilistically) is factored in, there's no gain, and in fact the total cost may have gone up. Thus, the actual probability of locating the target with the easier search is no greater, and may actually be less, than the probability of locating the target with the more difficult search once the probability of locating the easier search is factored in. In calculating the total probabilistic cost of using the easier search to find the target, we must compute the combined probability of finding the easier search and then, with it in hand, finding the original target.

All of this admits a precise mathematical formulation. Inherent in such a formulation is treating search itself as an object of search.[8] If this sounds self-referential, it is. But it also makes good sense. To see this, consider another example, this time a treasure hunt. Imagine searching for a treasure chest buried on a large island. We consider two searches, a more difficult search and an easier one (easier searches being those that successfully find targets with higher probability, more difficult ones being those that successfully find targets with lower probability). The more difficult search, in this case, is a blind search in which, without any knowledge of where the treasure is buried, you meander randomly about the island, digging here and there for the treasure. The easier search, by contrast, is to have a treasure map in which "x" marks the spot where the treasure is located, and where you simply follow the map to the treasure.

No doubt, it's great to have this treasure map. But where did you get that map in the first place? Mapmakers have made lots of maps of that island, and for every map that correctly marks the treasure's location, there are many many others that mark its location incorrectly or ambiguously. Indeed, for any place on the island, there's a map that marks it with an "x" (all but one of these maps will be incorrect). But there will also be many more ambiguous maps. Thus, for any pair

---

    8   Dembski and Marks, "The Search for a Search."

of places on the island, there's a map that marks both with an "x." Likewise, for any three places on the island, there's a map that marks all three with an "x." And so on. Such multiply marked maps will be ambiguous if one of the spots marked "x" corresponds to the treasure's location and will be flat wrong if none of them does. So how do you find your way among all these different maps to one that correctly (or perhaps ambiguously) marks the treasure's location? This line of reasoning shows how the original search for the treasure has been *displaced* to a search for a map that helps locate the treasure. Each map corresponds to a search, and locating the right map corresponds to a *search for a search* (abbreviated, in the Conservation of Information literature, as S4S).

Conservation of Information, in this example, would say that the probability of locating the treasure by first searching for a treasure map that accurately identifies the treasure's location is no greater, and may be less, than the probability of locating the treasure simply by blind search. This implies that the easier search (i.e., the search with treasure map in hand), once the probabilistic cost of finding the map is factored in, has not made the actual overall search any easier. In general, Conservation of Information says that when a more difficult search gets displaced by an easier search, the probability of finding the target by first finding the easier search and then using the easier search to find the target is no greater, and often is less, than the probability of finding the target directly with the more difficult search.

Conservation of Information, in focusing on the search for information needed to enhance search performance (i.e., the search for a search), suggests a relational ontology between search and objects searched. In a relational ontology, things are real not as isolated entities but in virtue of their relation to other things.[9] In the relational ontology between search and objects searched, each finds its existence in the other. Our natural tendency is to think of objects as real and search for those objects as less real in the sense that search depends on the objects searched but objects can exist independently of search. Yet objects never come to us in themselves but as patterned reflections of our background knowledge, and thus as targets of search.

---

[9] "The basic contention of a relational ontology is simply that the relations between entities are ontologically more fundamental than the entities themselves. This contrasts with substantivist ontology in which entities are ontologically primary and relations ontologically derivative." Quoted from Wesley J. Wildman, "An Introduction to Relational Ontology," typescript, May 15, 2006, available online at http://people.bu.edu/wwildman/pubs_articles. html (last accessed July 23, 2013). See also Christos Yannaras, *Relational Ontology*, trans. N. Russell (Brookline, Mass.: Holy Cross Orthodox Press, 2011).

Any scene, indeed any input to our senses, reaches our consciousness only by aspects becoming salient, and this happens because certain patterns in our background knowledge are matched to the exclusion of others. In an extension of George Berkeley's "to be is to be perceived,"[10] Conservation of Information suggests that "to be perceived is to be an object of search." By transitivity in reasoning, it would then follow that to be is to be an object of search. And since search is always search for an object, search and the object of search become, in this way of thinking, mutually ontologizing, giving existence to each other. Conservation of Information then adds to this by saying that search can itself be an object of search.

These considerations apply to evolutionary biology, which treats evolutionary search as a given, as an unsponsored gift, as something that does not call for explanation beyond the blind forces of nature. Yet insofar as evolutionary search renders aspects of a biological configuration space probabilistically accessible where previously, under blind search, they were probabilistically inaccessible (because too improbable), Conservation of Information says that evolutionary search achieves this increase in search performance at an informational cost. Accordingly, evolutionary search, when it improves on blind search, has itself to be found through a higher-order search (i.e., a search for a search, or S4S). Yet when this higher-order search is taken into account, evolutionary search proves no more effective at finding the target than the original blind search.[11]

---

[10]   "To be is to be perceived" (Latin "*esse est percipi*") is the motto that characterizes Berkeley's idealist philosophy. As mottos go, this is as good a short statement of his philosophy as exists. The closest I've been able to find to this motto in his writings, however, is the following: "[A]ll the choir of heaven and furniture of the earth, in a word all those bodies which compose the mighty frame of the world, have not any subsistence without a mind ... *[T]heir being is to be perceived or known*." George Berkeley, *Principles of Human Knowledge*, 26, emphasis added.

[11]   Because the idea of a higher-order search for a search (S4S) is so central to Conservation of Information, it is worth noting that this idea has independent support and was not simply invented to bolster Conservation of Information. Indeed, *hyperheuristics*, in which one searches a space consisting of heuristics (i.e., searches), is a well-developed area within operations research and computer science: "Hyperheuristics are yet another extension [to search] that focuses on heuristics that modify their parameters (online or offline) to improve the efficacy of solution, or the efficiency of the computation. Hyperheuristics provide high-level strategies that may employ machine learning and adapt their search behavior by modifying the application of the sub-procedures or even which procedures are used (operating on the space of heuristics which in turn operate within the problem domain)." Quoted from Jason Brownlee, *Clever Algorithms: Nature-Inspired Programming Recipes* (Raleigh, N.C.: Lulu, 2011), 9. See also Edmund K. Burke, Matthew Hyde, Graham Kendall, Gabriela Ochoa, Ender Özcan, and John R. Woodward, "A Classification of Hyper-heuristic

Given this background and motivation, we are now in a position to give a reasonably precise statement of Conservation of Information. It is this: *raising the probability of success of a search does nothing to make attaining the target easier, and may in fact make it more difficult, once the informational costs involved in raising the probability of success are taken into account.* Search is costly, and the cost must be paid in terms of information. Searches achieve success not by creating information but by taking advantage of existing information. The information that leads to successful search admits of no bargains, only apparent bargains that must be paid in full elsewhere.

Given that this is a book on metaphysics, this statement of Conservation of Information suffices for our purposes. Robert Marks and I have proved several technical Conservation of Information theorems.[12] Each of these looks at some particular mathematical model of search and shows how raising the probability of success of a search by a factor of q/p (> 1) incurs an information cost not less than $\log(q/p)$, or, equivalently, a probability cost of not more than p/q. If we therefore start with a search having probability of success p and then raise it to q, the actual probability of finding the target is not q but instead is less than or equal to q multiplied by p/q, or, therefore, less than or equal to p, which is just the original search difficulty. Accordingly, raising the probability of success of a search contributes nothing toward finding the target once the information cost of raising the probability is taken into account.

Conservation of Information, however, is not just a theorem or family of theorems but also a general principle or law. Marks and I call it the Law of Conservation of Information. This law vastly generalizes Medawar's law by that same name described in the last chapter. Once enough CoI theorems have been proved and once their applicability to a wide range of search problems has been repeatedly demonstrated (the Evolutionary Informatics Lab has, for instance, shown how such widely touted evolutionary algorithms as Avida, ev, Tierra, and Dawkins's WEASEL simulation all fail to create but instead merely redistribute existing information[13]), Conservation of Information comes to be seen not as a narrow, isolated truth but as a fundamental principle or law applicable to search in general. This is how we take Conservation of Information.

Approaches," in M. Gendreau and J.-Y. Potvin, eds., *Handbook of Metaheuristics*, 2nd edn. (New York, N.Y.: Springer, 2010), 449–68.

[12]   See the publications page at http://evoinfo.org (last accessed July 23, 2013). For a review article, see Dembski and Marks, "Life's Conservation Law."

[13]   See http://evoinfo.org/publications as well as http://evoinfo.org/ev, http://evoinfo.org/weasel, and http://evoinfo.org/minivida (last accessed July 23, 2013).

The theoretical apparatus underlying Conservation of Information is solid and has now appeared in a number of peer-reviewed articles in the engineering and mathematics literature.[14] Nonetheless, materialists, especially those committed to a mechanistic and nonteleological form of biological evolution, claim to see in Conservation of Information no great threat. So what, they say, if information output presupposes at least as much prior information input. All this information resides and moves within an *environment*. Insofar as the generation of information in nature requires explanation, the environment plugs all leaks. We may not understand the exact details and there may be other mechanisms besides natural selection. But there is no need to go outside the environment. The environment generates all of nature's information, including biological information. End of story.

The late Notre Dame philosopher of science Ernan McMullin made this very point to me over dinner at the University of Chicago in 1999, suggesting that the environment contains all the resources necessary to overcome any obstacles facing evolution. Yet if the environment supplies the information needed to drive biological evolution, where did the environment get that information? From itself? The problem with such an answer is this: Conservation of Information maintains that, without added external information, biology's information problem remains constant (breaks even) or intensifies (gets worse) the further back in the causal chain we trace it.

The whole magic of evolution is that it explains (or purports to explain) subsequent complexity in terms of prior simplicity.[15] For instance, it is no feat of evolutionary theorizing to explain how cave fish lost the use of their eyes after long periods of being deprived of light. Functioning eyes turning into functionless eye nubs is a devolution from complexity to simplicity. As a case of use-it-or-lose-it, it does not call for explanation. Evolution wins plaudits for purporting to explain how things like eyes that see can evolve in the first place from prior simpler structures that cannot see. Keep going back in time, and things get simpler and simpler. Eventually you get everything from nothing. In chapter 16, I cited Lawrence Krauss and Stephen Hawking for taking precisely this line.[16] By contrast, Conservation of Information says that there never was a prior state of primordial simplicity. According to CoI, any information

---

[14] Ibid. See especially Dembski, Ewert, and Marks, "A General Theory of Information Cost," available also online at http://www.worldscientific.com/doi/pdf/10.1142/9789814508728_0002 (last accessed July 23, 2013).

[15] "The one thing that makes evolution such a neat theory is that it explains how organized complexity can arise out of primeval simplicity." Dawkins, *Blind Watchmaker*, 316.

[16] Krauss, *A Universe from Nothing*; Hawking and Mlodinow, *The Grand Design*.

existing now had, absent external input (and there can be no external input if you're a materialist!), to exist in at least as intense a form at every point earlier in time going right back to the start (if there is a start; if there is no start, the intensification of information continues back in time indefinitely).

If evolutionary processes could ascertainably create biological information from scratch, then evolution from simplicity to complexity would be justifiable. But the evolutionary process as conceived by Darwin and extended by his successors is nonteleological.[17] Accordingly, it cannot employ the activity of intelligence in any guise to increase biological information. But without intelligent input, Conservation of Information entails that as we regress biological information back in time, the amount of information to be accounted for never diminishes and may actually increase.

Given Conservation of Information and an absence of intelligent input, biological information having the complexity we now see must have always been present in the universe in some form or fashion, going back even as far as the Big Bang. But where in the Big Bang, with a heat and density that rules out any life form in the early history of the universe, is the information for life's subsequent emergence and development on Planet Earth? Conservation of Information says this information, absent external input, has to be there, in embryonic form, at the Big Bang and at every moment thereafter.[18] So where

---

[17]   Neo-Darwinist Francisco Ayala, for instance, writes: "The functional design of organisms and their features would therefore seem to argue for the existence of a designer. It was Darwin's *greatest accomplishment* to show that the directive organization of living beings can be explained as the result of a natural process, natural selection, without any need to resort to a Creator or other external agent." Quoted from Francisco J. Ayala, "Darwin's Revolution," in *Creative Evolution?!*, eds. J.H. Campbell and J.W. Schopf (Boston, Mass.: Jones and Bartlett, 1994), 4, emphasis added.

[18]   Philosopher Holmes Rolston, without the benefit of a formal articulation of CoI, nails this point. He argues persuasively against the claim that all biological information was somehow front-loaded into the universe from the start. At the same time, as a nonmaterialist, he won't account for this information by appealing to a nonteleological form of evolution (cosmic, chemical, or biological). In a long but insightful quote, he writes,

> There are no humans invisibly present (as an acorn secretly contains an oak) in the primitive eukaryotes, to unfold in a lawlike or programmatic way ... On Earth, there really isn't anything in rocks that suggests the possibility of *Homo sapiens*, much less the American Civil War, or the World Wide Web, and to say that all these possibilities are lurking there, even though nothing we know about rocks or carbon atoms, or electrons and protons suggests this is simply to let possibilities float in from nowhere ... The information (in DNA) is interlocked with an information producer-processor (the organism) that can transcribe, incarnate, metabolize, and reproduce it. All such information once upon a time did not exist

is it? How is it represented? How does it unfold? The environment is sure to figure into any answer to these questions. Yet, merely invoking the environment as evolution's information source is, without further elaboration, empty talk, on the order of invoking the interstate highway system as the reason for Walmart's business success. There is, to be sure, some connection in both instances, but neither provides real insight or explanation.

To see more clearly why the environment is no panacea for biology's information problem, consider the following analogy. Imagine Scrabble pieces arranged in sequence to spell out meaningful sentences (such as METHINKS IT IS LIKE A WEASEL). Suppose a machine with suitable sensors, movable arms, and grips, takes the Scrabble pieces out of a box and arranges them in this way. To say that the environment has arranged the Scrabble pieces to spell out meaningful sentences is, in this case, hardly illuminating. Yes, broadly speaking, the environment is arranging the pieces into meaningful sentences. But, more precisely, a robotic machine, presumably running a program with meaningful sentences suitably encoded, is doing the arranging.

Merely invoking the environment, without further amplification, therefore explains nothing about the arrangement of Scrabble pieces into meaningful sentences. What exactly is it about the environment that accounts for the information conveyed in those arrangements of Scrabble pieces? And what about the environment accounts for the information conveyed in the organization of

but came into place; this is the locus of creativity. Nevertheless, on Earth, there is this result during evolutionary history. The result involves significant achievements in cybernetic creativity, essentially incremental gains in information that have been conserved and elaborated over evolutionary history. The know-how, so to speak, to make salt is already in the sodium and chlorine, but the know-how to make hemoglobin molecules and lemurs is not secretly coded in the carbon, hydrogen, and nitrogen ... Can one claim that what did actually manage to happen must always have been either probably probable, or, minimally, improbably possible all along the way? Push this to extremes, as one must do, if one claims that all the possibilities are always there, latent in the dust, latent in the quarks. Such a claim becomes pretty much an act of speculative faith, not in present actualities, since one knows that these events took place, but in past probabilities always being omnipresent ... Unbounded possibilities that one posits ad hoc to whatever one finds has in fact taken place – possibilities of any kind and amount desired in one's metaphysical enthusiasm – can hardly be said to be a scientific hypothesis. This is hardly even a faith claim with sufficient warrant. It is certainly equally credible and more plausible, and no less scientific to hold that new possibility spaces open up en route."

Holmes Rolston III, *Genes, Genesis and God: Values and Their Origins in Natural and Human History* (Cambridge: Cambridge University Press, 1999), 352–3, 357.

biological systems? That's the question that needs to be answered. Without an answer to this question, appeals to the environment are empty and merely cloak our ignorance of the true sources of biological information.

With a machine that arranges Scrabble pieces, we can try to get inside it and see what it does ("oh, there's the code that spells out METHINKS IT IS LIKE A WEASEL"). With the actual environment for biological evolution, we can't, as it were, get under the hood of the car. The best we can do, it seems, is achieve what Owen Barfield called "dashboard knowledge," a minimal knowledge that's practical and descriptive without understanding the deep structure of things.[19] Thus, with biological evolution, we see natural forces such as wind, waves, erosion, lightning, Brownian motion, attraction, repulsion, chemical bonding affinities, and the like. And we see slippery slopes on which organisms thrive or alternatively founder. If such an environment were arranging Scrabble pieces in sequence, we would observe the pieces blown by wind or jostled by waves or levitated by magnets. And if, at the end of the day, we found Scrabble pieces spelling out coherent English sentences, such as METHINKS IT IS LIKE A WEASEL, we would be in our rights to infer that an intelligence had in some way co-opted and coordinated the environment to insert information, even though we have no clue how.

Such a role for the environment, as an inscrutable purveyor of information, is, however, unacceptable to mainstream evolutionary theorists. In their view, the way the environment inputs information into biological systems over the course of evolution is eminently scrutable. It happens, so they say, by a gradual

---

[19]   "Take a clever boy, who knows nothing about the principle of internal combustion or the inside of an engine, and leave him inside a motor-car, first telling him to move the various knobs, switches and levers about and see what happens. If no disaster supervenes, he will end by finding himself able to drive the car. It will then be true to say that he knows *how to drive* the car; but untrue to say that he knows the car. As to that, the most we could say would be that he has an 'operative' knowledge of it—because for operation all that is required is a good empirical acquaintance with the dashboard and the pedals. Whatever we say, it is obvious that what he has is very different from the knowledge of someone else, who has studied mechanics, internal combustion and the construction of motor-cars, though he had perhaps never driven a car in his life, and is perhaps too nervous to try. Now whether or no there is another kind of knowledge of nature, which corresponds to 'engine-knowledge' in the analogy, it seems that, *if the first view of the nature of scientific theory is accepted*, the *kind* of knowledge aimed at by science must be, in effect, what I will call 'dashboard-knowledge.'" Quoted from Owen Barfield, *Saving the Appearances: A Study in Idolatry*, 2nd edn. (Hanover, N.H.: University Press of New England, 1988), 55. It becomes an interesting question whether, in an informational universe, scientific inquiry can do better than dashboard knowledge and, if so, how much better.

accumulation of information as natural selection locks in small advantages, each of which can arise by chance, this whole scenario playing out without the need for intelligent input. Let's now turn to this proposal.

Chapter 19

Natural Selection

Biological information presupposes the origin of life. Once life has originated, evolution can take existing biological information and augment it. Consequently, if evolution is indeed responsible for large-scale biological transformations, such as from "monad to man,"[1] it must have the ability to generate huge increases in the information content of living forms. There is, after all, a lot more genetic information in a human being than in a bacterium.[2] So how does evolution do it? How, as Richard Dawkins puts it, does "the information content of genomes increase in evolution"?[3] The conventional understanding of what causes biological information to increase over natural history is thoroughly Darwinian. In a word, *natural selection* is seen by the evolutionary community as the driving force for the elaboration of biological information once life has originated. Thus, according to Dawkins,

> In every generation, natural selection removes the less successful genes from the gene pool, so the remaining gene pool is a narrower subset. The narrowing is

---

[1] The phrase "monad to man" is Herbert Spencer's. Although Spencer meant by it to connect evolution to the idea of progress, the phrase underscores the vast transformation that organisms are supposed to have undergone over natural history, evolving from relatively simple single-celled beginnings to far more complex multicelled organisms that can reason, talk, and self-consciously reflect on what they are doing. See Michael Ruse, *Monad to Man: The Concept of Progress in Evolutionary Biology* (Cambridge, Mass.: Harvard University Press, 1996), 188.

[2] A mycoplasma bacterium, for instance, has around 500,000 DNA base pairs whereas a human being has 3 billion.

[3] Richard Dawkins, "The Information Challenge," http://www.skeptics.com.au/publications/articles/the-information-challenge (last accessed July 26, 2013). This article, published in the late 1990s, is an extended response to a question posed by an Australian film crew. Dawkins was asked for "an example of a genetic mutation or an evolutionary process which can be seen to increase the information in the genome." Though Dawkins has written much since then, and in more prominent venues, this seems to be his most considered statement on biology's information problem. For the segment of the interview with Dawkins where the Australian film crew raised this question, see http://www.youtube.com/watch?v=WmadkjPrjug (last accessed July 26, 2013).

nonrandom, in the direction of improvement, where improvement is defined, in
the Darwinian way, as improvement in fitness to survive and reproduce. Of course
the total range of variation is topped up again in every generation by new mutation
and other kinds of variation. But it still remains true that natural selection is a
narrowing down from an initially wider field of possibilities, including mostly
unsuccessful ones, to a narrower field of successful ones. This is analogous to the
definition of information with which we began: information is what enables the
narrowing down from prior uncertainty (the initial range of possibilities) to later
certainty (the "successful" choice among the prior probabilities). According to
this analogy, natural selection is by definition a process whereby information is
fed into the gene pool of the next generation.[4]

I offer this quote not only to make clear that Dawkins and I are using information
in the same way but also to underscore our main point of divergence, namely,
whether natural selection is a source of novel information (Dawkins) or merely
a mechanism for shifting around existing information (me).

In *The Blind Watchmaker*, Dawkins purports to show how natural selection
creates information. In that book, he gives his famous METHINKS IT IS LIKE
A WEASEL computer simulation.[5] A historian or literary scholar, confronted

---

[4]   Ibid. Dawkins prefaces this passage with, "Natural selection itself, when you think
about it, is a narrowing down from a wide initial field of possible alternatives, to the
narrower field of the alternatives actually chosen. Random genetic error (mutation), sexual
recombination and migratory mixing, all provide a wide field of genetic variation: the
available alternatives. Mutation is not an increase in true information content, rather the
reverse, for mutation, in the Shannon analogy, contributes to increasing the prior uncertainty.
But now we come to natural selection, which reduces the 'prior uncertainty' and therefore, in
Shannon's sense, contributes information to the gene pool."

[5]   Dawkins, *Blind Watchmaker*, 46–50. *The Blind Watchmaker* was published in 1986.
Variants of this simulation have appeared now for several decades and, indeed, continue to
appear, being touted as proof positive of the power of Darwinian evolution. The first instance
of this simulation that I know predated Dawkins's popularization of it and appeared in
Manfred Eigen and Peter Schuster, *The Hypercycle* (Berlin: Springer, 1979), 15–28. There
the target phrase was TAKE ADVANTAGE OF MISTAKE. David Berlinski identified the
illicit introduction of teleology in Eigen and Schuster's simulation (illicit from the point of
view of Darwinism). See David Berlinski, *Black Mischief: Language, Life, Logic, Luck*, 2nd
edn. (Cambridge, Mass.: Harcourt Brace Jovanovich, 1988), 345–50. Notwithstanding,
Bernd-Olaf Küppers, an Eigen student, continued to promote this simulation throughout
the late 1980s and into the 1990s. See Bernd-Olaf Küppers, *Information and the Origin of Life*
(Cambridge, Mass.: MIT Press, 1990), ch. 8. There Küppers's target phrase was EVOLUTION
THEORY. Essentially the same simulation appeared in Bernd-Olaf Küppers, "On the Prior
Probability of the Existence of Life," in *The Probabilistic Revolution*, vol. 2, eds. L. Krüger,

with the phrase METHINKS IT IS LIKE A WEASEL, would look to its human author, William Shakespeare, to explain it (the phrase is from *Hamlet*). An evolutionary theorist like Dawkins, by contrast, considers what it would take for an evolutionary process, simulated by an algorithm running on a computer, to produce this target phrase. All such algorithms consist of:

1. an initialization (i.e., a place where the algorithm starts—for Dawkins the starting point is any random string of letters and spaces the same length as METHINKS IT IS LIKE A WEASEL);
2. a fitness landscape (i.e., a measure of the goodness of candidate solutions—for Dawkins, in this example, fitness measures proximity to the target phrase so that the closer it is to the target, the more fit it becomes);
3. an update rule (i.e., a rule that says where to go next given where the algorithm is presently—for Dawkins this involves some randomization to existing candidate phrases already searched as well as an evaluation of fitness along with selection of those candidates with the better fitness);
4. a stop criterion (i.e., a criterion that says when the search has gone on long enough and can reasonably be ended—for Dawkins this occurs when the search has landed on the target phrase METHINKS IT IS LIKE A WEASEL).

Note that in these four steps, natural selection is mirrored in steps (2) and (3).

Do evolutionary algorithms create or generate novel information from scratch in the sense that, until the algorithm has acted, this information was completely absent? Or do they merely shuffle around existing information,

---

G. Gigerenzer, and M.S. Morgan (Cambridge, Mass.: MIT Press, 1987), 365–8. There his target phrase was NATURAL SELECTION. In *The Quantum Brain: The Search for Freedom and the Next Generation of Man* (New York: Wiley, 2001), 89–92, Jeffrey Satinover sought to demonstrate the power of evolutionary algorithms by showing how such an algorithm could generate the target phrase MONKEYS WROTE SHAKESPEARE. Satinover's algorithm was similar to Dawkins's except that Satinover used a few more techniques from the evolutionary computing tool chest (specifically, crossover and mating). Closer to the present, in 2010, RNA worlds researcher Michael Yarus reprised this simulation in *Life from an RNA World*, 64–8. There his target phrase was NOTHING IN BIOLOGY MAKES SENSE EXCEPT IN THE LIGHT OF EVOLUTION. I expect that the history of this simulation sketched here is grossly incomplete and that the evolutionary biology literature contains many more examples of it. Indeed, the lunatic vitality that infests these simulations suggests that the deconstruction of these simulations here via Conservation of Information, decisive though it is, will not end their endless recycling.

expressing and re-expressing it, but producing no genuine innovation? In fact, all the information that evolutionary algorithms output had first to be inputted into the fitness landscape (and sometimes also into the update rule). These algorithms therefore shuffle existing information rather than create novel information from scratch. Dawkins's algorithm confirms this point, privileging the target phrase by adapting a fitness landscape to it so that greater fitness is assigned to phrases that have more corresponding characters in common with the target.

But where did that fitness landscape come from in the first place? Such a landscape exists, potentially, for any phrase whatsoever, and not just for METHINKS IT IS LIKE A WEASEL. Dawkins's evolutionary algorithm could therefore have evolved to any phrase at all. The only reason it evolved to METHINKS IT IS LIKE A WEASEL is that he carefully chose the fitness landscape so that it assigned higher fitness to character sequences having more letters in common with it. Dawkins therefore got rid of Shakespeare as the author of METHINKS IT IS LIKE A WEASEL, only to reintroduce him as the (co) author of the fitness landscape that facilitates the evolution of METHINKS IT IS LIKE A WEASEL. Here is an actual computer run of his WEASEL program:

```
 0: WSC UDZHGQQFBSJCVKOBBXP AVND -- score: 3
 1: WSC UDZHGQQFBSJCVKOBAXP AVND -- score: 4
 2: WSC UDZHGQQFBSJCVKOBAXP AVED -- score: 5
 3: WST UDZHGSQFBSJCVKO AXP AVED -- score: 7
 4: MST UDZHGSQFBSHCVKO AXB AVED -- score: 8
 5: MST UDZHGSQFBSHCVKO AXBEAVED -- score: 9
 6: MST UDZHGIQFBSHCVKO AXBEAVED -- score: 10
 7: MST UDZHGIQFBSHCIKO AXBEAVED -- score: 11
 8: MDT IDSHGIQFBSHCIKO AXWEIVED -- score: 12
 9: MDT IDQH IQFBSNCIKN AXWEIVED -- score: 13
10: MDTHIDQH IQFBSNCIKN AXWEIVED -- score: 14
11: MDTHIDQH IQFBSQCIKN AXWEIVED -- score: 14
12: MDTHINQH IQFBSQCIKN AXWEIVED -- score: 15
13: MDTHINQH ITFBSQCIKN AXWEIVED -- score: 16
14: MDTHINQH ITFBSQLIKN AXWEIVED -- score: 17
15: MDTHINDH ITFBSQLIKN AXWEIVED -- score: 17
16: MDTHINDS ITFBSQLIKN AXWEIVED -- score: 18
17: MDTHINDS ITFBSQLIKN AXWEMVED -- score: 18
18: MDTHINLS ITFBSQLIKN AXWEMVEL -- score: 19
19: MYTHINLS ITFBSQLIKE AXWEMVEL -- score: 20
20: METHINLS ITFBSQLIKE AXWEMVEL -- score: 21
21: METHINLS ITFBSQLIKE AXWEACEL -- score: 22
22: METHINNS ITFBSQLIKE AXWEASEL -- score: 23
23: METHINNS ITFBSQLIKE AXWEASEL -- score: 23
24: METHINNS ITFBSQLIKE AXWEASEL -- score: 23
```

```
25: METHINNS ITFBSQLIKE AXWEASEL -- score: 23
26: METHINNS ITFBSQLIKE AXWEASEL -- score: 23
27: METHINNS ITFBSQLIKE AXWEASEL -- score: 23
28: METHINNS ITFBSQLIKE AXWEASEL -- score: 23
29: METHINNS ITFBSQLIKE AXWEASEL -- score: 23
30: METHINKS ITFBSQLIKE AXWEASEL -- score: 24
31: METHINKS ITFBSQLIKE AXWEASEL -- score: 24
32: METHINKS ITFBSQLIKE AXWEASEL -- score: 24
33: METHINKS ITFBSQLIKE ANWEASEL -- score: 24
34: METHINKS ITFBSQLIKE ANWEASEL -- score: 24
35: METHINKS ITFBSQLIKE ANWEASEL -- score: 24
36: METHINKS ITFBSQLIKE ANWEASEL -- score: 24
37: METHINKS ITFBSQLIKE ANWEASEL -- score: 24
38: METHINKS ITMBSQLIKE ANWEASEL -- score: 24
39: METHINKS ITMBSQLIKE A WEASEL -- score: 25
40: METHINKS ITMBSQLIKE A WEASEL -- score: 25
41: METHINKS ITJBSQLIKE A WEASEL -- score: 25
42: METHINKS ITJBSQLIKE A WEASEL -- score: 25
43: METHINKS ITJBS LIKE A WEASEL -- score: 26
44: METHINKS ITJIS LIKE A WEASEL -- score: 27
45: METHINKS ITJIS LIKE A WEASEL -- score: 27
46: METHINKS ITJIS LIKE A WEASEL -- score: 27
47: METHINKS IT IS LIKE A WEASEL -- score: 28
```

The run begins with a purely random sequence of 28 letters and spaces (in this case, WSC UDZHGQQFBSJCVKOBBXP AVND). This is the initialization, listed as generation 0. Future generations evolve from this starting point. Fitness is defined in terms of proximity to the target sequence (the target being METHINKS IT IS LIKE A WEASEL). Specifically, in the program run above, fitness is calculated as a score signifying the number of character matches with the target sequence. The initial sequence has a score of 3. As the program proceeds, the sequence changes, as does its score. A score of 28 is highest, signifying that every letter and space in a sequence matches the target sequence (making it identical with the target sequence). The program stops when, as sequences evolve, a sequence is reached having a score of 28. That's the stop criterion. To get from initial to final sequence, intermediate sequences are generated via the following update rule: take the current sequence, sloppily copy it 100 times, with a 5 percent mutation rate (i.e., chance of error) at each character, and then select the (randomly modified) copy with the best score, making it the new sequence for the next generation. In the present run, it took 47 generations to reach the target sequence.[6]

---

[6]   The actual run given and described here is taken from http://upload.wikimedia. org/wikipedia/commons/e/e7/Dawkins-Weasel.png (last accessed August 1, 2013). To

How does Conservation of Information apply to Dawkins's evolutionary algorithm? Straightforwardly. Obtaining METHINKS IT IS LIKE A WEASEL by blind search (e.g., by randomly throwing down Scrabble pieces in sequence) is extremely improbable, on the order of 1 in 10^{40} in a single trial. 10^{40} is ten thousand trillion trillion trillion. So even in a trillion trillion random trials, obtaining METHINKS IT IS LIKE A WEASEL with randomly tossed Scrabble pieces will remain extremely improbable (far worse than winning two state lotteries in a row). To overcome these odds, Dawkins proposes an evolutionary algorithm, his WEASEL program. It obtains this sequence with much higher probability and in relatively few trials (in the above example, only 47 generations with 100 mutated copies at each generation, or $47 \times 100 = 4,700$ trials total, were required to locate the target). With 20,000 such trials, it's almost inevitable that Dawkins's simulation will obtain the target sequence.[7] Compare this to blind search, which in a trillion trillion trials is still vastly unlikely to produce METHINKS IT IS LIKE A WEASEL.

So Dawkins's algorithm does a much better job, with much higher probability, of locating the target. But at what cost? According to Conservation of Information, Dawkins's algorithm incurs an even greater improbability cost than merely locating the target sequence by blind search. The problem here is accounting for the fitness landscape that rendered the evolution of METHINKS IT IS LIKE A WEASEL probable. Conservation of Information tells us that the necessary information was not internally created by the search algorithm but instead smuggled into it, a fact we can confirm independently, because Dawkins himself admits to smuggling it in. He is, after all, the program's designer.

When I raised this point with Dawkins in correspondence some years back, he conceded that this example is not true to biological evolution in that its criterion of optimization is a "distant ideal target," which introduces a teleology alien to the Darwinism that Dawkins promotes. "Life," he claimed, "isn't like that." But what, then, is life like? "In real life," according to Dawkins, "the criterion for

---

perform such runs online, with the ability to specify the target sequence and to vary the number of copies made at each generation along with the mutation rate, I recommend the Evolutionary Informatics Lab's Weasel Ware software at http://evoinfo.org/weasel (last accessed August 1, 2013). Once there, click on "simulation," and then adjust the parameters under "Proximity Reward Search." Note that what I called "copies" in the main text are called "offspring" in Weasel Ware.

[7]   Using the Weasel Ware software at http://evoinfo.org/weasel, I've never needed more than 20,000 trials (called "queries" in the program) to generate METHINKS IT IS LIKE A WEASEL when Proximity Reward Search is set at 100 copies ("offspring") and at a mutation rate of 5 percent. Compare the previous note.

optimisation is not an arbitrarily chosen distant target but SURVIVAL [*sic*]. It's as simple as that. This is non-arbitrary."[8] Survival is certainly a necessary condition for life to evolve. If you're not surviving, you're dead, and if you're dead, you're not evolving—period. But to call "survival," writ large and without qualification, a criterion for optimization seems a bit of a stretch.

Perhaps I'm reading Dawkins uncharitably. Presumably, what he really means is differential survival and reproduction as governed by natural selection acting on random variation. Let's say that this is what he means. Yet even on this more charitable reading, the information-generating powers of natural selection remain unjustified. Brown University biologist Kenneth Miller elaborates on this more charitable reading in *Only a Theory*. There he asks what's needed to drive the increase in biological information over the course of evolution. His answer? "Just three things: selection, replication, and mutation ... Where the information 'comes from' is, in fact, from the selective process itself."[9]

Miller's solution to evolutionary biology's information problem can be seen to fail even without the benefits of modern information theory. All that's required is to understand some straightforward logic, uncovered in Darwin's day, about the nature of scientific explanation in teasing apart possible causes. Indeed, biology's reception of Darwinism might have been far less favorable had scientists paid better attention to Darwin's contemporary John Stuart Mill. In 1843, sixteen years before the publication of Darwin's *Origin of Species*, Mill published the first edition of his *System of Logic* (which by the 1880s had gone through eight editions). In that work Mill lays out various methods of induction. The one that interests us here is his *method of difference*. In his *System of Logic*, Mill described this method as follows:

> If an instance in which the phenomenon under investigation occurs, and an instance in which it does not occur, have every circumstance in common save one, that one occurring only in the former; the circumstance in which alone the two instances differ is the effect, or the cause, or an indispensable part of the cause, of the phenomenon.[10]

---

[8]   Email from Richard Dawkins to me dated May 5, 2000. In *Blind Watchmaker* (p. 50) Dawkins elaborates slightly: "In real life, the criterion for selection is always short-term, either simple survival or, more generally, reproductive success." But my same criticism holds of reproductive success, namely, it is a necessary condition for life to evolve, but hardly sufficient.

[9]   Miller, *Only a Theory*, 77–8.

[10]   John Stuart Mill, *A System of Logic: Ratiocinative and Inductive*, 8th edn. (1882; reprinted London: Longmans, Green, and Co., 1906), 256.

Thus, according to Mill's method of difference, to figure out which of various
circumstances is responsible for an observed difference in outcomes requires
finding a difference in the circumstances. An immediate corollary is that
common circumstances cannot explain a difference in outcomes. Thus, if one
person is sober and another drunk, and if both ate chips, salsa, and popcorn,
this fact, common to both, does not, and indeed cannot, explain the difference.
Rather, the difference is explained, in this case, by one abstaining from alcohol
and the other drinking too much. Mill's method of difference, so widely used in
everyday life and also in science, is crucially relevant to evolutionary biology. In
fact, it helps bring some sense of proportion and reality to the inflated claims so
frequently made on behalf of Darwinian processes.

Case in point: Miller's overselling of Darwinian evolution by claiming
that "what's needed to drive" increases in biological information is "just three
things: selection, replication, and mutation." Mill's method of difference gives
the lie to Miller's claim. It's easy to write computer simulations that feature
selection, replication, and mutation (or SURVIVAL writ large, or differential
survival and reproduction, or any such reduction of evolution to Darwinian
principles)—*and yet these simulations go absolutely nowhere.* Taken together,
selection, replication, and mutation are not a magic bullet, and need not solve
any interesting problems or produce any salient patterns. That said, evolutionary
computation often does get successfully employed in the field of optimization,
so it is possible to write computer simulations that feature selection, replication,
and mutation and that do go somewhere, solving interesting problems or
producing salient patterns. But precisely because selection, replication, and
mutation are common to all such simulations, they cannot, as Mill's method
underscores, account for the difference.

One engineer who used evolutionary methods to solve optimization problems
liked to style himself as a "penalty function artist."[11] A penalty function is just

---

[11] "A common structure in evolutionary search is an imposed fitness function,
wherein the merit of a design for each set of parameters is assigned a number. The bigger
the fitness, the better. The optimization problem is to maximize the fitness function. *Penalty
functions* are similar, but are to be minimized. In the early days of computing, an engineer
colleague of mine described his role in conducting searches as a *penalty function artist*. He
took pride in using his domain expertise to craft penalty functions. The structured search
model developed by the design engineer must be, in some sense, a *good* model. Exploring
through the parameters of a poor model, no matter how thoroughly, will not result in a
viable design. In a contrary manner, a cleverly conceived model can result in better solutions
in faster time." From Robert J. Marks II, "Evolutionary Computation: A Perpetual Motion
Machine for Design Information," in W.A. Dembski and M.R. Licona, eds., *Evidence for God*
(Grand Rapids, Mich.: Baker, 2010), 94.

another term for a fitness landscape (though the numbers are reversed—the higher the penalty, the lower the fitness). Coming up with the right penalty functions enabled this individual to solve his engineering problems. Most such penalty functions, however, are completely useless. Yet any evolutionary computing environment in which penalty functions operate will feature Miller's triad of selection, replication, and mutation. So what is the difference-maker in Mill's (not Miller's) sense? Selection, replication, and mutation are held in common wherever penalty functions operate, so why do some penalty functions succeed and others (the vast majority) fail? The answer is obvious: the engineer, with knowledge of the problem he's trying to solve, carefully adapts the penalty function to the problem and thereby raises the probability of successfully finding a solution. He's not just choosing his penalty functions willy-nilly. If he did, he would be out of a job. He's an artist, and his artistry consists in being able to find the penalty functions that solve his problems.

Thus we see that computer simulations of evolution, merely by harnessing selection, replication, and mutation, cannot create novel information. Indeed, whatever information comes out of these simulations had, ultimately, to be created and inserted by a programmer (as through a penalty or fitness function). But what about evolution as it occurs not *in silico* but in the real world? Can real-life biological evolution, running solely off of selection, replication, and mutation (Miller's triad), drive increases in biological information? In fact, evolutionary biology faces the same obstacle to information generation as evolutionary computing. That obstacle is Mill's method of difference. In real-life biological evolution, selection, replication, and mutation are associated both with increases as well as decreases of biological information. Since these Darwinian processes are common to both, they cannot account for the difference.

Sol Spiegelman's experiment on the evolution of nucleotide sequences (DNA or RNA) illustrates the failure of Darwinian processes to create information in the biological real world. Spiegelman placed nucleotide sequences in a chemical environment featuring selection, replication, and mutation. Yet instead of the information in these sequences increasing, it steadily decreased over the course of the experiment. As Brian Goodwin explains,

> In a classic experiment, Spiegelman in 1967 showed what happens to a molecular replicating system in a test tube, without any cellular organization around it. The replicating molecules (the nucleic acid templates) require an energy source, building blocks (i.e., nucleotide bases), and an enzyme to help the polymerization process that is involved in self-copying of the templates. Then away it goes, making

more copies of the specific nucleotide sequences that define the initial templates. But the interesting result was that these initial templates did not stay the same; they were not accurately copied. They got shorter and shorter until they reached the minimal size compatible with the sequence retaining self-copying properties. And as they got shorter, the copying process went faster. So what happened with natural selection in a test tube: the shorter templates that copied themselves faster became more numerous, while the larger ones were gradually eliminated. This looks like Darwinian evolution in a test tube. But the interesting result was that this evolution went one way: toward greater simplicity.[12]

Mill's method of difference thus applies to both evolutionary computing and evolutionary biology. In both cases, the Darwinian evolutionary mechanism operates, but its operation is compatible with information being created as well as information staying constant or being destroyed. So, by Mill's method, that mechanism cannot account for the creation of information. Mill's method is an inconvenient truth for Dawkins and Miller, but it's a truth that must be faced. Unlike Dawkins and Miller, self-organizational theorist Stuart Kauffman understands the error in claiming that the Darwinian mechanism can generate biological information. As Kauffman observes, "If mutation, recombination, and selection only work well on certain kinds of fitness landscapes, yet most organisms are sexual, and hence use recombination, and all organisms use mutation as a search mechanism, where did these well-wrought fitness landscapes come from, such that evolution manages to produce the fancy stuff around us?"[13]

All the factors that Dawkins and Miller regard as crucial to the success of evolutionary processes are in fact common to all evolutionary processes, those processes that succeed and those that fail in creating information, so these common features cannot explain their success when indeed they do succeed. What, then, is the difference-maker? Where do all those "well-wrought fitness landscapes," as Kauffman puts it, come from that allow evolution "to produce the fancy stuff around us"? According to him, "No one knows."[14]

Kauffman's insight that purely Darwinian factors such as natural selection cannot account for the success of evolutionary processes in creating biological information is entirely in keeping with Conservation of Information. Indeed, he offers this insight in the context of discussing the No Free Lunch theorems, of

---

[12] Brian Goodwin, *How the Leopard Changed Its Spots: The Evolution of Complexity* (New York: Scribner's, 1994), 35–6.

[13] Kauffman, *Investigations*, 19.

[14] Ibid., 18.

which Conservation of Information is a logical extension.[15] The fitness landscape supplies the evolutionary process with information. Only finely tuned fitness landscapes that are sufficiently smooth, don't isolate local optima, and, above all, reward ever-increasing complexity in biological structure and function are suitable for driving a full-fledged evolutionary process.[16] So where do such fitness landscapes come from? Neo-Darwinian theory presupposes such fitness landscapes but does not explain them. Natural selection therefore is not, nor can it be, an explanation for the origin of biological information.

Natural selection is thus an information redistributor rather than an information generator or creator. Once this point is understood, an obvious question raises itself: What is the source (or sources) of the information in nature that allows its targets to be successfully searched? The most plausible answer, I submit, is *intelligence*.[17] On materialist principles, intelligence is not real but an epiphenomenon of underlying material processes. But if intelligence is real and has inherent causal powers, it can do more than merely redistribute information—it can also create it. Accordingly, this would make evolution in all its guises fundamentally teleological.[18] Indeed, the attempt to rid evolution of

[15]   Ibid., 19, where just before the quote by Kauffman cited above, he writes, "The no-free-lunch theorem says that, averaged over all possible fitness landscapes, no search procedure outperforms any other ... In the absence of any knowledge, or constraint, [read "information"] on the fitness landscape, on average, any search procedure is as good as any other. But life uses mutation, recombination, and selection. These search procedures seem to be working quite well. Your typical bat or butterfly has managed to get itself evolved and seems a rather impressive entity. The no-free-lunch theorem brings into high relief the puzzle."

[16]   See Dembski and Marks, "Life's Conservation Law," 390–91.

[17]   This intelligence can be God but need not be. Derived intelligences like us would also count. God, as an intelligence, can create information directly. But he can also create other intelligences that, like us, can in turn create information.

[18]   When I write of "evolution in all its guises," I'm merely acknowledging that, in the history of ideas, evolution has come in both explicitly teleological and explicitly nonteleological forms. On the teleological side, one will find views like (neo-)Lamarckism and orthogenesis. On the nonteleological side, one will find views like Epicureanism and (neo-)Darwinism. My argument is that however one conceives of evolution, if one demands of evolution that it increase biological information through successful targeted search, then evolution must be supplemented with teleology. In teleological forms of evolution, the teleology is already there. In supposedly nonteleological forms, the teleology must be added. In any case, I'm arguing that teleology is unavoidable, regardless of the protestations by evolutionists who think that evolution can make do without teleology. For different conceptions of evolution in the history of ideas, see Peter J. Bowler, *Evolution: The History of an Idea*, 3rd edn. (Berkeley, Calif.: University of California Press, 2003).

teleology then becomes a fool's errand. Conservation of Information shows that all such attempts end in smuggling teleology back into the evolutionary process.

The defining property of intelligence is its ability to create information.[19] Moreover, the type of information that intelligence is especially good at creating is information that finds needles in haystacks, that is, information that assists in targeted search. The ability of intelligence to create information should be more obvious and convincing to us than any claim of the natural sciences. Why? Because (1) we ourselves are intelligent beings who create information all the time through our thoughts and language and (2) the natural sciences themselves are logically downstream from our ability to create information (if we were not information creators, we could not formulate scientific theories, much less search for those that are empirically adequate, in which case there could be no science). Materialist philosophy, however, has all this backwards, making a materialist science primary and then defining our intelligence out of existence because materialism leaves no room for it (except as unintended motions and modifications of matter). The saner course would be to leave no room for materialism.

---

[19]   See Robertson, "Algorithmic Information Theory, Free Will, and the Turing Test."

Chapter 20

The Creation of Information

A leitmotif throughout this book has been that the ultimate source of information in the world is intelligence. Yes, material and mechanical processes can be conduits for information, taking preexisting information and, without direct oversight by intelligence, repackaging it. But, I've argued, intelligence is the ultimate source of information, both in signals that clearly evince purpose and in signals that appear random (randomness, as argued in chapter 16, being a byproduct of intelligence). I want in this chapter to expand on what it means for intelligence to create and impart information. I come at this question as a Christian for whom God, as creator, is the ultimate source of all there is, and thus of all the information in the world. My model for information creation, therefore, cannot be bottom up, as in trying to reconstitute information from material processes, but rather must be top down, as in trying to understand the creation of information from the vantage of a creative intelligence (in particular, the Christian God). Whether this approach seems forced or natural I will let readers decide.

To guide our discussion of information creation, I want to focus on what Claude Shannon, in his classic 1949 book on information theory, *The Mathematical Theory of Communication*, called the "schematic diagram of a general communication system":[1]

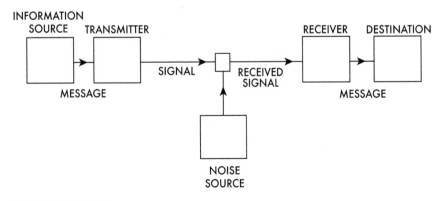

[1]   Claude Shannon and Warren Weaver, *The Mathematical Theory of Communication* (Urbana, Ill.: University of Illinois Press, 1949), 34.

This diagram is usually confined to humans sending signals across electronic communication channels. Nonetheless, it suggests a very general approach to information creation.

According to Shannon's diagram, information creation is essentially a speech act in which an intelligence, to advance a purpose, articulates an item of information and then broadcasts it. We obviously see this mode of creation in human speech acts. Nonetheless, speech acts, broadly construed, are able to characterize how intelligences create information quite generally. In our experience, information is created in any number of ways. Painters create information by applying dabs of paint to canvas, sculptors by chiseling away at stone, musicians by writing notes on lined sheets of paper, engineers by drawing up blueprints, etc.

Yet, in general, all such acts of information creation can be represented in language. For instance, a sufficiently elaborate set of instructions from a natural language can, with arbitrary precision, tell the painter where to apply the colors, the sculptor how to chisel the stone, the musician where to place the notes, the engineer how to draw up the blueprints, etc. Language, conceived as a speech act, in this way becomes the *universal medium* for creating information and thereby bringing purposes to realization. This is a linguistic picture of teleology. In this picture, purposes remain inert, ineffective, in limbo until appropriate items of information that advance the purpose are articulated and broadcast. Only in this way do purposes move from potentiality to actuality.

Speech acts are at once exclusionary and irrevocable. To say one thing is not to say others. Speech acts therefore exhibit the defining feature of information, that is, the inclusion of certain possibilities to the exclusion of others, in this case, the articulation and broadcasting of certain words rather than others. G.K. Chesterton saw such an inclusion–exclusion of possibilities as characteristic not just of speech acts but of all acts by intelligent agents. Addressing the will to action, whether divine or human, Chesterton wrote,

> Every act of will is an act of self-limitation. To desire action is to desire limitation. In that sense every act is an act of self-sacrifice. When you choose anything, you reject everything else ... Every act is an irrevocable selection and exclusion [*N.B.*: This matches precisely with the characterization of information throughout this book]. Just as when you marry one woman you give up all the others, so when you take one course of action you give up all the other courses.[2]

---

[2]   Chesterton, *Orthodoxy*, in *Collected Works of G. K. Chesterton*, vol. 1, 243.

An act of will is a decision. In this quote, Chesterton underscores the finality of decision, its irrevocability. It is no accident that the words *decision* and *homicide* share the same Latin root, the verb *caedere*, which means to cut off or kill.[3] Just as a homicide kills a human being, so a decision kills other options. After a decision, life is never the same again.

The decision to articulate and broadcast words exemplifies this finality. Once a word goes out, it cannot be taken back. Indeed, Shannon's diagram has no provision for putting the genie back in the bottle once a message has been sent down a communication channel.[4] Once the train has left the station, it cannot be recalled. This exclusionary and irrevocable aspect of speech holds not just for humans but, apparently, also for God. Any word spoken by any agent rules out those possibilities not spoken. Moreover, once the word is spoken, God himself cannot recall it. God can at best modify the original word's impact by adding further words.[5]

The Greek word for *word*, namely *logos*, offers some interesting insights to this discussion of information creation. For the ancient Greeks, *logos* was never merely a linguistic entity. Today, we often think of words as sequences of alphabetic characters written on sheets of paper or across computer screens. This is not what the ancient Greeks meant by *logos*. *Logos* was for them a much broader concept. Consider the following meanings ascribed to *logos* in Liddell and Scott's Greek–English lexicon: speech, reason, deliberation, evidence, inquiry, proportion, calculation, etc.[6] *Logos* was, for the ancient Greeks, an intensely rich notion spanning the entire life of the mind.

---

[3] The connection between decision and homicide is memorably described in Roy F. Baumeister and John Tierney, *Willpower: Rediscovering the Greatest Human Strength* (New York: Penguin, 2011), 86–7. The classic Latin dictionary by Lewis and Short, where a detailed definition of *caedere* can be found, is available online at http://archimedes.fas.harvard.edu/pollux (last accessed August 8, 2013).

[4] There's an interesting passage in the book of Daniel (6:15), which describes the law of the Medes and Persians as follows: "It is a law of the Medes and Persians that no interdict or ordinance that the king establishes can be changed." In our experience, laws can always be repealed. But there's a sense in which any law, once enacted, has an effect that even repealing it can never fully undo. Prohibition in the United States, for instance, was enacted in 1919 and repealed in 1933, but the damage done by it in distorting public sensibilities about alcohol and giving cover to organized crime has forever changed the American landscape.

[5] I've tackled this point at length in connection with how God addresses and redresses human sin. See my *End of Christianity: Finding a Good God in an Evil World* (Nashville, Tenn.: Broadman & Holman, 2009), part IV.

[6] Go to http://archimedes.fas.harvard.edu/pollux, select the Liddell-Scott-Jones drop down menu, and punch in "logos" (last accessed August 12, 2013).

The etymology of *logos* illuminates the role of intelligence in the creation of information. *Logos* stems from the Indo-European root *l-e-g*. This root appears in the Greek verb *lego*, which by the time of the New Testament typically meant "to speak." Yet the primitive Indo-European meaning of *lego* was to lay, from which it came to mean to pick up and put together, and from there to choose and arrange words, and therefore to speak. The root *l-e-g* has several variants. It appears as *l-o-g* in *logos*. It appears as *l-e-c* in *intellect* and *select*. And it appears as *l-i-g* in *intelligent*.

The word *intelligent* comes from the Latin rather than from the Greek. It stems from two Latin words, the preposition *inter*, meaning between, and the Latin (rather than Greek) verb *lego*, meaning to choose or select. The Latin *lego* stayed closer to its Indo-European root meaning than its Greek cognate, the latter referring explicitly to speech. According to its Latin etymology, intelligence therefore consists in *choosing between*. In an act of information creation, an intelligence chooses which possibility within a matrix of possibility to actualize. In the ultimate act of information creation, a supreme intelligence chooses which world among all possible worlds to actualize. The world so chosen becomes the real world. The real world then forms the backdrop for the matrices of possibility on which depend all subsidiary acts of information creation by created intelligences.

Making intelligence the ultimate source of information holds, unsurprisingly, little appeal to materialism. Materialism treats information as a property of matter. Thus, Shannon's communication diagram must, from the vantage of materialism, sit on top a purely material substrate. Matter, through its inherent (as opposed to externally imposed) structure and dynamics, therefore creates, transmits, and stores information. Moreover, intelligences, insofar as they create information, are themselves purely material entities, arranging and rearranging their material constituents through material processes and only thereby originating novel information. Intelligence, as with any other feature of the world, is, for the materialist, merely a consequence of matter arranging itself into different states. The same holds for information. For the materialist, there is no breaking free of matter.

Now, I come at the problem of information creation not as a materialist but as a Christian theist. Thus, for me, a nonmaterial trinitarian God is the supreme intelligence and ultimate reality. Moreover, this God creates via speech acts.[7] God

---

[7]   Both Genesis 1 and John 1 underwrite divine speech as the mode of God's creation. Note that this mode of creation is not unique to the Bible. Close in spirit to the biblical theology of creation is the Memphite theology of Egypt (eighth century B.C.) in which the

speaks and things happen. Or, alternatively, God communicates information and new possibilities are actualized. Accordingly, Shannon's communication diagram captures for me something very basic about reality. In fact, I would go so far as to say that if the trinitarian monotheism of Christianity is true, then Shannon's diagram is as accurate and succinct a summary of metaphysics and ontology as one can find. Indeed, I find in the triad on the left of that diagram (information source, message, and transmitter) a mathematical reflection of the Christian Trinity.

Of course, I realize that such an explicitly trinitarian interpretation of Shannon's diagram will be a stretch for many readers. Nonetheless, leaving aside trinitarian theology, one can still gain valuable insights into intelligent agency from the triadic mode of creation inherent in this diagram. Creation in Shannon's diagram is the creation and impartation of novel information. In this diagram, an intelligent agent forms an intention or purpose (at the information source or sender), articulates an item of information to advance that purpose (in the form of a message), and then broadcasts it (via a transmitter). The message, to be broadcast, must be energized in the form of a signal. As a signal, it crosses a communication channel to a receiver, where it induces a pattern and has a palpable effect (which, the sender hopes, realizes the original intention or purpose). All of this makes perfect sense in the context of ordinary human communication and, by extension, for communications by materially embodied intelligences generally (such as the transmission of radio signals to earth by intelligent aliens, if such aliens exist).

Materialists can therefore make a limited peace with Shannon's communication diagram. As they interpret the diagram, a material brain (whether human or otherwise) undergoing material motions acts as an information source, sending, by use of material energy only, a signal down a communication channel. Such a materialistic understanding of Shannon's diagram is fine as far as it goes. But what if materialism is false? What if information sources exist that are intelligent but not materially embodied (such as God, who traditionally is regarded as pure spirit and thus without a body)? In that case, no direct observational evidence of such an information source will exist (the source, because unembodied, cannot impinge directly on our senses). And yet, an intelligent information source

god Ptah "conceives the elements of the universe with his mind ('heart') and brings them into being by his commanding speech ('tongue')." Quoted from James B. Pritchard, *Ancient Near Eastern Texts Relating to the Old Testament*, 3rd edn. with suppl. (Princeton, N.J.: Princeton University Press, 1969), 4. Skeptic Michael Shermer attributes "divine edict creation stories" also to New World religions, notably those of the Maidu Indians and the Mayans. See Michael Shermer, *Why People Believe Weird Things* (New York: W.H. Freeman, 1997), 129.

can still be inferred if purely material processes cannot reasonably account for the information we do observe (recall the discussion in chapter 13 of the nonmaterial energy that such an information source would, in this case, have to use). Granted, if the information source is unembodied, then we do not have empirical access to the upper left portion of Shannon's diagram:

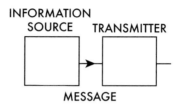

Nevertheless, we will ordinarily still have empirical access to the remaining portion of the diagram:

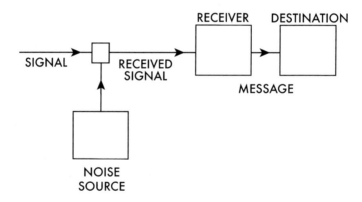

The challenge of communication theory is, from the received signal and through knowledge of the noise source, to recover the original signal. Noise distorts, and too much noise may block a signal from getting through. Even so, if noise does not completely overpower the signal, the message from an information source may still get through to the receiver.[8] It might seem that noise along a

---

[8]   The extraction of signals against a backdrop of noise is a major area in engineering, i.e., the field of signal processing. See, for instance, Robert N. McDonough and Anthony

communication channel means that the message received will necessarily be a corrupted version of the message sent. But that's not the case. To prevent corruption from entering, the received message requires that both ends of the communication channel employ *effective error correction*. Without error correction, noise will distort the received message. But with it, noise can in many instances be effectively prevented from distorting the received message.

We experience effective error correction every time we successfully send email messages to one another. All the communication channels that make up the Internet are subject to noise. The various file transfer protocols operating over the Internet employ error correction that effectively prevents noise from corrupting files in transmission. Without effective error correction, the Internet could never have gotten off the ground. With it, the Internet flourishes. Communication theory includes an entire branch for dealing with error correction: the theory of error-correcting codes.[9] Could it be that God's self-revelation in natural and human history has employed effective error correction? It would be interesting to understand what this might mean theologically (i.e., a theology of divine error correction), though that is a topic for another book.

Shannon's communication diagram is easily mined for theological resonances. Noise along the communication channel, for instance, can readily be identified with the distorting effects of evil on intentions that started out good at the information source. It then becomes an open question to what degree the noise source is autonomous, acts by its own warped intention, is perhaps sovereignly instituted by God, or has access to randomness that's beyond divine control (my own theology causes me to reject the latter option, though process and open theism would be receptive to it). As with divine error correction, these topics are best deferred. Instead of pursuing them here, I want to explore one final implication of Shannon's diagram, namely, that information creation by an intelligence is always a double creation.

The idea of creation as double creation goes back to antiquity. Plato expressed it in the *Timaeus* when he had the Demiurge (Plato's world architect) organize the physical world so that it conformed to patterns residing in the abstract world of ideas. Aquinas developed this thought with his notion of *exemplary causation*. An exemplary cause is a pattern or model employed by an intelligence for producing a patterned effect.[10] The preeminent example of exemplary causation

D. Whalen, *Detection of Signals in Noise*, 2nd edn. (San Diego, Calif.: Academic Press, 1995).

[9] Vera Pless, *Introduction to the Theory of Error-Correcting Codes*, 3rd edn. (New York: Wiley-Interscience, 1998).

[10] Gregory T. Doolan, *Aquinas on the Divine Ideas as Exemplar Causes* (Washington, D.C.: Catholic University of America Press, 2008).

within Christian theology is the creation of the world according to a divine plan, with that plan consisting of ideas eternally present in the mind of God.[11]

One of the best expressions of this principle of double creation that I've found, however, occurs not in the writings of theologians or philosophers. Rather, it appears in the work of businessman and leadership expert Stephen Covey: "*All things are created twice.* There's a mental or first creation, and a physical or second creation to all things."[12] Creation, in our common experience, begins with an idea, the first creation, and concludes with a thing, the second creation. Whatever is achieved needs first to be conceived. Creation, as a process, is thus bounded by *conception* at one end and *realization* at the other.

Shannon's communication diagram epitomizes this understanding of double creation. The diagram makes plain that the communication of information involves a fundamental duality: there's the information as it is originated and sent, and then there's the information as it is received and implemented. At the upper left triad of the diagram (information source, message, and transmitter), information is conceived. At the upper right triad of the diagram (receiver, message, destination), information is realized. In Covey's terminology, what happens on the left part of the diagram is the first creation; what happens on the right is the second creation.

Ordinarily, we expect the first and second creation to match up. For instance, if the first creation is an architectural blueprint and the second creation is the actual house, we expect the house to match up point for point with the blueprint. But what happens when there is a mismatch between the first and second creation? Covey, writing as a businessman, puts prime importance on getting the first creation right: "If you want to have a successful enterprise, you clearly define what you're trying to accomplish. You carefully think through the product or service you want to provide in terms of your market target, then you organize all the elements—financial, research and development, operations, marketing, personnel, physical facilities, and so on—to meet that objective."[13] As long as the second creation fulfills the promises of the first, there is no mismatch. But what if the second creation doesn't achieve anything like the promises set by the first creation? Covey considers this possibility and chalks it up to a failure in the first creation: "Most business failures begin in the first creation, with the

---

[11]   Compare the online Dictionary of Catholic Culture at http://www.catholicculture. org/culture/library/dictionary, s.v. "exemplary cause" (last accessed April 18, 2013).

[12]   Stephen R. Covey, *The Seven Habits of Highly Effective People* (New York: Simon & Schuster, 1989), 99. Emphasis in the original.

[13]   Ibid.

problems such as undercapitalization, misunderstanding of the market, or lack of a business plan."[14]

Covey faults the first creation for failure at the second creation. But that raises the question whether the second creation can fail through no fault of the first creation. This question is theologically intriguing. God, who presumably operates in the upper left triad of Shannon's communication diagram, is supposed to be perfect and thus incapable of making mistakes at the first creation. The first creation, as a conceptual act by God, would be completely under divine control. Thus, insofar as divine creation miscarries, it must miscarry at the second creation. But how can a perfect first creation fail at the second creation? This question, unaddressed by Covey in the context of human creation, cannot be avoided for divine creation. G.K. Chesterton, however, understood the problem and addressed it.

According to Chesterton, all creation entails separation. When a creator creates, the thing created is not identical with or even a prosthetic extension of the creator. Rather, in creating anything, the creator (divine, human, or otherwise), necessarily gives it a separate existence, "divorcing" oneself from it and thereby "setting it free." As Chesterton explains,

> It was the prime philosophic principle of Christianity that this divorce in the divine act of making (such as severs the poet from the poem or the mother from the new-born child) was the true description of the act whereby the absolute energy made the world. According to most philosophers, God in making the world enslaved it. According to Christianity, in making it, He set it free. God had written, not so much a poem, but rather a play; a play he had planned as perfect, but which had necessarily been left to human actors and stage-managers, who had since made a great mess of it.[15]

Chesterton here treats creation as a play whose production fails to match the quality of the script. God has written the perfect script, but the actors can't pull it off. In the idiom of double creation, God, as creator, exercises perfect control at the first creation but then cedes control at the second creation, permitting it to go haywire. This disjunction between first and second creation has, of course, profound implications for the problem of evil. God's will is done in heaven but less so on earth. God, in creating the world, has set it free (that freedom, presumably, entailing benefits that exceed its costs). In its freedom, the world

---

[14]   Ibid.

[15]   Chesterton, *Orthodoxy*, in *Collected Works of G.K. Chesterton*, vol. 1, 281–2.

has become prodigal, abandoning its divine moorings, and now needs to find its way back to God. According to Christian teaching, the Incarnation of Christ is God's means for winning the world back to himself, consistent with the world's freedom, without coercion.

Chesterton's insight that God, in creating the world, set it free resonates with Shannon's communication diagram. Implicit in that diagram is that the sender of a message loses control of the message once it is sent. Of course, the diagram does not strictly speaking demand such loss of control. Thus the sender might control all aspects of the communication channel as depicted in Shannon's diagram. But what would be the point, in that case, of sending any messages at all? With complete control of the communication channel, the sender would just be sending a message to oneself—like sending an email to oneself. Except perhaps for repeating a message, there is no point to such an exercise. The whole point of communication is to create novel information at one end of a communication channel and share it at the other end, where it does not exist until its receipt.

Chapter 21

A World in Communion

In this last chapter of the book, I want to sketch what the world looks like if the most basic thing happening in it is not the interaction of particles but the exchange of information. No fundamentally new ideas will be presented in what follows. Rather, I'll attempt to piece together the ideas developed in previous chapters into a coherent whole. I'll do this, very briefly, in a series of numbered points, underscoring key features of the informational view of reality that has been the focus throughout. I'll close with a parable, drawn from the game of golf, that ties together various elements of this book.

21.1 *Informational realism*. It's time to assign a name to the position developed throughout this book, according to which information rather than matter is the primary stuff of reality. In chapters 4 and 11, I referred to myself, in passing, as an "informational realist." It seems to me that the term *informational realism* aptly captures the view of information developed in the preceding chapters. The term underscores not only the primacy of information but also its reality. Information, as we have seen, is as real an object of study as nature has to offer. Information is a precisely defined measurable entity. Informational concepts have theoretical value in the sciences. They are not merely metaphors but insightful explanatory tools that probe the nature of nature.[1]

21.2 *Ontology*. Within informational realism, what exists? Informational realism is not informational monism, the view that information is identical with the totality of being. Informational realism, as the view that information is the primary stuff or fabric of reality, is a relational ontology, asserting that things exist insofar as they interact via information with other things. Informational

---

[1]   Informational realism relieves the following worry about information raised by University of Texas philosopher of biology Sahotra Sarkar: "It is incumbent upon those who think that informational concepts have theoretical value in biology (that is, they explain things rather than being merely metaphors) to produce an appropriate technical concept of information for biological contexts." Quoted from Sahotra Sarkar, *Doubting Darwin?* (Oxford: Blackwell, 2007), 119. Informational realism, as developed in this book, answers Sarkar's concern, not just for biology but for the sciences in general.

realism does not rule out informational monism—the things that exist may be, as it were, information "all the way down." But informational realism can also include sources of information that are not themselves items of information. For instance, in Judeo-Christian theology, God is not an item of information but rather the ultimate source of information, who, in a primal act of information separates out the actual world from all possible worlds.

21.3 *The exchange of information.* It is convenient to talk about the exchange of information in terms of a sender sending information down a communication channel to a receiver. Nonetheless, it is important to understand that this way of speaking is indeed only a convenience. Information at its most basic is always the actualization of one possibility to the exclusion of others. An exchange of information down a communication channel is really a correlation of such items of information. Thus, an item of information issuing from a sender and an item of information terminating at a receiver as well as any other intermediate items of information may exhibit a precise statistical correlation, with one item of information rendering others more or less probable. The exchange of information along a communication channel refers to such a correlation among different items of information.

21.4 *Freedom within constraint.* In answer to why things happen, materialism offers, in broadest strokes, the catchphrase *chance and necessity*. In other words, things happen by pure spontaneity or by inescapable compulsion or by some combination of the two. Informational realism, by contrast, suggests a different catchphrase to describe, again in broadest strokes, why things happen: *freedom within constraint*. When something happens, it happens by realizing one possibility to the exclusion of others. The possibility so realized and those excluded, however, don't range over the totality of all possibilities, but rather are restricted to a reduced set of possibilities, namely, the relevant matrix of possibility. A classic image of freedom within constraint comes from poetry, where a given meter sets the constraint within which the poet has freedom to create. But note, the very constraint that sets the boundary for freedom in one context can be the product of freedom in another. Thus a poet may write poetry (freedom) within dactylic hexameter (constraint). But before writing poetry, the poet must settle on which meter to use, chosen from a range of permissible meters appropriate to the poet's language. The choice of meter in this case becomes the act of freedom, and the range of permissible meters becomes the constraint.

21.5 *Necessity, chance, and design.* The freedom that operates within constraint can express itself in three ways. As necessity: the constraint may allow only one possibility. As chance: the constraint may allow multiple possibilities, whose occurrence is characterized by a probability distribution. As design: the constraint may allow multiple possibilities, with the one that occurs caused by an intelligence seeking to advance an end or purpose. Note that these three modes of explanation need not be mutually exclusive. Note also that chance and necessity, as described here, take on a different sense from what they mean within materialism, where they are basic and unanalyzable features of material reality. Within informational realism, both chance and necessity can be viewed as indirectly teleological. Thus necessity can be viewed as a consequence of an intelligence having selected a constraint that allows only one outcome. Moreover, chance can be viewed as a byproduct of intelligent or teleological activity (recall chapter 16). Design (treated quite generally and not merely as external design) is, of course, always directly teleological.

21.6 *What about matter?* In chapters 11 and 12, I referred to matter as a myth and as a convenience to thought. I did this in part to shake up our sensibilities, which at present assign too exalted a status to matter. Even though I retract nothing in what I wrote earlier about matter being a myth or convenience, I want also to give matter its due. Matter, in the form of particular material objects, is real. Such objects express their reality informationally. But, within informational realism, everything expresses its reality informationally (that includes mathematical objects, social realities such as money, spiritual agencies such as angels, etc.). So how does saying that an object is material add to our understanding? Material objects, in outputting information, operate within a particular set of constraints. Those material constraints, as we might call them, include laws of physics and chemistry as well as localization in space and time. For an object to be material therefore depends on whether its informational output is suitably constrained in this way.

21.7 *Nature and nurture.* Within materialism, nature and nurture account for all capabilities of organisms. After all, what else could influence an organism's capabilities, given the truth of materialism? Thus, when an organism is able to perform some feat, materialism assigns this capacity either to its material constitution as inherited from its parent(s) or to experiences that have impacted it from conception onward (in the form of learning, exercise, nutrition, etc.). Now, informational realism has no problem attributing some capacities of organisms to nature and nurture. In fact, it has no problem attributing all of them to nature and nurture so long as the information that nature and nurture provide to the organism is not limited, on a priori grounds, solely to material processes. Thus, for instance, it might be in the nature of certain organisms to tap into nonmaterial sources of information that guide them to, say, a particular mating site. The uncanny ability of certain birds and aquatic creatures to navigate thousands of miles to precise locations could conceivably result from nonmaterial sources of information.[2] I raise this as a possibility, and I would have no problem if a clear material basis could be found for such capacities (as in a heightened sensitivity of these animals to the earth's magnetic field). My point is simply that informational realism does not require that nature and nurture always be cashed out in purely material terms. Instead, an expanded view of nature and nurture is allowed within informational realism.

21.8 *Social vs. physical reality.* In *The Construction of Social Reality*, philosopher John Searle asks, "How can there be an objective world of money, property, marriage, governments, elections, football games, cocktail parties and law courts in a world that consists entirely of physical particles in fields of force, in which some of these particles are organized into systems that are conscious biological beasts, such as ourselves?"[3] Although Searle describes how humans (through collective intentionality, institutional facts, and status functions) construct social realities such as money and marriage, he is unable, in precise materialist

---

[2]   Consider, for instance, the following from Rupert Sheldrake: "[W]hen I was a Research Fellow at Clare College, Cambridge, my interest in pigeon homing reawoke, and I asked my colleagues in zoology how the pigeons did it. I soon found that no one really knew, an impression confirmed by reading the specialized papers and reviews in the scientific literature. Every reasonable hypothesis had been tried and seemed to have failed. I then saw this intriguing mystery concerned not only homing, but also migration. How do English swallows migrate in the autumn to South Africa, and then in spring return to England, even to the very same building where they nested the year before? Again, no one knew. I began to suspect that homing and migration might depend on a sense of power hitherto unrecognized by science. In particular, it seemed to me that there might be a direct connection between the birds and their home, rather like an invisible elastic band." Quoted from Rupert Sheldrake, *Seven Experiments That Could Change the World*, new edn. (Rochester, Vt.: Park Street Press, 2002), 33–4. Again, I'm not saying that such capabilities of animals cannot reasonably be accounted for in material terms—an adequate materialist explanation may indeed be forthcoming. What I am saying is that informational realism does not require materialistic explanations of such phenomena. Instead, informational realism is able to accommodate Sheldrake's "power hitherto unrecognized by science" and "invisible elastic bands" in terms of information from nonmaterial sources that guides these animals.

[3]   John R. Searle, *The Construction of Social Reality* (New York: Free Press, 1995), xi–xii.

terms, to trace these social realities to their presumed material underpinnings.[4] Informational realism, by contrast, offers a straightforward unification of social and physical reality. Both types of reality are informational; they simply operate according to different constraints. An even tighter unification is possible when informational realism is combined with theism. In that case, social realities constructed by humans mirror physical realities created by God. If you will, nature itself becomes a divinely constructed social reality, providing a stage (literally) on which humans construct their social realities.

I close with a parable to illustrate the scope of informational realism. Imagine that God were a golfer.[5] Golf is a social reality, constructed by humans. This reality, however, depends on grass, water, and other natural resources that allow for beautifully manicured golf courses as well as for all the equipment needed to play golf. Now God, though the creator of these natural resources and the possessor of supernatural powers, in playing golf agrees to play by the rules. God, therefore, must use existing commercially available golf balls and clubs. Only by applying force to the handle of the golf club and therewith hitting the ball with the club's head can God put the golf ball in motion. Thus God cannot cause wind to blow the golf ball where he wants or enlist a raccoon to toss it out of a sand trap.

Wherein, then, lies God's advantage in playing golf? Certainly, God can apply any force to the golf club's handle. Yet too much force will cause the club to buckle, or the golf ball to be hit so hard that it gets damaged, or both. So God, even as the consummate golfer, is limited in the amount of force he can apply to the club and therewith to the ball. Accordingly, God's advantage consists

---

[4]   Searle's failure to unify social and physical reality remained as complete as ever in his sequel to *The Construction of Social Reality*, namely, his *Making the Social World: The Structure of Human Civilization* (Oxford: Oxford University Press, 2010).

[5]   I'm indebted, indirectly, to Paul Nelson for this golf parable. Reporting on an American Scientific Affiliation conference that took place in 1995, Nelson summarized a talk by Kenneth Miller in which Miller cited a nun who had described God as "a really superlative pool player ... who lifts the triangular rack on the 15 balls, lines up the cue ball, and sinks all the balls with one shot." The nun referred to this pool player as her God, and Miller added "that's my God, too." Although I like this pool-playing parable, I don't think it is nearly as rich and insightful as the golf-playing parable presented here. For one thing, nature is absent from pool in a way that it isn't in golf (which depends on plant-infested golf courses). Also, the physical limitations on playing golf are much clearer than those on playing pool. It is not, for instance, clear to me that the physical dynamics of balls interacting on a pool table allow them all to be sunk with a single shot, especially if the collisions are not perfectly elastic. For Nelson's report on the 1995 conference, see http://www.arn.org/docs/asa795rpt.htm (last accessed October 22, 2013).

not so much in the magnitude of the force that he is able to impart to the ball (though he will have a strength advantage here over humans) as in knowing how, with arbitrary precision, to direct that force in light of all environmental factors that may influence the ball's trajectory. Armed with this knowledge and with the ability to implement it perfectly, God is guaranteed to defeat any human golfer, even scoring 18 holes in one on an 18-hole course provided that physical constraints do not prevent the ball from reaching the hole from the tee. But note, if the golf course is of gargantuan proportions, so that the distance from tee to hole is measured in miles rather than feet, even God will have a high score, requiring multiple strokes per hole.

In playing golf, God agrees to be constrained by the rules of golf. As a result, God's ability to play golf parallels our own. Like God, we are able to impart to the golf ball not just energy but directed energy. God, of course, is able to direct that energy much more precisely than we are. Thus God would be able to hit one hole in one after another. What is this directed energy? It is, of course, information. Of all the permissible ways that God might apply energy to the ball, God chooses a very narrow band within which the ball is sure to find the hole. In imparting directed energy to the ball, God is in fact imparting information, singling out one trajectory to the exclusion of others.

Golf, in this parable, is, of course, a metaphor for the world. The world is full of material objects that obey material principles, such as stars, planets, and landmasses on which golf is played. But it also contains patterned arrangements of material objects that obey clear teleological principles, such as living things, golf carts, and golfers themselves. It contains social realities, such as the game of golf, and mathematical objects, such as numbers used to score games of golf. And the world contains teleological processes that bring about what, on the basis of purely material principles, would have to be regarded as probabilistic miracles. Granted, no one has ever witnessed the probabilistic miracle of a golfer making 18 successive holes in one on a reasonably sized golf course. But nature seems to present us with other probabilistic miracles, such as the origin of life.

In this parable, I describe God as a supernatural being who, in playing golf, limits his supernatural powers by playing by the rules. The activities of a supernatural deity, when limited in this way, could, therefore, be indistinguishable from the activities of an immanent personal deity or even from the activities of an impersonal natural teleology, provided, in the latter case, that the activity belongs not to a social reality (like golf) but to the basic operations of nature. The divine golfer could, in this parable, therefore correspond to the teleological principles and laws that an atheist, like Thomas Nagel, finds congenial.

Of course, nothing in this parable prevents our divine golfer from being a full-throated supernatural deity. In that case, God may voluntarily choose to play by the rules, but he could also choose to do otherwise. Where it is physically impossible for a golf ball hit from the tee to land in the hole, such a deity could, by an act of supernatural power, cause the ball's trajectory to go through physically impossible contortions that, in the end, land the ball in the hole. Would God in that case be cheating? Some theists, taking a naturalistic bent, might say God would be cheating. Other theists, seeing God as the maker of all rules and thus as always within his rights to break or override them, might say God would not be cheating, perhaps even adding that God by definition is incapable of cheating. For my part, I don't offer this parable as a prescription for how God should or should not interact with the world—that's for God to decide.

I close this book with a final observation about the difference between materialism and informational realism. The weakness of materialism is that it artificially restricts the information sources that may be operating in the world. In particular, if information sources unacceptable to materialism do in fact exist, materialism will be sure to miss them. Conversely, the strength of informational realism is not that it requires nonmaterialist information sources to exist but that it allows them to be discovered and recognized if they do indeed exist. The importance of allowing the world to be itself may seem too obvious to need stating, but it does need to be stated because it is too easy to start with our preconceptions of how the world ought to be rather than to take the world as it is. Materialism is such a preconception. The informational approach to reality takes the world as it is.

Index

material(ist) age ix, 1
materialism 17(n1), 28, 48, 49(n4), 66, 81,
        106, 200
    alternatives to 6, 17
    analytical impulse behind 21–2
    appeal of 17
    beauty of 78
    bleakness of 5
    causal closure thesis of 113
    critique of 7, 17, 88
    Darwinian 48, 66–7, 142
    doubts about 4, 6
    fideistic 80
    information, approach to 77, 113, 191,
        203
    intelligence, approach to 48, 137–8,
        190, 199
    methodological, *see* methodological
        materialism
    nature, approach to 78, 105
    parsimony abused by 17–18(n2)
    as prejudice/preconception 28, 203
    reconstitutive 88; *see also* Tang problem
    reductionism of 4, 143
    vis-à-vis science 80, 123–4, 142, 186
    self-reference problems with 7
    teleology, approach to 57
    vs. theism 127
    truth of 145
    as working hypothesis 81
materialist
    culture 4
    imperialism i–ii
    principles 12
    worldview 4, 9, 11, 122
materialist-refuting logic 51–3, 60, 74–5
Mathematical Theory of Communication
        39(n3), 45(n6), 187
matrix/matrices of possibility 29–35, 46,
        88, 96, 129, 149, 190, 198
    for search 154, 156
    terminological justification 30(n2)
matter vii, xiii(n3), 16, 74–5, 88, 91, 199,
        202; *see also* embodiment
    as abstraction 79, 88, 96, 103

beauty of 8
as convenience 95, 97
as corporeal substance 79
definition of 97
empirical access to 78–9, 81
vs. energy 105–6
as inference 81
vs. information xix, 53, 77, 91, 94
information processing power of 115
as inherently informational 53(n16),
        75, 77–89, 92–3, 95–7, 103, 145
individuation of 21, 25
interaction of 8, 21
mysteriousness of 78
as myth 96(n9), 97, 199
normativity of 51
principles of operation of 9
as unreal 88
Maxwell-Boltzmann-Gibbs entropy, *see*
        entropy
McGrew, Tim & Lydia 128(n7)
McMullin, Ernan 169
measurement problem 86; *see also* quantum
        mechanics
mechanisms 20(n5), 49, 115–16, 146,
        152(n15), 169, 176, 184
Medawar, Peter 151
Media X (Stanford University) 2(n2)
medium 92–6, 100
message 92–6, 193
Metanexus Institute xvii
method of difference 181–4
methodological materialism 8, 80(n6), 81
Meyer, Stephen 52(n11), 60(n30), 86
Microsoft Windows 93–4
Mill, John Stuart 181–4
Miller, Kenneth 181–4, 201(n5)
Mind & Cosmos 47(n1), 52(n14), 65–75
mind 12, 66, 82, 92; *see also* brain
    information, connection with 20
miracles 8, 109, 120; *see also* probabilistic
        miracles
miraculous powers 32–3
modal logic 35
modal realism 26